THE ILLUSTRATED ENCYCLOPEDIA OF
MILITARY
HELICOPTERS

THE ILLUSTRATED ENCYCLOPEDIA OF
MILITARY
HELICOPTERS

A guide to over 80 years of rotorcraft, from the first types deployed
in World War II to the specialized aircraft in service today

FRANCIS CROSBY

LORENZ BOOKS

Contents

This edition is published by
Lorenz Books
an imprint of Anness Publishing Limited
info@anness.com
www.lorenzbooks.com
www.annesspublishing.com

A CIP catalogue record for this book is available from the British Library.

Publisher: Joanna Lorenz
Editorial Director: Helen Sudell
Senior Editor: Felicity Forster
Production Controller: Ben Worley

PUBLISHER'S NOTES
Although the information in this book is believed to be accurate and true at the time of going to press, neither the authors nor the publisher can accept any legal responsibility or liability for any errors or omissions that may have been made.
    The nationality of each helicopter is identified in the relevant specification box by the national flag that was in use at the time of service.

PAGE 1: **Mil Mi-24 attack helicopter.**
PAGE 2: **AH-64 WAH Apache Longbow.**
PAGE 3: **Boeing CH-47F Chinook.**
FRONT ENDPAPER: **Sikorsky SH-60F Seahawk.**
BACK ENDPAPER: **Boeing CH-47 Chinook.**

Introduction	6

A HISTORY OF MILITARY HELICOPTERS

Helicopter visionaries	10
Early pioneers	12
Juan de la Cierva	14
Autogyros of the world	16
James George Weir	18
Gyrogliders and rotorkites	20
Helicopters in World War II	22
Igor Sikorsky	24
Charles H. Kaman	26
Frank N. Piasecki	28
Soviet pioneers	30
Arthur Young (Bell Aircraft Corporation)	32
Stanley Hiller	34
Sikorsky R-4 Hoverfly	36
The Korean War	38
Air Sea Rescue (ASR)	40
Gyrodynes	42
The Suez Crisis	44
European helicopter development	46
The Malayan Emergency	48
The Vietnam War	50
Helicopters at sea	54
The helicopter cockpit	56
Rotor systems	58
Helicopter engines	62

Boeing CH-47 Chinook	64
Night Vision Technology (NVT)	66
Military heavy-lift helicopters	68
Anti-submarine helicopters	70
Soviet helicopters in Afghanistan	72
Gunships and attack helicopters	74
Bravo November	76
Operation Desert Storm	78
The anti-tank helicopter	80
AgustaWestland AH-64W Apache Longbow	82
US presidential helicopters	84
Helicopter assault ships	86
Tilt-wing and tilt-rotor	88
Vertical Unmanned Aircraft Systems (VUAS)	90

DIRECTORY OF MILITARY HELICOPTERS

Aérospatiale SE 3130 Alouette II	94
Aérospatiale SE 316 Alouette III	95
Aérospatiale SA 315B Lama	96
Aérospatiale SA 321 Super Frélon	98
Aérospatiale SA 330 Puma	100
Eurocopter AS 332 Super Puma/ AS 532 Cougar	102
Aérospatiale SA 341 Gazelle	104
Eurocopter AS 565 Panther	106
AgustaWestland AW109E Power	108

LEFT: **The Petroczy Karman-Zurovec PKZ 2 was powered by three Gnome rotary engines, and was first flown on April 2, 1918.**

Agusta A129 Mangusta/
  AgustaWestland AW129   110
AgustaWestland AW101 Merlin   112
AgustaWestland/Leonardo AW159
  Wildcat   114
Bell 47 H-13 Sioux   116
Bell UH-1 Iroquois   118
Bell UH-1D/H Iroquois   120
Bell OH-58 Kiowa/TH-67
  SeaRanger   122
Bell OH-58D Kiowa Warrior   124
Bell 209 AH-1 Cobra   126
Bell AH-1W SuperCobra   128
Bell CH-135/UH-1N/UH-1Y   130
Bell CH-146 Griffon   132
Bell Boeing V-22 Osprey   134
Boeing Vertol CH-46 Sea Knight 136
Boeing CH-47 Chinook   138
Boeing CH-47F Chinook   140
Boeing Vertol MH-47E/G   142
Boeing AH-64D/E Apache
  Longbow/Apache Guardian   144
Bristol Type 171 Sycamore   146
Bristol Type 192 Belvedere   148
Denel AH-2 Rooivalk   150
Eurocopter EC665/Airbus HAD
  Tiger   152
Eurocopter AS 550 Fennec/Airbus
  H125M   154
Eurocopter/Airbus UH-72 Lakota 156

Hiller OH-23 Raven   158
HAL Dhruv Mk 1 to 4   160
Hughes TH-55 Osage   161
Hughes OH-6A Cayuse   162
Hughes AH-64A Apache   164
Kaman H-43B Huskie   166
Kaman SH-2 Seasprite   168
Kamov Ka-25   170
Kamov Ka-27/Ka-29/Ka-31/Ka-32 172
Kamov Ka-50/Ka-52   174
MBB/Eurocopter Bo105   176
Mil Mi-1   178
Mil Mi-2   180
Mil Mi-4   182
Mil Mi-6   184
Mil Mi-8   186
Mil Mi-14   188
Mil Mi-24   190
Mil Mi-26   192
Mil Mi-28   194
NH Industries NH90   196
Piasecki YH-16 Transporter   198
Piasecki HUP Retriever/
  UH-25 Army Mule   199
Piasecki H-21 Workhorse/
  Shawnee   200
PZL W-3 Sokól   202
Robinson R22/R44   202
Saunders-Roe Skeeter   203
Sikorsky R-4   204

Sikorsky S-51   206
Sikorsky H-19 Chickasaw   208
Sikorsky CH-37 Mojave   210
Sikorsky H-34 Choctaw   212
Sikorsky SH-3 Sea King   214
Sikorsky HH-3E Jolly
  Green Giant   216
Sikorsky CH-54 Tarhe   218
Sikorsky CH-53 Sea Stallion   220
Sikorsky UH-60 Black Hawk   222
Sikorsky HH-60G Pave Hawk   224
Sikorsky SH-60 Seahawk   226
Sikorsky MH-60G Pave Hawk   228
Sikorsky CH-53E Super Stallion 230
Sikorsky MH-53J Pave Low   232
Sikorsky MH-53E Sea Dragon   234
Sikorsky Superhawk/
  CH-148 Cyclone   236
Sud-Ouest S.O. 1221 Djinn   238
Westland Whirlwind   240
Westland Wessex   242
Westland Sea King   244
Westland Wasp and Scout   246
Westland Lynx   248

Glossary   250
Key to flags   251
Index   252
Acknowledgements   256

ABOVE: **The Russian manufacturer Kamov championed and perfected the coaxial rotor system embodied in the Kamov Ka-27. The system removed the need for a tail rotor, which suited these compact machines for deck operations.**

ABOVE: **The design of the Sikorsky S-70 family of helicopters, designated the H-60 in US military service, dates back to the early 1970s, but many versions remain in widespread military use.**

Introduction

Although the word "helicopter" is derived from the ancient Greek *heli* (twisted, curved) and *pteron* (wing), the word we recognize today was not suggested until the 1860s in France, as *hélicoptère*. Both cultures are, however, pre-dated by the idea of flying in a way that we now associate with helicopters and a few fixed-wing aircraft. Successful helicopter designs are, compared to fixed-wing aircraft, relatively recent innovations. While thousands of monoplanes, biplanes, triplanes, bombers, scouts and fighter aircraft were being produced in World War I, helicopters were not developed in a concerted manner, and then only in a limited manner, until World War II.

From novel, unstable and frightening machines, helicopters have been developed to become incredibly sophisticated flying machines that can fly forward, backward, sideways and, of course, hover. If the military were initially slow to

ABOVE: **The Curtiss Bleecker helicopter standing in front of a hangar at the National Advisory Committee for Aeronautics (NACA) in Langley, Virginia, in 1926. The machine was one of many early experimental helicopters that lacked stability and suffered from extreme vibration.**

appreciate the potential of helicopters, they have been making up for that short-sightedness ever since. Helicopters have been developed for an incredible variety of military roles, including minesweeping, reconnaissance, rescue, casualty evacuation, gunship, tank-busting, anti-submarine warfare and heavy lifting. The helicopter has also been armed with guns and missiles, and even equipped to carry nuclear depth charges. The military troop-carrying role is among its most important, and the machine's unique capability enables military commanders to insert combat-ready troops into battle.

The civilian uses of the helicopter are no less impressive, and include firefighting, rescue, crop-dusting, law enforcement and of course being the transport of choice for the wealthy and famous. According to the American Helicopter Society (AHS), there are over 45,000 helicopters operating in the world today, and over three million lives have been saved by these aircraft in both peacetime and wartime operations since the first rescue at sea in 1944.

LEFT: **The Flettner Fl 282 Kolibri (hummingbird) was among the first helicopters in front-line military service during World War II. This example was captured from the Germans and tested in the US.**

While early designers may have grasped the broad concept of rotary flight, the power to get this kind of machine airborne simply did not exist. As engine technology developed, so did the ability to get designs from the drawing board into the air. Piston engine technology was accelerated during World War I, as was jet turbine technology during World War II.

Early military helicopters were powered by piston engines and gave sterling service, but the introduction of turboshaft engines dramatically boosted the helicopter's performance in terms of endurance and speed.

Better knowledge of aerodynamics, technical developments, computer-aided design and the creation of lightweight composite materials have led to a huge range of advances in helicopter design, which in turn have boosted all-round performance and lifting capability. Avionics and the incredible array of equipment and weapons that can be carried by a helicopter has made the type among the most expensive in the military inventory.

The helicopter is a versatile and vital asset in military inventories around the world, and plays a truly unique part in aviation that at the time of the Wright brothers' historic flight could only been predicted by a few true visionaries.

RIGHT: **The Bell OH-58D Kiowa Warrior has a distinctive Mast-Mounted Sight (MMS) above the rotor system.** BELOW: **Tilt-rotor aircraft such as the Boeing-Agusta BA609 combine the advantages of both rotor and fixed-wing aircraft.**

A History of Military Helicopters

In 1945, the Focke-Achgelis Fa 223 helicopter was flown by Luftwaffe crews during the defence of Nazi Germany on transport and supply missions. The German Navy had been operating the Flettner Fa 330 Bachstelze rotor glider from U-boats, and had operated the Flettner Fa 282 Kolibri reconnaissance helicopter from warships at sea. The Sikorsky R-4 entered service with the US military in April 1944, and was flown in Burma and the South Pacific. So began the age of the military helicopter.

During the Korean War more helicopter types entered service, and the military went on to gain vital experience of operations with the machine in battle conditions. The Vietnam War is known as "The Helicopter War" and, as the conflict escalated, more specific types were introduced, such as heavy-lift transports, gunships and attack helicopters. The Bell UH-1 Iroquois was the backbone of the force, being deployed for many roles, including casualty evacuation. In subsequent conflicts, the helicopter has been deployed at the forefront of the initial attack, and later to supply the advancing forces.

In naval service, the helicopter was initially used for rescue and supply duties. After gaining experience of operating the type at sea, it became obvious that the hovering ability of the machine made the type ideal for the anti-submarine warfare role. The helicopter has also become a vital asset to any modern amphibious assault force.

LEFT: **The Westland Sea King HAR.3 was a search and rescue version produced for the RAF. To provide more space in the fuselage, the cabin rear bulkhead was repositioned.**

ABOVE: **Leonardo da Vinci's 15th-century design was a flight of fancy that could not even fly in model form.** RIGHT: **In 1854, Sir George Cayley produced his "Aerial Top" to show the lifting power of the propeller.**

Helicopter visionaries

In common with many fields of human endeavour, the creation and development of what we now know as the helicopter began centuries ago as a concept in the minds of visionaries. These visionaries, apparently inspired by nature, had a notion of a craft somehow powered to achieve flight. While some sought to emulate the flapping wings of birds, others were inspired by the simple rotating seeds of trees such as the sycamore, which could fly for some distance with the correct wind conditions – as long as the seed continued to turn and wind generated lift, the seed could stay aloft.

Around 400BC, the Chinese are known to have been making special spinning tops consisting of slightly angled feathers fixed to the end of a stick which, when rapidly spun between the hands, generated lift that could carry the top upwards for free flight. These were just toys, but around AD 400, again from China, we have the first written reference of the notion of rotary wing aviation. A book entitled *Pao Phu Tau* refers to a person called "The Master" who describes flying cars made of wood from the inner part of the Jujube tree, powered by leather straps fastened to returning blades that set the machine in motion. This machine, however fanciful or theoretical, is close to what we understand today to be a helicopter.

For the first signs of an appreciation of helicopter principles in the Western world, we have to look to Ancient Greece and Archimedes, the inventor, mathematician and physicist who, in the 2nd century BC, perfected his rotating screw for use as

a water pump. As the screw was rotated inside a cylinder, the water in front moved, and simultaneously the water resisted and pushed back. This resistance principle also applied to the movement of a screw through air, which has fluid properties, to produce lift.

Many mistakenly believe it was Leonardo da Vinci who invented the first helicopter. He stated in his *Codex Atlanticus* that he had discovered a screw-shaped device made of iron, wire and starched linen, around 4m/13ft across, that would rise in the air if turned quickly by a team of four men. His theory for compressing the air for lift was in essence similar to that of today's helicopters. Genius though he was, the intriguing "Helical Air Screw" that Leonardo drew around 1483 (but not published for another 300 years) was, however, nothing more than a concept. Leonardo's plan to use just muscle power to revolve the rotor would never have been sufficient to operate a helicopter successfully, and there was no provision for dealing with the torque created by the turning blades. A scale model made in the early 21st century, even with the advantage of a lower weight than the full-size machine, could not raise itself in flight. Numerous experiments, inventions, technical developments and advances over the centuries following Leonardo did, however, ease the way for the development of the helicopter and vertical flight. The ability to produce robust precision mechanical parts came with the Industrial Revolution, and after that huge technological leap, the production of the helicopter as we know it today was inevitable.

In 1754, the "Father of Russian Science" Mikhail Lomonosov designed a machine with coaxial rotors to take meteorological instruments skywards to take readings. Perhaps inspired by the same principles as the Chinese feather toy of 2,000 years earlier, Lomonosov's model used two propellers rotating in opposite directions on the same level. Lomonosov demonstrated a model powered by a clock mechanism to the Russian Academy of Sciences in July 1754, but it is unsure whether his device flew unaided.

In 1768, French mathematician J. P. Paucton proposed a man-powered machine called a Pterophere, with two airscrews – one to provide lift for the machine in flight, and the second to provide forward propulsion. This machine was still based on the notion of "screws" boring through the air like a screw through wood. Then, in 1783, again in France, Launoy took the Chinese top concept that had been examined a few years earlier by Lomonosov, and produced a model consisting of two sets of rotors made of turkey feathers that rotated in opposite directions. This was demonstrated in 1784 in front of the Academy of Sciences, and succeeded in achieving free flight.

The last significant helicopter visionary was the British engineer Sir George Cayley, who famously built the first practical aeroplane in 1853, but had first sketched a twin-rotor helicopter in 1792. Cayley spent most of his life experimenting with flying machines, and carried out the first serious, experimentally based aeronautical research. In 1843, Cayley designed his "Aerial Carriage" which had four "rotors" arranged coaxially in pairs. However, Cayley was unable to find any steam engines that were light enough to help the design leave the drawing board and, hopefully, the ground.

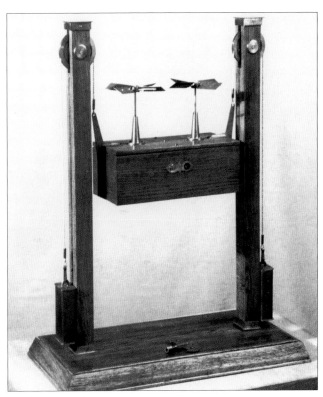

ABOVE: **Mikhail Lomonosov demonstrated this machine in 1754 to the Russian Academy of Science, to prove the lifting capacity of the propeller.**

Steam engines were always going to be too heavy, and internal combustion engines with sufficient powers would not appear for almost 50 years. Other rotorcraft experiments continued, but advances in glider design captured the imagination of most designers, who believed fixed-wing aircraft were the future.

LEFT: **A model of the "Aerial Carriage" designed by Sir George Cayley in 1843. The steam-powered machine was fitted with two lifting rotors, two rotating wings and two pusher-type propellers. The machine was never built.**

LEFT: **Paul Cornu, seated in his helicopter in 1907. The two rotors rotated in opposite directions to cancel torque. The machine was the first to have risen from the ground in free flight, using rotor blades instead of wings.**

Early pioneers

Many inventors and engineers from around the world contributed to the research and development that led to the design of the first successful helicopter.

Enrico Forlanini (1848–1930) was an Italian engineer, inventor and aeronautical pioneer who carried out considerable research into helicopters. In 1877 he developed a helicopter design in which superheated, high-pressure steam drove a pair of two-bladed, contra-rotating rotors. The steam was created as the helicopter was on its "stand" on the ground and pumped into a metal sphere on the aircraft. As the high-pressure steam was released, it drove the rotors. A scale model was demonstrated in a park in Milan, where it rose to a height of 13m/43ft from a vertical take-off, and hovered for 20 seconds.

In 1906, brothers Louis and Jacques Bréguet began helicopter experiments and meticulously tested airfoil shapes for rotors under the guidance of Professor Charles Richet. In 1907, they built the Bréguet-Richet Gyroplane No.1, which was one of the first recorded mechanical devices to actually hover. Their gyroplane had a small engine that provided just enough power to enable it to fly for around one minute in the late summer of 1907, in what is generally accepted as

the world's first vertical flight. As there was no means of control or stability, it required four men to steady it while it hovered 60cm/2ft off the ground.

A year later, again in France, bicycle maker and engineer Paul Cornu (1881–1944), was the first person to design and build a helicopter to achieve flight while carrying a passenger. Cornu's twin-rotor craft flew for some 20 seconds on November 13, 1907, rising to 30cm/12in in the air. A 24hp engine powered the helicopter, which had counter-rotating rotors. It is worth noting that both Cornu and Forlanini had both realized that without a tail rotor, a helicopter design would just spin on the rotor axis unless contra-rotation was employed. One can only imagine the countless heroic failures that led to this realization. Cornu, however, realizing that his design had no means of control in terms of forward or sideways motion, effectively reached his own technical dead end and abandoned this design after just a few flights.

Raul Pateras Pescara (1890–1966) was an Argentine lawyer and inventor who worked on seaplanes, engines compressors and helicopters. In 1919, Pescara built several true coaxial helicopter designs, which he described in the associated patent documents as a "rational helicopter". His designs were indeed

ABOVE: **Raul Pateras Pescara refined a coaxial rotor system that eliminated torque. This is the Pescara No 3 machine.**

ABOVE: **The design by Corrandino D'Ascanio had two counter-rotating coaxial rotors, each with a trailing elevator to vary the rotor blade angle of attack.**

pure helicopters, at least in theory, and from 1919 to 1923, no doubt benefitting from his own legal knowledge, he submitted around 40 related patents in several countries. Meanwhile, he had not neglected the technical developments at all, and refined the practical applications of his designs. His first machine weighed around 600kg/1,323lb without a pilot, and power was provided by one 45hp Hispano engine. Each of the two coaxial rotors was made up of 12 propeller blades (i.e. 24 in total), but the small engine simply could not lift the weight of the machine. A modified design with a much more powerful Le Rhône rotary engine did manage to just lift off the ground in May 1921.

Pescara's most successful design, the No.3 built in 1923, was, by January 1924, making flights of around 10 minutes' duration. The same coaxial rotor system was then fitted with a Hispano-Suiza engine providing the power. On April 18, 1924, Pescara achieved a new world record, with a flight of 736m/2,419ft covered in 4 minutes, 11 seconds (a speed of approximately 13kph/8mph) at a height of 1.8m/6ft. Most significantly, Pescara achieved forward motion by altering the pitch of the rotor blades in flight by warping, and the rotor head could be tilted to give the blades a degree of forward thrust. Pescara had successfully demonstrated the principles of cyclic and collective pitch control. Impressively, he appreciated how to make use of autorotation when his engine failed. Pescara never capitalized on his achievements in the helicopter world, and shifted his attention to the motor industry. His patents and associated royalties may, however, have been reward enough.

Étienne Oemichen was another French pioneer who began his experiments in 1920 by cleverly floating a balloon above a twin-rotor helicopter to provide extra lift for the machine. A subsequent Oemichen design had four lifting airscrews and five auxiliary propellers, and he flew this on April 14, 1924, powered by a 134kw/180hp Le Rhône engine, establishing a 360m/1181ft distance record – the first officially recognized by the Federation Aeronautique Internationale (FAI). Then, a few weeks later on May 4, Oemichen became the first person to fly a helicopter at least 1km/0.6miles, to set a closed-circuit record of 1.7km/5,550ft on a flight that reached a height of 15m/50ft and lasted 7 minutes, 40 seconds.

Corrandino D'Ascanio (1891–1981) was fascinated by aviation from an early age and, after qualifying as a mechanical engineer, he joined the Italian Army where he was soon involved in military aviation. After World War I he began to consider the challenges of control in helicopters, and filed a number of related patents. In 1925, he co-founded a company which, in 1930, produced the large D'AT3 that had two double-bladed, counter-rotating rotors. Control was achieved by using auxiliary wings or servotabs on the rotor blade trailing edges. Additional control of pitch, roll and yaw came from three small propellers mounted on the airframe. The D'AT3 set international speed and altitude records. The Depression halted helicopter research and D'Ascanio went to work for Piaggio, developing high-speed adjustable-pitch propellers. During World War II, having been made a General in the Regia Aeronautica (Italian Air Force), he restarted helicopter development in 1942. Post-war Italy was forbidden the research or development of military and aviation technology, so D'Ascanio became involved in the development of a cheap, easy-to-manufacture motor scooter, and designed the iconic Vespa scooter of which many millions have been built since 1946.

LEFT: Juan de la Cierva designed and built his first autogyro, the C.1, in 1920. He used the fuselage from a French-built Deperdussin monoplane, and fitted his own rotor system. The machine did not fly, but during ground trials it did prove the concept of autorotation.

Juan de la Cierva

Juan de la Cierva was born in Murcia, Spain, in 1895, and he is acknowledged as the inventor of the autogyro. He began designing and building aircraft from the age of 17, when he completed rebuilding a Sommer biplane which he re-engined and improved, naming it the BCD-1 El Cangrejo (crab). The aircraft is considered to be the first to be built in Spain. His final fixed-wing design was the C-3 built for a 1918 Spanish military competition for new aircraft. The large tri-motor biplane was completed in May 1919, but crashed in testing. The pilot had flown the aircraft too slowly, and it had stalled before crashing. A disappointed de la Cierva was inspired to consider alternative ways of flying at low speeds, and experiments with model helicopter designs led him to develop what he called, and trademarked, the "Autogiro". In de la Cierva's autogyro designs, the rotor was drawn through the air by a conventional propeller driven by an engine, while the rotor generated lift to sustain level flight, climb and descend.

In 1920, de la Cierva's journey to creating a viable autogyro design began with the Cierva C.1, which was a Deperdussin fixed-wing aircraft mounted with two contra-rotating rotors that provided lift and, by counter-rotating on a single drive shaft, helped eliminate torque that would affect stability. In testing, the C.1 simply would not fly, however it proved the principle of autorotation as it taxied.

BELOW: The experimental C.8 autogyro was flown in the 1928 King's Cup Air Race before being used to make demonstration flights around continental Europe. The machine was flown to Paris from London in September 1928, and is now preserved at the Musée de l'Air et de l'Espace, Le Bourget, France.

His next design was the C.2, which had only one rotor with five blades. This was put on hold as funds ran out, so de la Cierva designed the Cierva C.3, which was completed in June 1921. It had a three-blade rotor as well as a rudder and elevator for yaw and pitch control, while lateral control was dictated by what came to be known as collective pitch. This meant the angle of attack of the rotor blades would be changed at the same time. The design was shown to be too complex, and the C.3 only made a few short flights. He then revisited the C.2. which was finally completed in 1922. While lateral control was improved, sustained flight still eluded the autogyro pioneer.

These early experiments had fallen foul of asymmetric lift, which caused the aircraft to tilt during take-off. Lift between the advancing and retreating rigid rotor blades was not equal as they rotated, and de la Cierva's brilliant solution was the development of the flapping hinge. This allowed the rotor to rise and fall depending on the direction in which the blades were moving. Blades moving with the aircraft in forward motion rose because of the higher lift, but this also served to decrease their angle of attack. The blades travelling in the opposite direction to the autogyro would fall because of the lower lift, which increased their angle of attack. The rising and falling action, known as flapping, and the resulting increase and decrease of the angle of attack balanced the lift created on each side of the aircraft. Hinged blades also eliminated the gyroscopic effect caused by the rigid blades.

The Cierva C.4 incorporated hinged rotors, ailerons mounted on outriggers to the side of the aircraft for lateral control, while pitch and yaw control came from rudder and elevators. On January 17, 1923, the C.4 flew successfully, and performed the first controlled flight of an autogyro. Just three days later, an inflight engine failure demonstrated just how safe the autogyro could be, compared to fixed-wing aircraft. During the flight, the C.4 went into a steep nose-up attitude after the engine failed when the aircraft was just 11m/35ft off the ground. While a fixed-wing aircraft would have stalled and probably crashed, the C.4 beautifully demonstrated the principle of autorotation, and slowly and safely descended to the ground.

The Cierva C.6 had a four-blade rotor with flapping hinges, and used an Avro 504K fuselage and fixed-wing aircraft controls for pitch, roll and yaw. Having conducted his groundbreaking work in Spain, and following a successful demonstration tour with the C.6 in 1926, de la Cierva relocated to Britain where, in partnership with the Scottish industrialist James G. Weir, he established the Cierva Autogiro Company. He then focused on designing and producing the rotor systems, while the airframes were built by other aircraft constructors.

His autogyro designs continuously improved, and when fitted with more powerful engines, achieved higher performance. He had to overcome innumerable technical challenges along the way – as the autogyro pioneer, he was effectively writing the rule book as he went. In the Cierva C.19 the problem of getting the rotors up to speed was finally solved with a direct drive from the engine to the rotor, which was then disconnected prior to the take-off run.

As his autogyros achieved success, they inspired other engineers, who were then able to bring their expertise to benefit de la Cierva. His autogyros, as well as serving with the Royal Air Force in World War II, were built under licence in many countries, including France, Germany, Japan, the Soviet Union and the USA. Juan de la Cierva died in the crash of a Douglas DC-2 shortly after take-off from Croydon Airport on December 9, 1936, but his technical legacy was considerable.

ABOVE: **The experimental C.29 had an enclosed cabin that seated five, and was the heaviest and largest autogyro produced by Cierva at that time.**

LEFT: **Test pilot Frank Courtney (to the right of the aircraft wearing goggles and cap), talking with officials and reporters at Farnborough Aerodrome before taking Cierva's sixth autogyro design for a flight on October 19, 1925.**

Autogyros of the world

Juan de la Cierva's work influenced autogyro designs across the world. The first autogyro made in the Soviet Union was the KASKR-1 "Red Engineer" based on the Cierva C.8. and, like the C.8, featured an Avro 504 fuselage. Built by Kamov and Skrzhinskii (hence the KA plus SKR in the designation), the machine was first tested in September 1929, and proved to have control and power issues. It was rebuilt as the KASKR-2 with a more powerful engine, and was flown successfully in 1931, leading to later Soviet rotorcraft development.

In the USA, the Kellett Autogiro Corporation was set up in 1929 with a licence from Cierva. Early models were basically the same as those produced in the UK. The KD-1, the first non-experimental rotary-wing aircraft in US Army service, was very similar to the Cierva C.30, but with a US-built engine.

The requirements of the US military called for Kellett to revise the design, so the YO-60 with an enclosed cockpit was very much an original design. The KD-1B (civil version of the YO-60) was used by Eastern Airlines to launch the first US rotary-wing airmail service in July 1939.

In Germany during the mid-1930s, Flettner was experimenting with both helicopters and autogyros. The Fl 184 autogyro, designed for the German Navy, was used for anti-submarine and reconnaissance missions, but the prototype caught fire in flight, and the company then resolved to focus on helicopter development. Elsewhere in Germany, the Focke-Achgelis company, having built up their rotorcraft knowledge as licensed builders of Cierva autogyros, were applying this experience to the building of experimental helicopters.

The Kayaba Ka-1, built in Japan, is worthy of note because it is believed to have been the first military rotorcraft to be armed and used operationally. In common with many military powers, the Imperial Japanese Army could see the value of the autogyro as army co-operation/artillery-spotting aircraft. In 1939, a Kellett KD-1A two-seat autogyro was imported from the USA for evaluation. Soon after its arrival in Japan, the autogyro was written off during trials, and what was left of it was handed over to Kayaba, who were conducting autogyro research. Employing some reverse engineering techniques, the US-built machine was studied closely, leading to the production of the Ka-1 two-seat observation autogyro. The Japanese-built machine was powered by a 240hp Argus engine (225hp Jacobs engine in the US-built machine) driving a two-blade propeller,

LEFT: **In 1935, the Kellett YG-1 (KD-1A) was flown on evaluation trials for the US Army at Langley Field, Virginia. A total of seven, fitted with an enclosed cockpit and powered by a Jacobs R-755 radial piston engine, were built for the US Army, and designated XO-60.**

LEFT: **The Pitcairn PAA-1 Autogyro was flown at Langley Research Center as part of the National Advisory Committee for Aeronautics (NACA) experimental rotor blade research programme.**

and had a three-blade rotor. In mid-1941, after successful testing, the Ka-1 was produced as an artillery co-operation aircraft. Once Japan was at war, the autogyro's performance also interested the Imperial Japanese Navy, who were suffering increasing shipping losses from Allied submarine actions. To counter this, the Ka-1 was modified for anti-submarine duties, operating from converted merchant ships and land bases. Changes included the deletion of one of the crew positions to allow space for carrying a small depth charge.

Developments by the US company Bensen attracted the interest of the post-war US military. Led by Russian immigrant Dr Igor Bensen who, having studied captured wartime German rotorcraft, produced the Bensen B-7 "homebuild" rotorkite. In late 1955, Bensen tested the powered B-7M, a true autogyro.

Refinements led to the B-8M that was produced in its thousands for civilian use. As the X-25, it was considered by the US Air Force, which was losing valuable aircrew over Vietnam and wanted to examine integrating an autogyro or rotorkite into ejection seats. The Discretionary Descent Vehicle (DDV) programme would allow aircrew to deploy the craft as they descended, and thereby have more control over where they would land. No full-scale tests ever took place, and the end of the Vietnam War also ended the programme's proposed imaginative use of the autogyro principle.

BELOW: **The A.V. Roe-built Cierva C30A was produced in 1936, and was powered by an Armstrong Siddeley Civet radial piston engine. This aircraft entered Royal Air Force service as DR624.**

LEFT: **The rotor on the W.2 was linked to the engine by an auxiliary driveshaft. This allowed the rotor to be spun to give an improved take-off performance. The sole surviving W.2 is on display at the National Museum of Flight, East Fortune, Scotland.**

James George Weir

Air Commodore James George Weir (1887–1973) was a pioneering Scottish aviator and industrialist who financed Juan de la Cierva's development of the autogyro, and helped establish the Cierva Autogiro Company Limited.

Weir had served as a British Army officer from 1906, for part of that time in the Royal Artillery, and this experience would have given him a true appreciation of the value of using aircraft for battlefield observation and artillery spotting. On November 8, 1910, Weir was awarded Royal Aero Club Aviator's Certificate No. 24, having taken his test in a Blériot Monoplane at Hendon. This aviation experience led to his transfer to the embryonic Royal Flying Corps (RFC). He remained a serving officer until his retirement from the military in 1920.

In 1926, Weir helped to establish and then became chairman and managing director of Cierva. He came from a family of industrialists – his father and uncle had founded G & J Weir Ltd in 1871, a company which was a major manufacturer of specialized pumping equipment for the shipbuilding industry.

During World War I, the company manufactured munitions and built aircraft, including the Royal Aircraft Factory FE.2.

While the Cierva company, backed by Weir, marketed and refined Cierva's designs, a parallel family of autogyros was created by the Weir company, using Cierva patents and their considerable industrial capacity to produce the machines at their Cathcart, Glasgow, factory, as well as the engines, without the anxiety of development costs. G & J Weir designed and built four experimental autogyros from 1933–37, after which the company went on to produce the twin-rotor W.5 and W.6 helicopters before development was halted by the increasing industrial demands of World War II.

In 1932, Cyril Pullin joined Weir's aircraft department as chief designer, specifically to develop single-seat autogyros. Pullin had been a very successful motorcycle racer, winning the Isle of Man TT in 1914 while working for Douglas Motorcycles. In the late 1920s, he formed a motorcycle company to manufacture the Ascot-Pullin 500 and the Pullin-Groom light motorcycle. As an inventor, he had developed a number of helicopter engine patents in the 1920s, which were listed by the Douglas company.

The first Weir autogyro was the W.1 of 1933, powered by a Douglas 0-75 Dryad engine. The W (Weir) prefix was used on rotorcraft through to the Cierva W.14 Skeeter. The improved single-seat W.2, powered by a Weir 0-92 Flat Twin air-cooled engine, designed by Pullin and G. E. Walker, first flew in March 1934. The design had some stability problems, and the addition of tail surfaces led to the W.3, powered by a Weir Pixie four-cylinder in-line engine.

The W.3 included a Cierva "jump-start" design feature, in which the rotor was engaged to the Weir Pixie engine through a direct-drive shaft to generate lift without forward propulsion. Once airborne, drive from the engine was then

LEFT: **An improved tailplane assembly, with three fins, was fitted on the W.3 to overcome the stability problems that had been experienced on the W.2.**

LEFT: **The two-seat W.6 retained the outrigger configuration of the earlier Weir design. During testing, the helicopter attracted interest from the British military establishment. The pilot was Raymond Pullin, eldest son of the designer.**

changed to the tractor propeller for forward flight. This was the last autogyro manufactured by Weir. From 1938, the company concentrated on helicopters, which they believed had greater development potential, especially for carrying passengers.

The first helicopter design was the small, single-seat W.5 made in part from autogyro components. It had a plywood box-section outrigger on each side of the fuselage, with two-blade rotors on each hub. Powered by a Weir Four engine, cooled by a specially designed engine-driven blower unit, the W.5 was first flown at Dalrymple, Scotland, on June 7, 1938, with Raymond Pullin, the eldest son of Pullin, at the controls. This helicopter, the first in Britain to fly successfully, pioneered the now-standard helicopter safety feature of autorotation, in which the rotor can be disengaged from the engine in the event of power failure. The W.5 was controlled only by cyclic pitch, and there was no collective pitch; vertical control was achieved by varying rotor speed. The W.5 could be flown at up to 161kph/ 70mph. More than 100 flights were made between June 1938 and July 1939, at which point development was halted.

When Dr J. A. J. Bennett was chief technical officer of Cierva from 1936–39, he developed a rotary-wing design, the C.41. This was revived in April 1946 by the Fairey Aviation Company Limited, where Bennett became head of the rotary-wing aircraft division. The C.41 was developed as the Fairey Gyrodyne.

The W.6 design retained the outrigger configuration of the W.5, but was improved by using steel tubing to construct the fuselage and outriggers. A three-bladed rotor was mounted on each outrigger. The machine was powered by a de Havilland Gipsy VI engine. This pioneering two-seat helicopter first flew on October 27, 1939, and one of the early passengers was Sir (later Marshal of the Royal Air Force) Arthur Tedder, who at that time was Director General for Research in the Air Ministry. This was a clear indication of the level of official

interest in this helicopter, and in the military applications of rotary-wing craft in general. As World War II escalated, the Weir company ceased helicopter development to increase production of more vital equipment that would make a more immediate contribution to the war effort.

By 1944, however, the company was working on the design of the Cierva W.9, a large single-rotor helicopter that used jet thrust to counter torque effect. Like the earlier W.5, the W.9 did not have collective pitch and used rotor speed to control vertical movement. When the prototype crashed during testing in 1946, further development of the project ceased.

The Weir-Cierva team next produced the large and impressive W.11 Air Horse, first flown in December 1948. Proposed as a crop-dusting platform, among other uses, the helicopter was unusual in having three rotors mounted on outriggers, driven by a single Rolls-Royce Merlin engine housed in the fuselage. The largest helicopter of the time, the first W.11 crashed during testing, and the project was scrapped. As a result, G & J Weir Ltd decided to withdraw all funding, and all helicopter development plans were passed to Saunders-Roe (Saro), including those for the W.14 Skeeter. This machine is usually thought of as a Saro design, but was in fact the last of the Weir-Cierva helicopters.

RIGHT: **First flown in June 1938, the W.5 pioneered the autorotation facility that is now standard on helicopters. This allows a safe descent in the event of engine failure. Note the plywood box-section outriggers housing the driveshafts, which transfer power from the engine to the rotors.**

ABOVE AND RIGHT: **The experimental Rotachute was designed to enable paratroops to be deployed accurately in enemy territory. Towed into the air by a truck, the machine was tested extensively throughout 1942.**

Gyrogliders and rotorkites

A rotorkite, also known as a gyroglider, is a simple and unusual flying machine – essentially a towed, engineless autogyro in which the forward motion that turns the rotors is provided by a towing vehicle. Like an autogyro or helicopter, it relies on lift created by the rotors in order to fly. Considerable research into rotorkites and potential military applications was carried out during World War II, and one design, the Focke-Achgelis Fa 330, did see operational service with the German Navy.

German submarines sat low in the water and, as the crew could not see more than a few miles around even in perfect weather, were always at risk from fast-moving enemy warships. The Fa 330 Focke-Achgelis Bachstelze (wagtail) was developed to be towed by a winched cable in the air behind a U-boat, to extend the range of vision. By mid-1942, sea trials proved that the Fa 330 could work, but only the Type IX U-boat could tow the machine fast enough for flight, and only then in low-wind conditions.

The simple airframe consisted of two 6.35cm/2.5in diameter steel tubes forming an inverted "T". While one tube was the "fuselage" of the aircraft with the pilot's seat and instruments (altimeter, airspeed indicator and rotor tachometer), the other

tube served as the rotor mast. The pilot simply moved the control column for direct pitch and roll control, and used foot pedals to move the large rudder to control yaw. The rotor blades consisted of a steel spar supporting plywood ribs skinned with fabric-covered plywood.

When not assembled, the Fa 330 was stored in two long watertight compartments built into the U-boat's conning tower. One tube contained the blades and tail, and the other the fuselage. In calm conditions, four crewmen could assemble the entire aircraft on the deck of a submarine in just three minutes.

As the U-boat moved ahead, the airflow would begin to spin the rotor, resulting in autorotation, the movement of relative wind through the rotor blades which caused them to turn with enough speed to generate lift and carry the machine aloft. To speed up take-off, a deckhand could pull hard on a rope wrapped around a drum on the rotor hub to spin the rotor.

The Fa 330 was towed by a cable around 150m/492ft long, and "flew" 120m/394ft above the surface, where visibility was around 46km/29 miles compared to just under 10km/6 miles from the conning tower of a U-boat. Normal flight was 205rpm at a standard towing speed of 40kph/25mph, while a minimum

LEFT: **The Focke-Achgelis Fa 330 provided a simple solution to a serious problem facing German, and indeed all, wartime submarine commanders – the need to know what threats or targets may be over the horizon.**

speed of 27kph/17mph was required to maintain autorotation. The pilot talked to the submarine using an intercom system via a wire wrapped around the towing cable.

In the event of an attack that would cause the U-boat to dive, both the pilot and machine were expendable, although the pilot was equipped with a parachute. Allied air-cover was so good in the North Atlantic that only U-boats operating in the far southern parts of the Atlantic and the Indian Ocean deployed the Fa 330. Use of the Fa 330 assisted U-boat U-177 to intercept and sink the Greek cargo ship *Eithalia Mari* on August 6, 1943.

Meanwhile, in Britain, the talented Raoul Hafner was investigating alternative means of accurately deploying paratroopers. He led the rotorcraft team of the Airborne Forces Experimental Establishment (AFEE) at Ringway Aerodrome, now Manchester International Airport.

In October 1940, work began on the Rotachute, which was a simple steel tube frame where the pilot sat, open to the airstream, a two-blade 5m/15ft rotor, a rubber-mounted skid and a tapered fairing behind the pilot that stabilized the machine in flight. The self-inflating rear fairing was made entirely of rubberized fabric, typifying the budget approach to the design, which could have been produced cheaply in vast numbers. The rotor hub was rubber-mounted, which dampened vibration, and two-axis control was by a single lever fixed to the hub.

Tests with ever-larger models proved the concept, and one of the launch options considered was to release a number in a stream from the top of a large aircraft. The Rotachute itself weighed just 23kg/50lb and could carry 109kg/240lb, which could have included a soldier, a machine-gun, ammunition

ABOVE: **Simple to manufacture and easy to assemble, the Fa 330 was stored in containers on the outside of the U-boat conning tower.**

and a parachute. The size of the rotor made the Rotachute the smallest man-carrying vehicle capable of controlled flight built at that time. The first full-size test flights took place in early 1942, and refinements and improvements led to the Rotachute III that, by the end of 1942, was reaching altitudes of up to 1,189m/3,900ft and flight durations of up to 40 minutes. The Rotachute was never put into service.

The same team went on to develop the Rotabuggy, essentially a Jeep-type military vehicle combined with an autogyro. A 12m/41ft diameter rotor was attached, along with a tail assembly for stability in flight. Trials began in November 1943, and the Rotabuggy was eventually to reach glide speeds of 72kph/45mph. Free flight trials after being towed aloft by a Whitley bomber saw the machine reach a speed of 113kph/70mph at an altitude of 122m/400ft for up to ten minutes. Despite progress, the development of large vehicle-carrying assault gliders rendered the Rotabuggy obsolete, and the project was abandoned. The war ended before the concept of a Rotatank could be developed. This very heavy machine with a rotor diameter of 46m/152ft would have required two aircraft in tandem to tow it, but the design never progressed beyond the prototype stage.

ABOVE LEFT AND LEFT:
The Rotachute team went on to develop the Rotabuggy, a Jeep-type vehicle fitted with a rotor. A Rotatank concept never saw service.

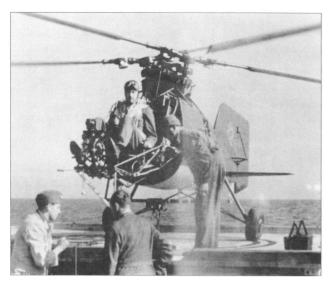

ABOVE: The single engine of the Focke-Achgelis Fa 223 Drache (dragon) drove two three-blade rotors. LEFT: The Flettner Fl 282 Kolibri entered German Navy service, and was flown off the gun turret of a German warship.

Helicopters in World War II

It is an often overlooked fact of aviation history that a small number of helicopter types did see active service, on both sides during World War II, and were far more than just experimental machines. The service of the Sikorsky R-4 is described elsewhere in this book, but two German designs are worthy of mention here.

Germany explored and developed a number of helicopter design beyond the ubiquitous Cierva-derived autogyros that many nations utilized in some form. Impressed by the potential of the Focke-Wulf Fw 61, the German Air Ministry instructed Henrich Focke to develop the Fw 61 design into one that could carry a 700kg/1,500lb payload. Having established the new company Focke-Achgelis with pilot Gerd Achgelis, they designed an enlarged Fw 61, initially designated Fa 226 Hornisse (hornet), that could carry up to six passengers. This design, the first-ever transport helicopter, was ordered by German national airline Lufthansa in 1938, before its first flight. In 1939, the type was then redesignated Fa 223, and entered military service as the Drache (dragon).

Although it retained the twin-rotor arrangement of the Fw 61, the Fa 223 had a fully enclosed cabin and freight/luggage bay, and was powered by a single BMW Bramo engine mounted in the centre of the tubular-steel airframe. The V1 prototype's first untethered flight took place in August 1940, and testing showed it to have the best performance of any helicopter to that date (it had a top speed of 182kph/113mph, a climb rate of 528m/1732ft per minute, and attained an altitude of 7,100m/23,300ft). The Fa 223 Drache was, however, a long way from entering front-line service, as the rulebook for operating helicopters effectively had yet to be written. Although numerous variants were proposed, just one multi-purpose version was developed. The pilot and observer sat side-by-side, and two steel tube outriggers extended from the fuselage side to carry the two non-overlapping three-bladed rotors.

BELOW: The Sikorsky R-4 was the world's first large-scale, mass-produced helicopter, and the first helicopter to enter service with the US military, as well as the Royal Air Force and Royal Navy.

Production was consistently disrupted by Allied bombing, but the type's capability was proven by demonstration flights, including the lifting of a complete Fiesler Storch (stork) aircraft and operations over 1,600m/5,200ft above sea level and over great distances. In January 1945, three Fa 223s were assigned to the Luftwaffe's only wartime operational helicopter unit, Transportstaffel (Transport Squadron) 40 (TS/40) in Bavaria – two of these pioneering machines were seized by the Allies at the end of the war, and these or derivative machines were flown post-war by the USA, Britain, France and Czechoslovakia.

The Flettner Fl 282 Kolibri (hummingbird) was developed by German aeronautical scientist and helicopter pioneer Anton Flettner. Having built his first helicopter in 1930, Flettner produced the Fl 265 that first flew in 1939, and from this developed the Fl 282, designed from the outset for military use. Intended to carry a pilot and an observer, the design was judged to have so much potential for naval use that no fewer than 30 prototypes and 15 pre-production machines were ordered simultaneously to accelerate development and production.

The pilot sat in front of the rotors in a typically open cockpit while the observer sat in a single compartment aft of the rotors, facing backwards. Small, fast and agile, Luftwaffe fighter pilots found it hard to keep the small helicopter in their gunsights in mock attacks. The Fl 282 could land on a ship, even in heavy seas. Mass production was ordered, but Allied bombing of the factories meant that only the prototypes were produced. Nevertheless, 24 of these aircraft entered service with the German Navy in 1943 for escort service, flying off the gun turret of a ship to spot submarines, and to perform resupply missions in even the worst weather conditions. The Fl 282 was designed so that the rotor blades and landing gear could be removed and the helicopter could be stowed on a U-boat, although it is not known if this happened. This pioneering military helicopter served in the Baltic, North Aegean and the Mediterranean. Only three of these helicopters survived the war, as the rest of the machines were destroyed to prevent capture by the Allies. Two of the surviving machines went to the USA and Britain, while the third went to the Soviet Union. Anton Flettner moved to the USA after the war, and became chief designer at the Kaman Aircraft Corporation.

ABOVE: **The Doblhoff WNF 342 was developed for the German Navy. The type was powered by a petrol engine which drove a small propeller and an air compressor to supply air to the pulse jets on the tips of the rotor.**

ABOVE: **A Flettner Fl 282 V – one of 30 prototype machines built.**
BELOW: **This production version of the Fl 282 was fitted with a rear cockpit to carry an observer.**

Igor Sikorsky

gor Ivanovich Sikorsky (1889–1972) was one of aviation's true pioneers, whose talents led to extraordinary developments in both fixed-wing and rotary aviation. He was born in Kiev on May 25, 1889, to a mother and father who were respectively a physician and psychology professor. He was absorbed by science and aviation from an early age, and his parents encouraged his interests. As a boy he built and flew model aircraft and helicopters, while hearing of the trailblazing work of people such as the Wright brothers. He attended the Imperial Russian Naval Academy, and went on to study engineering in Paris and then mechanical engineering in Kiev. His later studies were, however, curtailed by his passion for all things aviation, which took him back to Paris to learn more of the embryonic science of aeronautics.

Back in Kiev, he built his first helicopters, but the two machines failed to lift their own weight. Frustrated by the lack of available engine power and the limitations of his knowledge of rotary flight at that time, Sikorsky then turned to fixed-wing aircraft. Success came swiftly, and having been appointed

head of the aviation subsidiary of the Russian Baltic Railroad Car Works, he designed the world's first four-engine aircraft – Russky Vityaz. Sikorsky's ambitious design included an enclosed cabin, lavatory, upholstered chairs and an exterior walkway around the nose, where braver passengers could take an inflight stroll. An even-larger aircraft followed in 1913, the Ilya Muromets, of which military versions saw action in World War I – it was the first strategic bomber. Sikorsky moved to France when the Bolshevik Revolution gripped Russia, and was soon at work on a bomber aircraft. This was never built as the war ended so, eager to find an outlet for his skills and passion, Sikorsky moved to the USA in 1919.

He struggled to find a position and then, in 1923, with financial backing from fellow immigrants who knew of his reputation from Russia, the Sikorsky Aircraft Corporation was born. The company produced a series of pioneering, successful, record-breaking flying boats that were used on routes around the world. In 1929, the Sikorsky Company became a subsidiary of United Aircraft & Transport Corporation, the predecessor of United Technologies. Sikorsky, now firmly established in the industry, returned to the challenge of helicopters. Since his early experiments almost three decades earlier, rotary craft understanding had advanced considerably due to experimental work in many other countries around the world. Designers now had a good understanding of the basic principles, including the workings of transmission and reduction gear boxes, and the collective and cyclic pitch required

RIGHT: **The Sikorsky XR-4 hovering at the Stratford, Connecticut plant during its first flight. Note the original horizontal-mounted tail rotor and open space frame-type structure for the aircaft.**

LEFT: The Sikorsky S-52 was operated by the US Navy and the US Marine Corps as the HOSS-1. The HOSS-1G was operated by the US Coast Guard.

to control vertical and horizontal flight respectively. Sikorsky appreciated the vital importance of these dynamic components, and had the genius to build on these findings and developments. Over the years he had continued to record and patent ideas for possible designs and, in 1938, United Aircraft backed his plans to build a new helicopter, the Vought-Sikorsky VS-300. The airframe was manufactured from welded steel tubing and was not covered. The cockpit was open and not fitted with instruments.

On September 14, 1939, Sikorsky, wearing his trademark Homburg hat, flew the tethered VS-300 a few feet off the ground, and gave the world the first practical single-rotor helicopter. It is also interesting to note that the design was developed purely with company money and had no government support. Breaking new ground in helicopter development was not easy, and the design was far from right first time – the vibrating, clattering machine was nicknamed "Igor's Nightmare" by some of the ground crew for good reason. The 8.5m/28ft three-blade main rotor and the first anti-torque rotor at the rear, for example, were not sufficient to allow the pilot complete control. However, after a long process of methodical refinements, modifications and experimentation with a number of configurations, Sikorsky settled on a single main rotor with cyclic pitch control and an anti-torque tail rotor.

By 1941, the VS-300 had broken all helicopter records, and the design was to characterize Sikorsky helicopters henceforth and effectively set the template for the vast majority of all the world's helicopters. The success of the VS-300 led to military contracts, and in 1943 large-scale manufacture of the R-4 (derived from the VS-300) made it the world's first production helicopter. The company went on to produce the R-5, R-6 and the S-51 series, and were soon famous as a specialist helicopter manufacturer. Igor Sikorsky received countless academic, scientific and industry awards acknowledging his remarkable contribution to aviation. He continued to work long after others would have retired, and died at home on October 26, 1972, at the age of 83, after working a normal day at his office.

BELOW: In 1941, Sikorsky fitted floats (also called pontoons) to the Sikorsky VS-300, making the first practical amphibious helicopter and opening up another area of application.

LEFT: The slender greenhouse-type cockpit of the Sikorsky S-51 was a distinguishing feature of the machine. The type was the first Western helicopter to be widely exported.

Charles H. Kaman

Charles Huron Kaman (1919–2011), in common with many aviation pioneers, was passionate about making flying models as a teenager, and he set national duration records for hand-launched model gliders. His dream of becoming a professional pilot was thwarted by deafness in one ear, so the young Charles decided to enter into aviation by another route. He graduated top of his aeronautical engineering class in 1940, and went to work for Hamilton Standard in the propeller performance unit. It was there that he met Igor Sikorsky, and was inspired by what he saw of his pioneering work with helicopters.

All designers face the challenge of the helicopter's fundamental stability and control problems. Kaman's simple goal was to make helicopters safer and easier to fly. Working at home in the evenings and at weekends, Kaman devised an innovative solution to the problem of torque. He developed an all-new concept of rotor control based on servo-flaps – small tabs added to the trailing edge of each rotor blade to give the pilot the ability to change the angle of attack of the blades and improve stability. He also proposed a unique arrangement in which twin rotors were intermeshed – this would generate increased lift and eliminate the need for a tail rotor, as torque would no longer be an issue.

By 1945, he was ready to strike out on his own, and with finance of just $2,000 from two friends, he founded the Kaman Aircraft (later Corporation) in his garage at his mother's home in West Hartford, Connecticut. From these modest beginnings, Kaman built a billion-dollar company, producing helicopters with an enviable reputation that went on to set numerous performance and altitude records.

RIGHT: **The experimental K-125 was Kaman's first helicopter, and utilized intermeshing rotors as well as the patented servo-flap rotor system. First flown in January 1947, it led to a series of production helicopters.**

ABOVE: **Charles H. Kaman with the test rig he built to run his first full-scale rotor assembly. A gifted engineer, Kaman patented his unique servo-flap rotor control system while he was still a young man.**

Kaman's first helicopter, the K-125, was an intermeshing, contra-rotating twin rotor, and first left the ground on January 15, 1947, during a short tethered flight. Within a few months, the K-125 had its first free flight, in which the test pilot took the helicopter straight up to an altitude of 15m/50ft and was soon executing figures-of-eight in the air at speeds of up to 97kmh/60mph. Subsequent developments led directly to the hugely successful HH-43 Huskie helicopter, which flew with the US Navy, US Marine Corps, US Air Force and a number of overseas air arms. In December 1951, a modified K-225 became the first helicopter to be powered by a gas-turbine engine.

Kaman's later SH-2 Seasprite multi-mission naval helicopter which, interestingly, did not have intermeshing rotors, flew more than 1,000,000 hours in service with the USN

LEFT: The HOK-1 Huskie was operated by the USMC during the Vietnam War for liaison, observation and rescue missions. ABOVE: Many versions of the Kaman HH-43 Huskie served with the US military.

in anti-submarine warfare, anti-shipping and search and rescue. Kaman's designs proved very popular with the US military, due in no small part to the reputation that the helicopters had for performance and quality. In 1954, Kaman developed the first twin-turbine helicopter; in 1957, he designed and produced the first electrically powered helicopter drone. Kaman was always interested in business diversification and, among other successful ventures, he used his knowledge of music and plastics to produce the famous Ovation series of guitars, and formed the Kaman Music Corporation.

Charles Kaman received many awards and distinctions for his contributions to aviation, including the National Aeronautical Society Wright Brothers Memorial Trophy, the National Medal of Technology and the US Department of Defense (DoD) Distinguished Public Service Medal. He was inducted into the United States Hall of Honor at the National Museum of Naval Aviation, and is an Honorary Fellow of the Royal Aeronautical Society in Britain.

The HH-43 Huskie was flown on more rescue missions during the Vietnam War than all other helicopters combined, and Kaman was especially proud of the fact that his helicopters had been used to save an estimated 15,000 lives in the second half of the 20th century.

LEFT: In 1992, Kaman introduced the K-1200 K-MAX, the first helicopter specifically designed for repetitive medium-lift operations. Two K-MAX aircraft have been modified for unmanned operations to conduct military resupply or humanitarian missions in high-threat environments.

Frank N. Piasecki

Frank N. Piasecki, pilot, aeronautical and mechanical engineer, and pioneer in the development of transport helicopters and vertical lift aircraft, founded the hugely influential Piasecki Aircraft Corporation and Piasecki Helicopter Corporation.

Piasecki was born in Philadelphia, USA, on October 24, 1919, the only son of Polish immigrants. After school, he went on to study mechanical engineering at the University of Pennsylvania, before earning his Bachelor of Science degree from the Guggenhiem School of Aeronautics of New York University in 1940. Prior to attending university, Piasecki had been employed by the Kellett Autogryo Company and the Aero Service Corporation, both based in Philadelphia. After he graduated, he became a designer at Platt-LePage Aircraft Corporation, and then later worked as aerodynamicist for the Edward G. Budd Manufacturing Company, Aircraft Division.

ABOVE: **The Piasecki HRP-1 Rescuer was named the "Flying Banana" by aircrews, due to the distinctive shape of the machine.**

During 1940, the 21-year-old Piasecki, along with other fledgling engineers from the University of Pennsylvania, founded the PV Engineering Forum, which they ran in addition to their day jobs. The Forum ultimately became what is known today as the Rotorcraft Division of the Boeing Company. Piasecki, always keen to be in the thick of testing and leading by example, flew the first PV Engineering Forum helicopter, the PV-2, on April 11, 1943. The PV-2 was only the second successful helicopter to fly in the United States, so Piasecki was a pioneer of the truest kind. This trail-blazing single-seat, single-rotor helicopter with anti-torque tail rotor used full cyclic rotor control with dynamically balanced blades, and is

LEFT: **The PV-3 was procured as the HRP-1 Rescuer by the USN, USMC and the USCG. The airframe was fabric-covered, and the machine was powered by a Pratt & Whitney R-1340-AN-1 radial piston engine.**

now preserved by the National Air and Space Museum of the Smithsonian Institution in Washington, DC.

The technical achievement of this pioneering flight attracted the attention of the US Navy, who were aware of the potential that helicopters had for naval operations. The USN awarded Piasecki a contract for the construction of his ambitious design for a large tandem rotor helicopter capable of carrying heavy loads internally. In March 1945, just 13 months later, again with the intrepid Piasecki at the controls, the world's first successful tandem rotor helicopter, the XHRP-1, took to the air. This machine, nicknamed the "Flying Banana", was the first-ever helicopter designed for the US Navy, and it was the forerunner of the modern tandem rotor helicopters in service. There were a number of people experimenting with helicopter designs at this time, but few got it as right as Frank Piasecki who, in the XHRP-1, created a helicopter capable of carrying as many passengers as similarly powered fixed-wing aircraft, and three times the weight of any helicopter flying at the time.

Piasecki played a large part in proving the helicopter to be an equal of fixed-wing aircraft and not a poor relation. His innovative tandem rotor design is considered to be pivotal in transforming the helicopter from at worst a novelty, at best a small aerial observation platform, into an aircraft with extensive military and civilian applications. The tandem rotor configuration was Piasecki's signature, and led to the development of the CH-46, the US Marine Corps primary assault helicopter for four decades, and the mighty Chinook, which continues to play a front-line role for numerous air arms around the world.

In 1946, the PV Engineering Forum became the Piasecki Helicopter Corporation, with Piasecki as both President and Chairman of the Board of Directors. Piasecki initiated further design studies that led to remarkable production transport helicopters including the HRP Rescuer series, HUP Retriever series, H-21 and H-16.

The Piasecki Helicopter Corporation was sold to the Boeing Airplane Company and its name was changed to the Vertol Division, but in the late 1950s, Piasecki and his fellow original founders formed the Piasecki Aircraft Corporation (PiAC) to continue research work on new Vertical Take-Off and Landing (VTOL) aircraft. PiAC developed a series of unique

experimental aircraft, including the Sea-Bat, an omni-directional VTOL Remotely Piloted Vehicle (RPV). By having two pairs of tilting propellers with no cyclic control but with dual differential collective control, the Sea-Bat was omni-directional.

Piasecki was the first man to qualify as a helicopter pilot with the US Civil Aeronautics Administration prior to receiving a fixed-wing pilot's licence. He did most of the test flying on his early helicopter designs, and was awarded numerous patents and awards for his work as a helicopter pioneer.

Frank Piasecki, a true pioneer in the vertical aviation industry, and one of the original inventors of the helicopter, died on February 11, 2008, aged 88 years.

ABOVE: **Piasecki later developed the 16H-1 Pathfinder high-speed compound aircraft. It was part helicopter, part fixed-wing aircraft, and was powered by a tail-mounted ducted propeller ring tail.**

Soviet pioneers

The first Soviet-designed autogyro was the KASKR-1 built by the pioneering designers Nikolay Ilyich Kamov and Nikolai K. Skrzhinsky. It made its maiden flight on September 25, 1929, with I. V. Mikheyev as pilot and Kamov in the rear cockpit. While their first design resembled a Cierva C.8 autogyro, in 1930 the designers produced the KASKR-2, based on the KASKR-1. Members of the Air Force Scientific and Research Institute participated in the evaluation of this autogyro, which made around 80 test flights. Among the team working on the autogyro was the gifted Mikhail Mil, who was a student of the Novocherkassk Polytechnical Institute and a protégé of Kamov.

In 1931, Kamov began working with the dedicated autogyro design group as part of the Central Aero and Hydrodynamics Institute (TsAGI) for Soviet autogyro development. Within two years he was heading one of the brigades that made up the group, while Mil was heading up another.

Progress in the work on autogyros within TsAGI, in turn, had a noticeable influence on the speed of achievements in helicopter design within the Institute. In 1932, the first Soviet experimental helicopter, the TsAGI 1-EA, a single-rotor machine with a rigid main rotor, was developed and flown to altitudes in excess of 600m/1,969ft. This design was followed by a number of improved experimental helicopters.

While autogyro research aided helicopter development, the experience gained from helicopters in turn influenced autogyro design. The A-7 which first flew in 1937 owed much to the helicopter experience gained within TsAGI. At the beginning of 1940, aircraft factory No. 290 was established and tasked with autogyro production with Kamov as chief designer and director, while Mil was appointed as his deputy.

The industrial, economic and military pressure caused by the war highlighted the relative importance of the autogyro compared to bomber and ground-attack aircraft, however, so production was terminated. A massive amount of rotary aircraft

TOP: **The Mil V-12/Mil-12 that first flew in July 1968 is the largest helicopter ever built. Only two prototypes were built, and this is the second, preserved at the Russian Air Force Museum at Monino.** ABOVE: **The Kamov Ka-22 Vintokryl was a turboshaft-powered convertiplane that first appeared in public in July 1961. The engines mounted at the wingtips powered both rotors and propellers.**

design expertise had nevertheless already been accumulated, including main rotor blades with tubular steel spars, rotor head with articulated blade attachments, automatic flapping damping of the rotor blades and a system for rotor thrust control. Mil later stated that they were just one step away from creating a viable helicopter, and just needed to perfect a gearbox to transmit the drive from the engine to the main rotor. As World War II neared its end, it was the helicopter with its ability to hover, fly very slowly if required and land and take-off vertically that captured the imagination of the military of the victorious nations, including the Soviet Union – the autogyro was effectively forgotten, and Kamov and Mil concentrated on helicopter designs.

The Kamov OKB (design bureau) was established in 1945, with specific responsibility for developing a contra-rotating rotor system for helicopters. Kamov developed a way of successfully mounting two rotors on one mast. As each rotor moved in

LEFT: **The Kamov Ka-10 (NATO identifier Hat) was developed from the Ka-8 as a light observation helicopter. An improved version, the Ka-10M – fitted with two tailfins and the more powerful Ivchenko AI-4G piston engine – was built and first flown in 1950.**

opposite directions, this innovative solution neutralized the torque effect of the rotor shaft and removed the requirement for a stabilizing tail rotor.

Kamov first used the system on a production helicopter in the Ka-15, which entered Soviet Navy service in the early 1950s. The large Ka-18 was developed from the Ka-15, and saw service with Aeroflot. The coaxial rotor system was to be a signature feature on most of Kamov's designs. In 1947, Mil was appointed to head the Helicopter Laboratory at TsAGI. This later became the Mil Moscow Helicopter Plant,

designing 15 types of helicopter in over 200 variants, which went on to be built in their thousands. It is estimated that every fourth helicopter in the world today is of Mil origin. Mil died in 1970, but the OKB continued using his name. In 1971, his Mil Mi-12 won the Sikorsky Prize as the world's most powerful helicopter.

Kamov continued to lead his business until his death in 1973. Proud of his company's achievements, he set up a company museum in 1971. Between them, Kamov and Mil exerted a profound and long-lasting influence on the world of aviation.

LEFT: **The Kamov Ka-226 (NATO identifier Hoodlum) is a small, twin-engined utility helicopter. In place of a conventional cabin, the type has an interchangeable mission cargo pod.**

Arthur Young (Bell Aircraft Corporation)

Arthur Middleton Young (1905–95) was a brilliant and extraordinary character. He was an inventor, cosmologist, philosopher, astrologer and a helicopter pioneer. From an early age, Young grappled with philosophical matters such as the nature of reality, and decided that to develop the mental tools needed for this demanding intellectual pursuit he would first study mathematics and engineering. In his final year at Princeton University, Young devoted himself to philosophy and devising a comprehensive theory of the universe. Unable to develop his theory to his own satisfaction, a frustrated Young decided instead to set himself a goal in which solutions could be tested. Young visited the US Patent Office to consider areas of research that might interest him, including television and 3D film. However, it was the development of the helicopter that caught his attention

ABOVE: **In the Bell 47, Arthur Young and his team created the world's first commercially viable helicopter and a design classic. Numerous manufacturers had previously rejected his designs.**

– up to that point these machines had not been perfected, and Young was confident that research and testing could provide the solution. He devoted the next 19 years to working on helicopter design and development.

After graduation in 1927, Young returned to the family estate in Radnor, Pennsylvania, where for the next 12 years he worked alone on developing and perfecting helicopter design. Young was a wealthy young man, so was not driven to cut corners or rush his development because of some financial imperative. At that time, helicopters were still considered to be something of a novelty, and no manufacturer would have supported all his years of research and experimentation. As a boy he had been a gifted and prolific modelmaker, and he tested his theories on a succession of model helicopters built in a barn converted into an aeronautical laboratory.

The models were made from hobby store supplies and were powered by elastic bands or small electric motors. By 1937, Young was using a 20hp outboard motor to power complex geared rotor assemblies. He experienced many technical failures but, as he said in a later interview, "the experience gained in calculating stress and building parts proved invaluable". He also appreciated the need for trial and error in trying to master helicopter stability: "this meant I had to have flights and have wrecks". Young wanted to solve as many technical issues as possible using models. This was how he had a major breakthrough and developed the stabilizer bar that kept his

LEFT: **The Bell 47B was a record-breaking model which is now preserved by the Smithsonian Air and Space Museum. The machine was used in service for 57 years.**

LEFT: **The prototype of the XHSL-1 (Bell Model 61) first flew in March 1953, and was designed to meet an urgent US Navy requirement for an anti-submarine warfare helicopter. Development problems resulted in limited production and service.**

LEFT: **The Bell XV-3 (Bell Model 200) tilt-rotor aircraft was first flown in August 1955, and featured an engine mounted in the fuselage with drive shafts to transfer power to two-bladed rotor assemblies mounted on the wingtips.**

model machines and then full-size helicopters in stable flight. Young also developed a functioning remote control system that enabled him to fly the model around and out of his barn.

A number of manufacturers had turned down the chance to view Young's findings, until a friend's chance remark got him an appointment in 1941 with the Bell Aircraft Company in Buffalo, New York. Having presented his data and his models, Bell agreed to build two full-scale prototypes. Young and his small team were given a facility remote from the main Bell plant, where they could develop and test the revolutionary machine in secret.

The first prototype Bell 30 was built in just six months, and Arthur Young himself, though not a pilot, took the controls for the first tethered flights. On June 26, 1943, the tethering cable was removed, and pilot Floyd Carlson took the Model 30 on its maiden flight. Igor Sikorsky visited the plant to see Young's machine for himself, and when the Bell 30 gave public demonstrations, it caused a sensation, flying inside large buildings and demonstrating precision

manoeuvres in front of stunned crowds. As the design was refined and World War II was drawing to an end, Bell Aircraft saw the helicopter as a way of keeping their peacetime order books full, so were keen to develop commercially viable helicopter designs.

Having perfected experimental machines, Young's team then focused on the design which became the Bell 47. On March 8, 1946, the type received Helicopter Type Certificate H-1 as the world's first commercial helicopter. The Type 47 had a 27-year manufacturing history, and over 5,000 military and commercial machines were built in 20 versions in the US and under licence overseas. It was considered to be such an iconic and influential design that an example was added to the permanent collection of New York's Museum of Modern Art in 1984.

Young felt that he had found the solution in developing a viable helicopter, so he left Bell in 1947, returned to philosophy, and founded the Institute for the Study of Consciousness in Berkeley.

LEFT: **The Hiller YROE-1 Rotorcycle was a single-seat ultralight foldable self-rescue and observation helicopter, designed in 1953 to a military requirement.**

Stanley Hiller

Stanley Hiller Jr was born in San Francisco in 1924 and showed an early flair for technical innovation and business, having designed and produced a range of small, fast model racing cars powered by model aircraft engines. By the age of 17, his company Hiller Industries was producing 350 miniature cars each month, and turned over $100,000 a year. To improve the strength of his model cars, Hiller invented a die-casting machine that increased the strength of aluminium castings used in their construction. During his short academic career at the University of California at Berkeley, Hiller's technical innovation came to the attention of the US military, and Hiller Industries was soon producing aluminium parts for fighter aircraft. Ever the businessman, in his spare time Hiller designed cast aluminium kitchen utensils to keep his small factory busy when war-related orders were completed.

Hiller's father Stanley Sr was also an engineer and inventor who had built and flown his own aircraft in 1910, so when Hiller was asked to reflect on his remarkable achievements from an

ABOVE: **The Hiller UH-5 that led to the Hiller 360 was initially unstable in trials until it was fitted with the patented Rotormatic Control System – two small paddles which acted as a control rotor.**

early age, he said: "I was fortunate in my choice of a father." Hiller had been considering helicopter designs for some time. As a 15-year-old he had read about Igor Sikorsky's rotary wing experiments, and believed he had a solution to the torque-induced instability that plagued early helicopter designs. He believed that contra-rotating coaxial rotors were the answer and would eliminate the need for a tail rotor and associated complex drive mechanism. The teenager tested the theory by dropping a model coaxial helicopter from his father's ninth-storey office window, and proved his theory. His determination to develop the coaxial concept drew him away from university, and he focused on the production of a 45kg/100lb model which, when demonstrated, convinced the US military to commission Hiller to build a full-size coaxial helicopter, the XH-44 Hiller-Copter. Although he had never flown a helicopter before, or even seen one fly, on July 4, 1944, Hiller conducted the test flight of the XH-44, an all-metal single-seat helicopter powered by a 90hp petrol engine, coaxial rotors and no tail rotor. This first successful flight of a helicopter in the western US and the first-ever flight of a coaxial helicopter in the US made Hiller famous. He was hailed in the international press and became the youngest person to receive the Fawcett Aviation Award for major contributions to the advancement of aviation.

The Hiller business grew, and was associated with the giant Kaiser Company for a time. In 1945, he formed United Helicopters and focused on the post-war commercial helicopter market with the Hiller UH-4 Commuter helicopter, a two-seat personal helicopter with coaxial rotors.

Hiller then developed the Rotormatic Control System, which reverted to a single rotor that achieved stability with a greatly simplified tail-rotor configuration. This design was the basis of the influential Hiller 360, only the third helicopter certified by the US Civil Aeronautics Administration (CAA). By now operating under the name of Hiller Aircraft Company, it was the first company in the US to produce helicopters without military sponsorship, his backers sharing his view that the machine would revolutionize utility operations in,

RIGHT: **On July 4, 1944, Hiller flew his XH-44 design and himself into aviation history – performing the very first flight of a coaxial helicopter in the USA.**

among other markets, agriculture, crop spraying and rescue. Worldwide marketing led to orders from the French, who ordered the production version, the UH-12, for medical evacuation in the Indo-China war, and the type proved very capable under difficult jungle conditions. Hiller had been urging the US Army to consider the UH-12, and the outbreak of the Korean War finally led to large orders. Hiller Aircraft was soon delivering a helicopter a day for the Korean front line, and in US military service the type was designated the OH-23 Raven.

Stanley Hiller was a gifted leader who encouraged creativity in his team, so Hiller Aircraft had the reputation as the people to go to who could make often demanding operational requirements a reality. The OH-23 series became the first helicopter of any type to be approved for 1,000 hours of operation between major overhauls. As early as 1947, Hiller's creative group had experimented with rotor systems that tilted forward for higher speed horizontal flight, and the company was an early pioneer in pure jet lift concepts. By 1951, the company was flying the two-seat Hornet powered by ramjets (designed by the company) on the rotor blade tips.

Hiller Aircraft Corporation's imagination seemed to know no bounds, and other projects included the Hiller Flying Platform for the US Army, using ducted propellers to lift its operator, who only needed to lean in the direction he wanted to go. The Hiller XROE-1 Rotorcycle was an ultra-light one-man helicopter that could be parachuted behind enemy lines, assembled in nine minutes and take off to fly like a standard helicopter. In 1956, Hiller developed a high-speed vertical take-off and landing (VTOL) aircraft to transport troops and equipment into inaccessible combat locations. The tilt-wing X-18 was fitted with a wing that could pivot through 90 degrees so that the propellers would act like helicopter rotors. Although no orders resulted, the data generated were vital for later VTOL research projects.

ABOVE: **The Hiller YH-32 Hornet was powered by Hiller HRJ-2B ram jet units mounted on the tips of the rotor blades. A total of 14 were built for the US Army.**

In 1968, Stanley Hiller merged Hiller Aircraft into what became the Fairchild Hiller Corporation, and left aviation to set up a what was to become a hugely successful management consultancy that turned ailing companies around. He died aged 81 on April 20, 2006.

RIGHT: **The Fairchild Hiller FH-1100 light helicopter was designed for the US Army Light Observation Helicopter (LOH) competition. A Hughes design was chosen, but the type was successfully marketed by Hiller as the FH-1100 civilian helicopter.**

Sikorsky R-4 Hoverfly

The Vought-Sikorsky VS-316 was developed from the VS-300 and, under the US Army Air Forces (USAAF) system for Rotorcraft, was designated as the XR-4. The machine was first flown on January 13, 1942, and was delivered to the USAAF for evaluation on May 30, 1942. The R-4 was flown operationally during World War II over the jungles of the Burmese border region and areas of the South Pacific. The type entered service with the Royal Air Force as the R-4 Hoverfly. Many of these aircraft were to be passed to the Royal Navy to train Fleet Air Arm pilots to fly helicopters.

RIGHT: **This cutaway of the Sikorsky R-4 clearly shows the tubular steel rear fuselage and tail boom structure. In early models, as a weight-saving measure, these were simply covered with doped and painted fabric in the same way as most World War I aircraft. Even the rotor blades on the early R-4s were fabric-covered.**

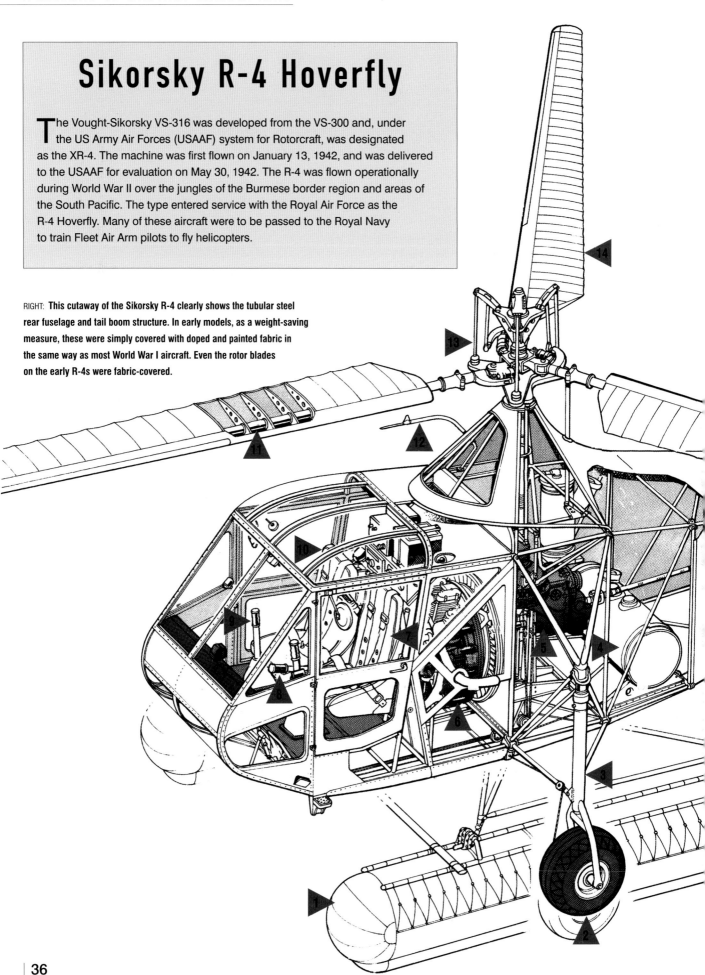

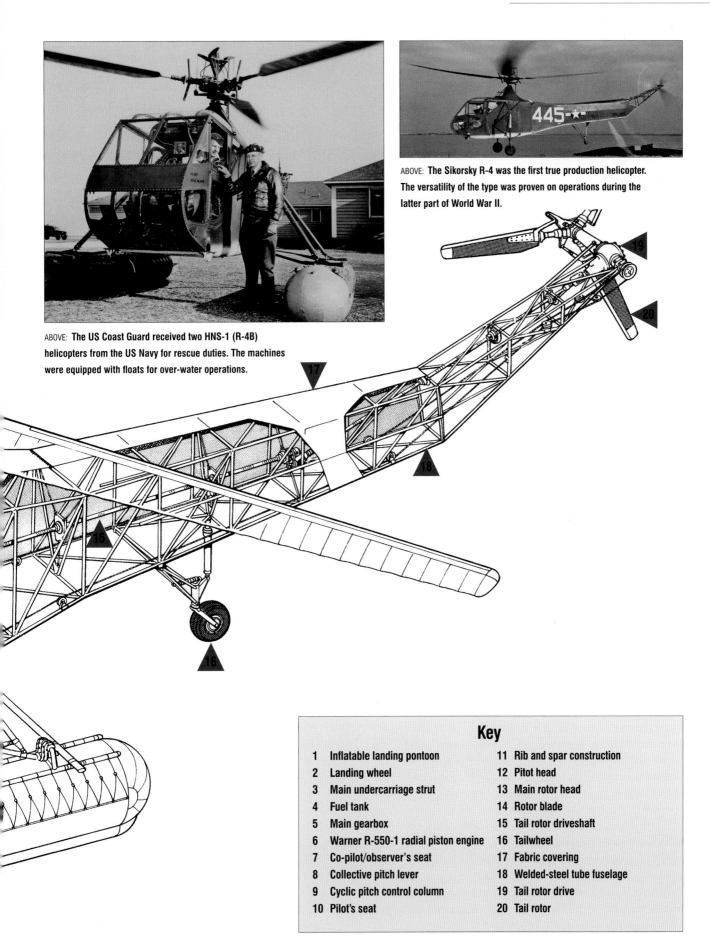

ABOVE: The Sikorsky R-4 was the first true production helicopter. The versatility of the type was proven on operations during the latter part of World War II.

ABOVE: The US Coast Guard received two HNS-1 (R-4B) helicopters from the US Navy for rescue duties. The machines were equipped with floats for over-water operations.

Key

1	Inflatable landing pontoon	11	Rib and spar construction
2	Landing wheel	12	Pitot head
3	Main undercarriage strut	13	Main rotor head
4	Fuel tank	14	Rotor blade
5	Main gearbox	15	Tail rotor driveshaft
6	Warner R-550-1 radial piston engine	16	Tailwheel
7	Co-pilot/observer's seat	17	Fabric covering
8	Collective pitch lever	18	Welded-steel tube fuselage
9	Cyclic pitch control column	19	Tail rotor drive
10	Pilot's seat	20	Tail rotor

LEFT: **The Sikorsky H-19 Chickasaw first flew in November 1949, and after rapid development entered operational service. The US Army's 6th Transportation Helicopter Company (THC) was equipped with 12 of the type, and arrived in Korea during March 1953. The machines were used for light transport and casualty evacuation.**

The Korean War

In early August 1950, when US Marine Corps forces were rushed into action to help defend the Pusan perimeter against a North Korean assault, their Brigade Commander was flown in a Marine Observation Squadron 6 (VMO-6) Sikorsky HO3S-1 helicopter to assess the terrain, find a location for a command post and visit unit commanders. Although British, US and German forces were all operating helicopters by the end of World War II, helicopters were still seen as something of a novelty, and critics focused on their limitations rather than their many unique strengths. The US military's use of helicopters in the Korean War (1950–53) saw the type prove beyond doubt to be a vital element in the inventory of any military force.

Four main helicopter types were used in the Korean War, some in a number of different versions serving with different arms of the US forces – the Sikorsky H-5 and H-19, the Bell H-13 and the Hiller H-23.

The Sikorsky H-5/HO3S was a four-seat utility helicopter used by the US Air Force, US Navy and US Marine Corps during the Korean War. First into action were HO3S helicopters, from the aircraft carriers USS *Valley Forge* (CV-45) and USS *Philippine Sea* (CV-47), positioned offshore to support the retreating UN troops. These machines operated as plane guards to recover aircrew from the sea in the event of a landing or take-off accident.

Helicopters were also assigned to USN cruisers and battleships, and began to be used for spotting and directing the fall of the ships' big gun shells on land; this dramatically boosted accuracy and effectiveness. The HO3S was also used for mine spotting. The USAF 3rd Air Rescue Squadron (ARS),

based in Japan, possessed nine H-5s at the beginning of the war, and they were soon in use evacuating casualties. These helicopters were also being used to rescue downed aircrew from the sea, and in many cases snatching them back to safety under the very noses of the enemy. This hazardous form of mission resulted in the loss of a number of Sikorsky helicopters and their crews to enemy fire.

ABOVE: **The Sikorsky H-5, fitted with two external stretcher-carrying pods, enabled the US military to transport wounded troops back from the front line for treatment. The type also provided a new means of extracting personnel from behind enemy lines or from the sea before being captured.**

LEFT: **A Bell H-13 Sioux with personnel of a Mobile Army Surgical Hospital (MASH).** BELOW: **A Sikorsky H-19 Chickasaw operated by the US Army is being used to deliver ammunition to a hilltop artillery position.**

The number of helicopters available in Korea far outstripped demand, and commanders were soon asking for the deployment of larger, more capable machines to move troops and supplies. The Sikorsky H-19 Chickasaw was an eight-seat utility helicopter used by the USAF, USN, US Army, and USMC during the war. Experimental YH-19s had arrived in Korea in March 1951, and within 24 hours were being used to evacuate casualties.

The USMC Helicopter Transport Squadron 161 (HMR-161), which had arrived in Korea on August 30, 1951, was equipped with 15 of the USMC version, the HRS-1. During the last year of the war, HMR-161 expanded the role of USMC helicopters, and used them for air assault, air transport to support an attacking force, and for tactical redeployments. Meanwhile, the US Army's 6th Transportation Helicopter Company (THC), equipped with 12 machines, arrived in Korea in March 1953, and these were used mainly for light transport and for casualty evacuation (CASEVAC). In this role, the H-19 could carry six stretchers and one medical attendant.

The two-seat Bell 47 was widely used by the US Army and USMC during the war. The USMC version, the HTL-4 (as the H-13), arrived in Korea as part of Observation Squadron 6 (VMO-6) and served in throughout the war. Four US Army H-13B Sioux from the 2nd Army Helicopter Detachment (AHD) arrived in Korea in December 1950, and became the first US Army helicopters to serve in Korea. Although the primary role was battlefield observation and reconnaissance, in the first month of operation alone, they were used to move over 500 casualties from the combat zone. This led to the development of the H-13C equipped to carry two stretchers externally. The 801st Medical Air Evacuation Squadron (MAES) evacuated more than 4,700 casualties in December 1950, and were awarded a Distinguished Unit Citation (DUC).

The three-seat Hiller H-23 Raven served in Korea in relatively small numbers, but also inevitably served in the CASEVAC role as well as a battlefield observation and surveillance platform.

While its tactical value is not in question, the importance of the CASEVAC helicopter in Korea cannot be overstated. The unforgiving and difficult terrain in question meant that the time taken and the nature of transporting the injured in vehicles would have undoubtedly resulted in the deaths of many wounded US troops. Instead, casualties could be quickly removed to a safe location such as a Mobile Army Surgical Hospital (MASH), or possibly a hospital ship moored nearby off the coast.

LEFT: **Some helicopters, such as the Sikorsky HH-3E Jolly Green Giant, have a watertight boat-like hull to enable the machine to land directly on the water.**

Air Sea Rescue (ASR)

Before helicopters were available for the role, if a person had to be rescued from the sea, this could have been achieved in a number of ways. First, boats could sail towards the person in need of rescue, provided they knew the location. Fixed-wing aircraft could search huge tracts of ocean looking for survivors and drop dinghies, emergency supplies and even rigid lifeboats, and then direct rescue boats. If the sea conditions were right, flying boats or amphibious aircraft could land in the sea close to the victims, pick them up and fly them to safety. The helicopter combines the best of all these approaches, and can perform in conditions where fixed-wing aircraft cannot, then hover over the casualty, lift them to safety and, if required, fly them to a ship or even to a hospital on land.

Air sea rescue (ASR), also known as search and rescue and sea air rescue (both of which are abbreviated to SAR), is the coordinated search for and then rescue of the survivors or victims of an emergency at sea. Military SAR was developed to save downed aircrew as well as the crews of surface vessels and submarines, but in peacetime these assets are frequently used to rescue civilians. As soon as working helicopters were introduced in the 1940s, their application in ASR was a priority for many naval commanders who were also quick to appreciate that helicopters could perform many other tasks when not involved in rescue operations. A Sikorsky S-51 was used to carry out the first successful helicopter rescue at sea on November 29, 1945, when test pilot Dimitry Viner broke off from a demonstration flight for the US Navy and lifted two seamen to safety from a ship in

ABOVE: **The PZL Anakonda is the SAR version of the PZL W-3 Falcon operated by the Polish Navy, and the first helicopter to be completely designed and manufactured in Poland.** RIGHT: **The Westland Sea King helicopter was the main type of rescue helicopter in service with the RAF and Royal Navy for over three decades.**

RIGHT: The Canadian Armed Forces operate CH-149 Cormorant search and rescue (SAR) helicopters. The helicopter has three powerful hoists – two for rescue and a third for cargo. A sophisticated ice protection system allows the type to be operated in cold Arctic conditions.

LEFT: Pilots of the RAF are currently trained at the Search and Rescue Training Unit (SARTU) at RAF Valley on Anglesey, using the Bell UH-1 designated HT-1 Griffin.

distress not far from the Sikorsky airfield. Equally, helicopters are able to rescue people who may be trapped in inaccessible places – among rocks, for example.

The Korean War was the first conflict in which downed aircrew had a reasonable chance of being quickly found and rescued from the sea. In Britain, the Royal Air Force were keen to be able to rescue their aircrew, who may have parachuted into the seas around the UK. The world's first dedicated peacetime ASR unit was No. 275 Squadron, reformed for the task in 1953 at RAF Linton-on-Ouse. Equipped with Bristol Sycamore helicopters, No. 275 was tasked with providing ASR cover over the North Sea. The aircraft were painted bright yellow, which established a colour scheme that remains in use on many rescue helicopters around the world today. Other types joined the RAF's rescue services around the UK – 1956 saw the arrival of the Westland Whirlwind for the task. These were in turn replaced by the Westland Wessex HAR.2, which brought the added safety feature of multi-engine operations – especially reassuring

when flying a search mission over large area of open sea. In August 1978, the Westland Sea King entered service, and after the Falklands War a number of machines from RAF Coltishall were deployed in support of RAF and Royal Navy fighter operations from Stanley Airfield, and were always on standby to rescue any downed British aircrew.

Although some rescue helicopters could land directly on water to carry out a rescue, due to a watertight hull, others, including some early Bell designs, were fitted with pontoons so that the helicopter could operate on both water and land. Most helicopters are equipped with a rescue winch and a crew member generally termed "rescue swimmer", who will jump into the water to help the survivor get into the hoisting harness.

Today, the Royal Air Force maintains a year-round, 24-hour search and rescue service operating from six locations covering the entire UK and large areas of coastal waters. For complex operations, the helicopters will operate in conjunction with a maritime patrol aircraft to coordinate a major rescue operation from the air.

LEFT: **The Fairey Jet Gyrodyne, a modification of the second prototype FB-1 Gyrodyne, was built to develop the pressure-jet rotor drive system.**

Gyrodynes

A gyrodyne is a type of rotorcraft that has a rotor system driven by an engine for take-off and landing, like a helicopter, but it also has one or two propellers mounted on the wing(s) for propulsion, while also having an anti-torque function. In forward flight, the spinning rotor provides lift and keeps the aircraft in the air.

Dr James Bennett developed the gyrodyne while he was Chief Engineer at the Cierva Autogiro Company, and patented the concept in 1939. Bennett's design study finally became a reality in 1945; when employed by Fairey Aviation, he updated and developed his concept and produced the Fairey Gyrodyne. It was a compact, aerodynamically refined rotorcraft weighing just over 2,000kg/4,410lb, and was powered by an Alvis Leonides radial piston engine that drove the rotor and a single starboard wing-tip mounted propeller as required. The rotor enabled the Gyrodyne to be hovered like a helicopter, while the propeller provided thrust for forward flight. A test flight on December 4, 1947, led to a period of intensive testing and evaluation, which included an attempt to set a new world helicopter speed record in a straight line. Just days before attempting another closed-circuit record in April 1949, a mechanical fault in the rotor caused the first prototype to crash, killing the crew.

The Gyrodyne had already secured an order from the British Army for use in Malaya, in preference to the Sikorsky S-51 Dragonfly and Bristol Sycamore, but the crash investigation delayed production, and the sales opportunity was lost. The heavily modified second prototype did not fly again until January 1954, and was by now called the Jet Gyrodyne, with the rotors driven by tipjets fed with air from compressors driven by the Alvis Leonides radial engine. Pusher-type propellers, now mounted at the tip of each stub wing, provided yaw control as well as thrust for forward flight. Fairey had not, however, built the Jet Gyrodyne as a new type, but used the machine to gather flight data in support of Fairey's Rotodyne project.

The Fairey Rotodyne was developed to satisfy the long-standing interest in a vertical take-off airliner that could operate from city centres and airports with equal ease. Fairey was confident that they had proved the concept with the Jet Gyrodyne, and built the Rotodyne which had short, fixed shoulder-mounted wings each with a Napier Eland turboprop engine for forward propulsion. The engines also produced compressed air which was fed to tipjets to be mixed with fuel and burned to drive the rotors for take-off, landing and

LEFT: **G-APJJ is the sole complete survivor of six Fairey Ultralights built, and is preserved at the Midland Air Museum in the UK. Air from the engine's compressor was bled to the rotor tips, where it was mixed with fuel and ignited.**

LEFT: **The Sikorsky X-2 was an experimental compound (gyrodyne) helicopter, which is thought to have been the fastest helicopter-type aircraft ever built. All performance data gained during flight testing were to be used for the Sikorsky S-92 Raider project.**

hovering. The rotors autorotated during flight cruise when all engine power was applied to the propellers. No anti-torque correction system was required, although propeller pitch was controlled by the rudder pedals for low-speed yaw control. Cockpit controls included cyclic and collective pitch levers, as found in a conventional helicopter.

The Fairey Rotodyne made its first flight on November 6, 1957, piloted by Chief Helicopter Test Pilot Sqdn Ldr W. Ron Gellatly and Assistant Chief Helicopter Test Pilot Lt Cdr John G. P. Morton. The first successful transition from vertical to horizontal flight and back was achieved on April 10, 1958. In testing, the Rotodyne also demonstrated that it could be hovered with one engine shut down, and also could be landed as an autogyro.

Tipjet drive and unloaded rotors produced a much better performance than that of a pure helicopter. The machine could be flown at 324kph/201mph, and pulled into steep climbing turns without demonstrating any adverse handling.

The proposed mode of operation for the Rotodyne was that it would take off vertically from a city centre location with all lift coming from the tipjet driven rotor, and then would increase forward airspeed with all power from the engines being transferred to the propellers while the rotor autorotated. In this mode, the wings would be taking as much as 50 per cent of the aircraft's weight. The Rotodyne would then cruise at 280kph/174mph to another city location, where the rotor tipjet system would be restarted for a vertical landing. When the Rotodyne landed and the rotor stopped moving, the blades drooped downwards from the hub. To avoid striking the tail fins on start-up, the fins were angled down to the horizontal, and would be raised up once the rotor was at running speed.

RIGHT: **The Fairey Rotodyne was a compound gyroplane transport aircraft. High noise levels from the rotor tipjets spelt doom for this innovative project.**

British European Airways (BEA), the RAF, New York Airways and the US Army were all interested in placing substantial orders for the Rotodyne, and a larger version was also being designed. However, increased costs, British aviation industry mergers, problems with engines, and finally a withdrawal of government funding doomed this very interesting project. Other companies have experimented with gyrodyne principles since then, and in recent years there has been a renewed interest in the concept.

LEFT: **HMS *Theseus* with Westland Whirlwind and Bristol Sycamore helicopters of the Joint Experimental Helicopter Unit (JEHU), which operated alongside Royal Navy helicopters. Note the French hospital ship in the background.**

The Suez Crisis

In 1956, the Suez Crisis erupted over Egyptian President Nasser's decision to nationalize the strategically important Suez Canal. The Anglo–French military response proved to be one of the final chapters for the British Empire. Britain's Prime Minister at the time was Anthony Eden, and when

he died in 1997, *The Times* newspaper noted, "He was the last prime minister to believe Britain was a great power and the first to confront a crisis which proved she was not." The military actions are also remarkable because they included the first helicopter-borne assault landing.

The Suez crisis began on October 29, 1956, when Israeli forces attacked Sinai. British and French combat aircraft carried out bombing and anti-shipping attacks over the following days as a prelude to an invasion of the Canal Zone. While some French and British troops were parachuted in and other British personnel came ashore on World War II-vintage landing craft, the Royal Marines of 45 Commando were taken into battle by a mixed fleet of Royal Navy, Army and Royal Air Force helicopters.

The Joint Experimental Helicopter Unit (JEHU), had been set up in 1955, and was the first joint British Army/RAF unit established since the end of World War II. Its role was to examine how best to transport troops by helicopter from RN ships. Having practised using a runway marked out as a carrier deck on dry land, the unit had first landed on a moving carrier in October 1955. The Suez crisis gave the unit an opportunity to put theory into practice, and it was positioned on board the light-fleet carrier HMS *Ocean*, complementing the helicopters of No. 845 Naval Air Squadron (NAS) on board HMS *Theseus*. The helicopters were also there, however, to serve in the rescue role. On November 3, a Westland Wyvern fighter-bomber was hit by Egyptian gunners during a ground-attack mission and the pilot had to eject, landing in the sea less than 5km/3 miles from an Egyptian shore battery. Fleet Air Arm (FAA) fighter aircraft mounted an air patrol overhead, while a Royal Navy helicopter was deployed to rescue the pilot from the sea.

LEFT: **The versatility of the helicopter proved invaluable during the crisis, being used to transport supplies to and from the invasion fleet.**

At 16:00 on November 6, the helicopter crews on both carriers were given orders to begin the assault, and all were airborne within five minutes, as the first wave of the force of almost 500 commandos was carried to the landing zone at Port Said. Eight RN Whirlwind HAR.22s took part, together with a further six Whirlwind HAR.2s from the JEHU and six Bristol Sycamore HC.14s.

The helicopters returned immediately to the ships to pick up the next wave and, in around 90 minutes, 435 commandos together with some 2,337kg/5,152lb of equipment had been carried ashore. While the helicopters continued to deliver supplies, British and French casualties were flown back to the ships. One injured marine was back on board just 20 minutes after he had left, which illustrates the remarkable leap in casualty evacuation (CASEVAC) and treatment that helicopters represented. A Royal Navy helicopter also carried

ABOVE: **A flight of six Bristol Sycamore helicopters transporting troops of 45 Commando Royal Marines during the assault on Port Said.**

out the first combat rescue when the pilot of a Hawker Sea Hawk fighter-bomber, Lt Stuart-Jervis, had to eject.

International, mainly US, pressure forced a ceasefire, and the British and French forces ultimately withdrew. History judges the Anglo–French military action to have been pointless, but the campaign did showcase the remarkable versatility of the helicopter and its many military applications. It also persuaded British military chiefs that commando-carrying, dedicated amphibious warfare ships equipped only with helicopters were an essential component of the Fleet.

BELOW: **British helicopters were also used to transport Egyptian wounded to hospital ships for treatment. A Westland Whirlwind prepares to depart Port Said.**

LEFT: **Not all helicopter development in Europe was successful. This strap-on helicopter was designed by Frenchman, George Sablie.** ABOVE: **The Aerotécnica AC-12, designed by Jean Cantinieau in France, had a distinctive spine above the cockpit, which carried the engine ahead of the rotor assembly. The type was first flown in 1954, and 12 machines were delivered to the Spanish Air Force as the EC-XZ-2.**

European helicopter development

Helicopters are often thought of as an US invention, but although many European companies began by licence-building US machines, technical vision and innovation was also very evident in Europe.

British helicopter development made little significant progress until 1944 when the Bristol Aeroplane Company established a Helicopter Division, later to become Bristol Helicopters. The company's first helicopter was the Sycamore, which was in some ways more technically advanced than the early Sikorsky machines, and won export orders. The Bristol team then went on to develop the twin-engine tandem rotor Bristol Type 173 that became the Belvedere. Meanwhile, Westland was manufacturing a modified Sikorsky S-51 under licence as the Dragonfly for the British military and export customers. In 1960, Bristol Helicopters was absorbed by Westland, which was already established as the main British helicopter manufacturer. Westland went on to manufacture other Sikorsky types through to the Sea King.

Westand soon began to co-operate with French aerospace companies, and this led to the hugely successful Gazelle and later the Lynx. Italian company Agusta and Westland joined together to develop the design that ultimately produced the versatile and successful Merlin. Today the companies have merged as AgustaWestland.

Two French companies, Sud-Est and Sud-Ouest, developed a range of exciting helicopter projects in the late 1940s and early 1950s. Sud-Ouest built the tipjet Djinn, while Sud-Est developed the record-breaking Alouette series of helicopters. Sud-Ouest and Sud-Est were later merged into Sud-Aviation, which itself became part of Aérospatiale. It was this team that developed the Puma that is still in service today.

In 1992, Aérospatiale joined with the German helicopter manufacturer Messerchmitt-Bölkow-Blohm (MBB) to create Eurocopter Holdings. Both companies were already participating in the four-nation NH Industries NH90 military helicopter project, in partnership with Agusta and Fokker.

ABOVE: **The French-built Sud-Ouest SO-1120 Ariel III. Note the single fin and rudder tail assembly. Additional directional control was provided by turbine exhaust gases blown over the fin.**

ABOVE: **The Agusta A.101 was a large transport helicopter built only as a prototype and was first flown on October 19, 1964. Flight testing and development continued until 1971, when the project was abandoned.**

LEFT: **The Nord 500 was a single-seat tilting-duct research aircraft. Two were built in France, the second flying in 1968. Two five-blade ducted propellers and the wing on which they were mounted could be tilted horizontally.**

The post-war German helicopter industry had unlikely origins. In 1956, a civil engineering company moved into aviation, and formed Bölkow-Entwicklungen KG. In 1957, the company decided to investigate the possibility of designing its own helicopter trainer to capitalize on the then greatly expanding market. The P102 prototype was built, and was then produced as the Bo102. It was constructed as a training airframe that was never intended to fly, and it sold well. Having built one flying example, the team then developed more marketable helicopters, including the ultimately very successful Bo105 that featured an innovative rigid rotor system. After a succession of mergers, including one with the famed Messerschmitt company, the operation was finally known as Messerschmitt-Bölkow-Blohm (MBB).

The Agusta company in Italy (now part of AgustaWestland) is the European helicopter company with the longest aviation lineage. It was founded in 1923 by Count Giovanni Agusta, who had flown his first aircraft in 1907 and built aircraft until World War II. Post-war, Agusta switched to motorcycle manufacture, and then from 1952 the company became involved with helicopters, building Bell, Sikorsky, Boeing and McDonnell Douglas products under licence. The company, however, had ambitions to design and build its own helicopters, and these have included the Agusta A109 and the A129 Mangusta anti-tank helicopter – the first attack helicopter to be designed and produced in Western Europe.

It was the end of the Cold War and the associated budgetary limitations and high development costs of new technology that encouraged many companies to amalgamate and produce specific aircraft, or to merge entirely. This is the only way that the European helicopter industry has a real chance of competing with US and Russian military helicopter manufacturers.

LEFT: **The Eurocopter AS 350 Écureuil (Squirrel in RAF and AAC use) and AS 355 Ecureuil 2 were designed in the early 1970s as a replacement for the Aérospatiale Alouette II (lark).**

The Malayan Emergency

During World War II, Malayan communist anti-Japanese guerrillas had been supported by the British, and after the end of the war these same guerrillas attempted to seize power in Malaya. Britain's response was to declare a State of Emergency in June 1948, and rush reinforcements to the country. At any given time, some 3,000 guerrillas were fighting against a combined force of around 350,000 troops, police and militia. The emergency continued for 12 years, and since much of the fighting took place in deep jungle, progress was slow. The introduction of helicopters made a huge difference to the British military effort. Entering service as a CASEVAC asset, the helicopters were soon in use transporting troops quickly to launch surprise attacks. This new type of air mobility enabled the British military to fight a different kind of war.

Malaya was one of the first operational deployments of a Royal Air Force helicopter unit – the Far East Air Force (FEAF) Casualty Evacuation Flight (CEF). This was formed in response

ABOVE: **The Bristol Type 175 Belvedere was operated by No.66 Squadron in Malaya from June 1962, providing heavy-lift support for British forces on ground operations.**

to a request made to the Chiefs of Staff in March 1949 for the provision of helicopters to evacuate any casualties resulting from a planned increase in operations against terrorists in the more remote jungle areas. As a result, the CEF was formed in April 1950, and equipped with three (only three were ever built) Westland Dragonfly Mk2 helicopters based at Changi, Singapore, from May 1950. Their first CASEVAC operation was to recover a British soldier who had been shot during an ambush and flown from a water-logged airstrip at Segamat on June 14. The first CASEVAC operation from a jungle clearing followed just five days later.

The CEF was re-equipped with the more capable Dragonfly HC.4 which, like the Mk2, was a dedicated CASEVAC version built for the RAF and fitted with all-metal rotor blades.

LEFT: **Westland Whirlwind HAR.4s of No.155 Squadron near Kuala Lumpur airfield. During the Malayan emergency, the squadron was primarily deployed on CASEVAC duties.**

ABOVE: **Men of 22 Special Air Service Regiment (SAS) guiding a Bristol Sycamore HR.14 of No.194 Squadron to land in a jungle clearing at Ula Langat, near Kuala Lumpur, November 1957.** RIGHT: **Troops of the Special Air Service deploying from a Whirlwind HAS Mk22 of the Royal Navy.**

The helicopters, of course, were also used for purely military missions, including reconnaissance, the tactical movement of British troops, and delivery of military supplies and equipment.

The success of the CEF led to it being elevated to full squadron status as No.194 in February 1953. The Dragonfly helicopters were in constant demand, and from early June 1953 were supplemented by aircraft from No.848 Naval Air Squadron (NAS) equipped with early Sikorsky-built S-55 Whirlwind. No.194 Squadron operated the Dragonfly Mk4 until October 1954, when it began to receive the Bristol Sycamore Mk14, and finally phased out the last Dragonfly in July 1956. In April 1957, it was reported that these machines had flown 10,000 hours, one aircraft alone having flown for 1,000 hours.

In October 1954, helicopter operations were further strengthened by the introduction of the Westland Whirlwind Mk4 to equip No.155 Squadron formed at Kuala Lumpur airfield, which had now become the main helicopter operations base. By the end of 1956, No.155 and No.194 were equipped with 17 Whirlwind and 14 Sycamore helicopters, but a reduced threat and continuing problems with the Whirlwind led to the only helicopters operating in Malaya being the Sycamores of No.194. In February and April 1959, two fatal accidents involving Sycamore helicopters led to the remainder of the force in Malaya being grounded.

On June 3, 1959, No.194 and No.155 Squadrons were disbanded, and No.110 Squadron re-formed at Butterworth with the remaining Whirlwinds from No.155. On July 31, 1960, after the squadron was re-equipped with the Bristol Sycamore

Mk14, the Malayan Emergency was declared to be at an end. The celebratory flypast over Kuala Lumpur included three Sycamore Mk14s.

The British helicopter force in Malaya pioneered most of the short-range military helicopter transport roles, and from June 1950 to July 1960 these RAF and RN helicopters carried out 4,759 evacuations, moved 127,425 troops, 17,865 passengers and 1,226,034kg/2,699,327lb of cargo. These figures are all the more remarkable when one remembers that the first-generation helicopters were only capable of transporting five soldiers and a maximum of 363kg/800lb at a time.

ABOVE: **A Westland Whirlwind being recovered from a swamp after a forced landing in a jungle area near Kuala Lumpur.**

The Vietnam War

While the Korean War (1950–53) was to prove the military value of the helicopter, Vietnam was the first war that could not have been waged without the type. From the first US helicopter combat missions captured by television news crews to the chaos of the final US withdrawal from Saigon rooftops in 1975, Vietnam was the first true helicopter war.

US forces faced an unusually complex challenge in South-east Asia. While fighting to support the Republic of Viet Nam in a battle against a communist-backed insurgency, US forces had to establish a very modern fighting force in an underdeveloped environment with challenging terrain while facing Viet Cong (VC) guerrilla tactics and conducting conventional operations against well-trained regular units of the Viet Nam People's Army (North Vietnamese Army). Helicopters were vital to US operations, and thus began the development of the US air mobility force.

Among the first types operated by the US Army in South Vietnam were Bell HU-1A Iroquois "Hueys" that arrived in April 1962, before the US was officially involved in the war. These supported the Army of the Republic of South Viet Nam (ARVN), but were flown by US crews. In October that year, the first armed Hueys, equipped with 2.75in rockets and 0.30in machine-guns, began operations as gunships for escort missions in support of the transport helicopters.

Piasecki H-21 Shawnee helicopters were used to ferry ARVN troops into battle against VC forces in 1962. When troop-carrying helicopters first appeared in action,

ABOVE: **The Bell UH-1A Iroquois Huey is an iconic symbol of the Vietnam War due to the presence of the type in great numbers.** BELOW: **A US Marine Corps Sikorsky HUS-1 flying over South Vietnam. The type was extremely vulnerable to ground fire.**

LEFT: **A Bell UH-1A Iroquois fitted with chemical spraying equipment. Operations included the eradication of mosquitoes, destroying Viet Cong farm crops, and tree defoliation.**

the VC troops fled, but at the Battle of Ap Bac in 1962 they stood firm and shot down five US helicopters, while damaging many others. Later Communist combat training manuals were to show the best techniques for shooting down helicopters by using small arms as a form of improvised anti-aircraft fire, shooting ahead of the target to allow for forward speed to increase the chance of hitting the aircraft. The manuals also detailed the most vulnerable parts of the machine (tail rotor, rotor head and engine), where the most devastating mechanical damage could be inflicted.

The Bell UH-1 Iroquois was the workhorse of the war, and according to the Vietnam Helicopter Pilots Association (VHPA), those in US Army service flew 7,531,955 hours between October 1966 and 1975. Operations with the Bell AH-1G Cobra accumulated 1,110,716 flight hours in the war. As a result, some sources, including the VHPA, assert that these two types have more combat flight time than any other aircraft in the history of warfare, if one includes exposure to actual hostile fire. For example, Allied bombers in World War II were certainly flown on long missions, but were not exposed to enemy fire for the entire time. In Vietnam, helicopters were rarely flown above 458m/1,500ft, and thus were always at risk from enemy ground fire.

LEFT: **South Vietnamese paratroopers running to board two Piasecki CH-21 Shawnee helicopters for a mission in the Mekong Delta. A large number of the type were shot down by enemy ground fire.**

The Bell UH-1 was upgraded and improved, based on combat experience gained, and was instrumental in enabling the US military to develop airmobile warfare tactics. A typical air assault mission would see UH-1 helicopters dropping infantry deep inside enemy territory while gunships would escort an attack force of up to 100 transport helicopters. In a matter of minutes, battalions of US troops could be inserted behind enemy lines, ready for combat. The troops were deployed without having to fight for positions, or being too dispersed along a wide battlefront, and could be withdrawn as required. This meant that ground would not be taken, but it allowed strategists to deploy military assets over large areas and engage the enemy at designated places.

The statistics detailing the use of helicopters in the war are staggering. A total of 2,197 US helicopter pilots and 2,717 crew members were killed from all services including those from Air America, an "airline" operated by the Central Intelligence Agency (CIA). Some 500,000 MEDEVAC missions

ABOVE: **The HH-3E Jolly Green Giant was used for combat rescue, and featured protective armour, self-sealing fuel tanks, a retractable inflight refuelling probe and a high-speed hoist.**

were flown and over 900,000 casualties were airlifted. As a result of these operations, the average time lapse between battlefront to hospitalization was less than one hour, resulting in significantly improved survival rates for casualties.

Militarily, the helicopter allowed US forces unprecedented mobility. Without the aircraft it would have required three times as many troops to secure the 1,287km/800-mile border with Cambodia and Laos. About 12,000 helicopters were deployed to Vietnam with a peak strength of some 4,000 in 1970, of which around 2,600 were Bell UH-1s. A total of 5,086 helicopters were lost in service over Vietnam, including over 1,000 in 1968.

Mention must also be made of Royal Australian Air Force (RAAF) and Royal Australian Navy (RAN) helicopter operations in South Vietnam. Although small in scale

RIGHT: **Sikorsky CH-53 from HMH (Marine Heavy Helicopter Squadron) 462 on a mountainside base in Vietnam in 1968. At this stage in the war, the USMC squadron was tasked with the tactical retrieval of downed aircraft and movement of heavy equipment.**

ABOVE: **Helicopters enabled US forces to operate from a variety of locations, including smaller warships.** RIGHT: **Inflight refuelling from aircraft such the Lockheed C-130P Hercules enabled Combat Search and Rescue (CSAR) helicopters to range far and wide over South-east Asia.**

compared to US operations, the overall contribution of these two services in the conflict is often and quite wrongly overlooked by historians outside Australia.

The RAN formed the Royal Australian Navy Helicopter Flight Vietnam (RANHFV), and the first element arrived in October 1967. Trained for anti-submarine warfare, the crews had to learn how to drop and recover troops in high-risk combat areas. The RANHFV was integrated with the US 135th Assault Helicopter Company tasked with the tactical movement of combat troops, supplies and equipment. During a one-year operational tour, RAN crews commonly logged a combined total of between 9,000 and 12,000 flying hours. The RANHFV ceased offensive operations on June 8, 1971, and by the time the unit left the country, hundreds of offensive operations had been flown. A total five personnel were killed and 22 wounded in action from a complement of 200.

An element of No.9 Squadron RAAF had arrived in Vietnam in June 1966, complementing to the RAAF's fixed-wing commitment of military transports and, later, bombers. Equipped with UH-1Bs, the RAAF helicopters transported infantry, equipment and supplies, and dropped propaganda leaflets over enemy territory. The aircraft were used to spray their base to eradicate mosquitoes but, more offensively, to spray chemicals on Viet Cong farmland to interrupt the enemy food supply. In 1967, after re-equipping with the more capable UH-1H, No.9 worked more closely with its RAN counterparts, transporting troops to and from patrols, and undertaking battlefield casualty evacuations. By the time No.9 finally left Vietnam in December 1971, six personnel had been killed in action.

LEFT: **The Sikorsky HUS-1 was widely used in Vietnam by the USMC, and although the US Army operated the CH-34 Choctaw the type was not used in the war.**

LEFT: **A US Navy Sikorsky HO3S-1 of Helicopter Utility Squadron HU-1 taking off from the battleship USS *New Jersey* (BB-62) off Korea on April 14, 1953.**

Helicopters at sea

As the helicopter was developed for military use, its value as a naval, particularly anti-submarine weapons platform, was exploited specifically. Planners could see the value of an aircraft that could take off vertically from a relatively small space while carrying troops or weapons. Initially, only aircraft carriers could cope with the large weapons and equipment-laden helicopters such as the Sikorsky S-58 but, after trial operations, it was confirmed that smaller warships – mainly frigates tasked with defending other ships, if modified or ideally designed for purpose from the outset – could operate these vital aircraft effectively. By operating an ASW helicopter, these ships could extend a navy's anti-submarine capability far beyond the fleet the frigates were there to protect from enemy attack.

During the Cold War, Soviet submarines were considered to be a major threat as they had the ability to attack NATO fighting ships, just as the German Navy U-boats had for a time wreaked havoc with Allied shipping in the Atlantic during World War II. As missile technology improved and submarines were developed to fire nuclear missiles at the West while submerged, it became even more important to be able to detect and destroy enemy submarines in war.

The Royal Navy has always been at the forefront of helicopter-borne anti-submarine capability, and the RN's Type 81 Tribal class of frigate commissioned between 1961 and 1967 were the first designed from the outset to operate a helicopter. On the Tribal class, this would be a single Westland

RIGHT: **A Kamov Ka-27PS (NATO identifier Helix) from the Ukrainian Navy landing on the flight deck of USS *Taylor* (FFG-50) in the Black Sea during Exercise Sea Breeze, 2010.**

LEFT: An AgustaWestland EH-101 Merlin on the deck of HMS *Iron Duke* (F234).
ABOVE: A South-African-built Atlas Oryx M2 landing on the deck of USS *Swift* (HSV-2).

Wasp equipped to carry two homing torpedoes, but could also be armed with SS.11 wire-guided missiles to attack small surface vessels.

The Type 81-class ships were complemented by the Leander-class frigates, the last of 26 of which entered service in 1971. These ships had a helicopter hangar for the anti-submarine warfare Westland Wasp.

From the early 1960s, the RN also operated Type 12 frigates, the Whitby class, designed as an ocean-going convoy escort. The Type 12s were used as fast fleet anti-submarine warfare escorts and were also equipped with a Westland Wasp.

On April 25, 1982, the Argentine submarine *Santa Fe* was spotted and attacked first by a Royal Navy Westland Wessex from the destroyer HMS *Antrim* (D18). HMS *Plymouth* (F126), a Type 12, then launched its Wasp HAS Mk1 while HMS *Brilliant*

(F92), which carried two Lynx helicopters, launched one of its helicopters to join the attack. Two other Wasps from the RN Antarctic ice patrol ship HMS *Endurance* (A171) also took part in the attack. Anti-shipping missiles were fired at the submarine from the helicopters, causing damage that forced the vessel to be withdrawn. Two interesting historical facts to note are that the Wasp had already been retired from RN service when it was brought back into service for the Falklands War. Also, when the RN sailed south to retake the Falklands, it was carrying nuclear depth charges that would have been helicopter-dropped if required.

Today the Royal Navy operates Type 23 frigates, first conceived in the late 1970s to specifically counter Soviet nuclear submarines operating in the North Atlantic. First commissioned in 1989 in the anti-submarine role, these ships have become multi-purpose fighting ships reflecting both the demands of the world today and ever-shrinking defence budgets. The Type 23s will be replaced by Type 26 Anti-Submarine Warfare and Type 31 general purpose frigates in Royal Navy service, but until then will continue to operate Agusta Westland AW159 Wildcat or EH101 Merlins. The RN believes the Type 23 weapons system reaffirmed its reputation as a leader in anti-submarine warfare.

LEFT: **Civil-registered Super Puma helicopters operate from Military Sealift Command (MSC) transport stores ships, and are used for Vertical Replenishment (VertRep) of other US Navy vessels.**

The helicopter cockpit

The helicopter is a the world's most versatile flying machine, but very complex and difficult to fly – a pilot must be able to coordinate in three dimensions and must constantly use both hands and feet simultaneously to keep the aircraft under control.

The cockpit of a helicopter is at first glance similar to that of a fixed-wing aircraft, but closer inspection reveals significant differences. Helicopters do not have the same control wheels or columns, and usually no throttle controls. The other significant point to note is that in most helicopters the pilot-in-command flies the machine from the right-hand seat, whereas on the flight deck of a fixed-wing aircraft the captain flies the aircraft from the left-hand seat.

In the cockpit, the cyclic stick (control column) is operated to tilt the main rotor to raise or lower the nose and to make the aircraft bank to the left or right. The collective pitch control is positioned to the left of the pilot's seat, and is operated to change the pitch angle of the main rotor blades to decrease or increase lift for take-off, landing and flight altitude.

A helicopter does have a conventional rudder for directional control, but is fitted with an anti-torque tail rotor. The pedals operated by the pilot's feet are not unlike those in the cockpit of a fixed-wing aircraft, and are positioned in the same place. The pedals control the pitch of the tail rotor blades to provide

TOP: **The AW101 Merlin in service is equipped with high-definition colour display screens.** ABOVE: **The much simpler all-analogue dial instrument panel of the Sikorsky S-51.**

directional control while the machine hovers and is in forward flight. Helicopter and fixed-wing aircraft pilots have to receive the same technical information, such as airspeed, attitude (in relation to the horizon), altitude, compass heading and rate of climb and descent, to fly safely and efficiently. Engine performance, including fuel and oil consumption, is vital to the operation of both types of aircraft. The helicopter is also equipped with a torque indicator to show the amount of engine power being applied to the main rotor blades.

Analogue (dial-type) instruments were a standard fitment in all cockpits for many years, but many of the types now in service are fitted with all-glass cockpits. All-important flight data, navigation and weapons information is displayed on small, flat Liquid Crystal Display or Video Display Unit (LCD or VDU) screens. Most military helicopters have basic analogue flight instruments as a stand-by in the event of an electronics systems failure. Other equipment in the cockpit of modern military helicopter is fitted to provide communications and navigation information, with specialized warning equipment for defence and targeting for offensive weaponry.

BELOW: **The AgustaWestland AW139 has a Honeywell Primus Epic modular/ integrated glass cockpit, offered to customers in four different mission- optimized configurations. Maintenance personnel may use the cockpit displays or a laptop computer to perform aircraft rigging, sensor calibration and avionics systems diagnostics.**

ABOVE: **The very basic instrument panel of the Mil Mi-8. Note the collective, bottom left, the cyclic in front of the seat, and the foot pedal control bar.**

LEFT: The pilot of an AgustaWestland Merlin in Royal Navy service carrying out his pre-flight checks. The complex rotor systems fitted on modern military helicopters can survive much greater damage than those of earlier machines.

Rotor systems

Autogyro pioneer Juan de la Cierva investigated, developed and tested many of the fundamentals of the rotor (the system of rotating aerofoils) that lifts and keeps a helicopter off the ground. A helicopter rotor is powered by the engine, through the transmission (the mechanism transmitting mechanical energy) to the rotating mast (a metal shaft) extending up from and driven by the transmission. At the top of this mast is the rotor hub, the attachment point for the individual rotor blades.

The pitch of main rotor blades can be varied cyclically throughout its rotation to control the direction of rotor thrust and select the part of the rotor disc where the most thrust will be developed – for example front, side and back. The collective pitch varies the magnitude of rotor thrust, increasing or decreasing thrust over the entire rotor disc at the same time. The differences in blade pitch are controlled by tilting and/or raising or lowering what is known as the "swash plate" with the flight controls.

The swash plate generally consists of two closely spaced concentric plates separated by bearings, the top one of which rotates with the mast, while the other does not. The rotating plate is also connected to individual rotor blades, and the non-rotating plate is connected to links which are moved by the pilot – the collective and cyclic controls. The swash plate can move vertically and tilt. Through shifting and tilting, the non-rotating plate controls the rotating plate, which in turn controls the pitch of each individual rotor blade. Most

BELOW LEFT: The Cierva W.11 Air Horse was the largest helicopter in the world when it first flew in 1948. The three rotors mounted on outriggers were driven by a single engine mounted inside the fuselage.
BELOW: The Yakovlev Yak-24 had a tandem rotor layout, not typical for Soviet helicopters. The engines were linked so that each could drive one or both rotors, but this caused severe vibration in the airframe.

LEFT: **The rotor head of a Sikorsky S-92. This helicopter features an active vibration control system that provides comfortable flight and acoustic levels. This system also extends airframe life by reducing fatigue loads on the airframe.**

helicopters maintain a constant main rotor speed, so only the rotor blade angle of attack is used to adjust thrust. The mighty Mil Mi-6, for example, has a main rotor turning at a very slow 120rpm during flight.

Helicopter main rotor systems are classified depending on how the main rotor blades are attached and move relative to the rotor hub. Essentially there are three basic types: fully articulated, rigid and semi-rigid.

Cierva developed the fully articulated rotor for systems with three or more blades. Each rotor blade is attached to the rotor hub through a series of hinges which allow each blade to move independently. The horizontal hinge, called the flapping hinge, enables the blade to move up and down, and this movement (flapping) is designed to compensate for dissimilar lift and

ensures a steady, level take-off. The flapping hinge can be at varying distances from the hub, and there may be more than one flapping hinge. A vertical hinge, called the lead-lag or drag hinge, allows the rotor blade to move back and forth. The purpose of the drag hinge and dampers is to compensate for acceleration and deceleration and, by changing the pitch angle of the blades, the thrust and direction of the main rotor disc can be controlled.

A rigid rotor is usually a hingeless rotor system where blades are flexibly attached to the rotor hub. Rigid rotors are either of the feathering or flapping type. In a flapping rigid-rotor system, each blade flaps, drags and feathers (depending on the design) about flexible sections of the root. The flapping rigid-rotor system is mechanically simpler than the fully articulated rotor system.

LEFT: **The Kaman HH-43 Huskie had an unusual intermeshing contra-rotating twin-rotor system.** ABOVE: **The Russian-built Kamov Ka-25 has folding three-blade coaxial rotors.**

ABOVE: The McDonnell Douglas MD 520N is fitted with the NOTAR anti-torque system, which increases operational safety and reduces external noise.

Loads from flapping and lead/lag forces are accommodated by bending rather than through hinges. By flexing, the blades compensate for the forces that previously required rugged hinges. The result is a rotor system that has less of a delay in control response because the rotor has much less oscillation.

The semi-rigid rotor is also known as a teetering or seesaw rotor. This system is always composed of two blades (such as on a Bell UH-1) which meet just under a common flapping, or teetering, hinge at the rotor shaft. This allows the blades to flap together in opposite motions, like a seesaw. The semi-rigid description comes from the fact that it does not have a lead-lag hinge. The rotor system is rigid in-plane, because the

blades are not free to lead and lag, but they are not rigid in the flapping plane (through the use of a teetering hinge). The rotor is therefore not rigid, but neither is it fully articulated, so it is termed "semi-rigid".

Most helicopters have a single main rotor, but a separate rotor is also required, rotating in the vertical plane to overcome torque, the effect that causes the body of the helicopter which is attached to the engine to always turn in the opposite direction of the rotor. To eliminate this effect, some type of anti-torque control must be designed into the helicopter to allow the aircraft to maintain a heading and to provide yaw control. The three most common types of anti-torque controls are the tail rotor, ducted fan and NOTAR (no tail rotor).

The tail rotor is a small propeller mounted to rotate at or near the vertical at the end of the tail boom of a typical single-rotor helicopter. The tail rotor's position and distance from the aircraft's centre of gravity allows it to develop thrust in the opposite direction from the rotation of the main rotor, and thereby balances the torque effect. The tail rotor is far less complex than the main rotor, as it requires only collective changes in pitch to vary thrust. It is controlled by the pilot using foot pedals, which also provide directional control by

LEFT: The semi-rigid rotor system is used on helicopters such as the Bell UH-1 Iroquois and Bell AH-1 Cobra.

allowing the pilot to rotate the entire helicopter around its vertical axis and, in doing so, change the direction in which the machine is pointed.

Originally conceived by Sud Aviation in France, a ducted fan can be used in place of a tail rotor and built into the aircraft tail with the fan housing being part of the aircraft, as in the case of the Gazelle. A ducted fan can typically have eight to 18 blades, compared to the two to four of a standard type of tail rotor, and can have irregular angular spacing, allowing it to run at lower noise levels. Although heavier and more expensive to build, the ducted fan is less prone to foreign object damage or tail strike as the aircraft is taking off or landing, and is less likely to cause injury on the ground. Fenestron and Fantail are trademarked names for individual manufacturers' ducted fan designs.

The third anti-torque option is NOTAR, an acronym trademarked by Hughes Helicopters for NO TAil Rotor. The use of directed air to provide anti-torque control was tested as early as 1945 on the British-built Cierva W.9, but Hughes (later McDonnell Douglas) engineers revisited the concept in the mid-1970s. Although the principle took time to refine, it is quite simple, and provides directional control in the same way a wing develops lift. A variable pitch fan driven by the main rotor transmission forces low-pressure air through two slots on the right-hand side of the tail boom. This causes the downwash from the helicopter's main rotor to hug the tail boom, producing lift, and directional control which is supplemented by a direct jet thruster and vertical stabilizers. Three McDonnell Douglas production helicopters currently use the NOTAR system: the MD 520N (a NOTAR variant of the Hughes/MD500 series), the MD 600N (a larger version of the MD 520N), and the MD Explorer.

ABOVE: **The conventional tail rotor on an Aérospatiale Puma generates thrust to counteract the main rotor torque and directional control.**

LEFT: **"Fenestron" is the trademarked name of the integrated ducted fan assembly fitted to the Eurocopter EC120B. Comparing the two systems, the enclosed fan is much safer for ground operation, and is also quieter.**

LEFT: **Vietnam, 1966. Ease of engine maintenance is a key design consideration. The Sikorsky S-58 had unique clamshell covers that gave easy access to the engine. Note the engine is mounted at an angle.**

Helicopter engines

A helicopter's size, performance and its applications are all determined by the number, size and type of engine used. Without the right powerplant a helicopter is simply a large ornament, and the correct engine is as vital as the rotor that keeps the aircraft in the air. Incredibly powerful steam engines were available in the 19th century, but the power from even, by necessity, the smallest, lightest examples was not sufficient to allow for manned helicopter flight.

It should be remembered that although Forlanini was astounding people with his contra-rotating steam-powered model in 1877, it was just that – an experimental model and a long way from carrying a man off the ground. Just as it was with fixed-wing aircraft, it was the arrival of the internal combustion engine in the late 19th century that started to turn the dream of manned helicopter flight into reality. Increasingly powerful, more compact engines began to be developed which, it was hoped,

could produce enough power to lift their own weight and a helicopter and pilot off the ground. Early helicopter designs used custom-built engines or rotary engines that had been designed for fixed-wing aircraft, but more powerful motor car and radial engines soon replaced these in the plans of aspiring helicopter designers. Even so, what held back helicopter development more than anything else was the overall lack of power required to overcome the machine's weight in vertical flight.

It was when the compact, horizontally opposed flat engine was developed that helicopter designers found a lightweight powerplant that could be readily adapted to small experimental helicopters. As soon as the helicopter design was perfected, then the designers, on a quest for bigger and more capable helicopters, returned to the trusted radial engine. The Wright Cyclone R-1820 was a development of an engine that first ran in 1925. The engine was used to power wartime fixed-wing

LEFT: **One of two General Electric T64-GE-7 turboshaft engines on a Sikorsky CH-53E Super Stallion.**

LEFT: **The Aérospatiale Alouette II (lark) was the first production helicopter powered by a turboshaft engine instead of a piston engine, which was considerably heavier.**

aircraft, including the Boeing B-17 Flying Fortress bombers and even tanks such as the famous Sherman. A Wright Cyclone R-1820 mounted diagonally below the cockpit also powered the early versions of the Sikorsky S-58/H-34 Choctaw.

In the UK, the Alvis Leonides, first run in 1936, was chosen to power the Westland Dragonfly by direct drive immediately beneath the rotors. Later versions of the Westland Whirlwind were also powered by inclined-drive versions of the same engine. These helicopters were later re-engined with the lighter and more powerful Bristol Siddeley Gnome turboshaft. The arrival of the jet engine immediately opened a wealth of possibilities for designers, once it was modified and developed into a turboshaft which optimized shaft power rather than jet thrust. Crucially, the turboshaft engine was able to be scaled to the size of the helicopter being designed, so that virtually all but the lightest of helicopters are powered by turbine engines today.

In December 1951, the Kaman K-225, predecessor to the HH-23 Huskie, had been the first-ever turboshaft-powered helicopter to fly. Kaman replaced the piston engine with a Boeing 50-2 turboshaft to demonstrate the potential of jet-powered helicopters to the US Navy.

German wartime jet development expertise was harnessed by the Lycoming company who, in 1951, appointed Anselm Franz. He had led the design of the Junkers Jumo 004, the world's first turbojet engine, to enter production, which then went on to power the Messerschmitt Me 262 jet fighter and Arado Ar 234 bombers in combat. Franz was taken on to develop the T35 turboshaft for helicopters. Around 20,000 of these engines were made in turboshaft and turboprop versions. The turboshaft was used to power the Bell AH-1 Cobra, UH-1 Iroquois and Kaman H-43B Huskie.

French manufacturers explored tipjet propulsion – the 1949 SNCASO 1100 Ariel I used a piston engine to drive a compressor that pumped air under pressure to tip burners to spin the rotors. It was the Sud-Ouest Djinn (genie), with simpler cold tip jets that expelled compressed air without a combustion chamber, that proved to be a success. The French Alouette II (lark) fitted with a Turboméca engine became the first production helicopter to be turboshaft-powered.

The jet engine made helicopters fly better, faster and for longer, and removed the need to carry dangerous, low-flashpoint, gasoline-based fuels. Fewer moving parts meant engine failure was a rare occurrence compared to piston-powered machines. A turboshaft-powered helicopter can usually be ready to lift off within just a minute of engine start.

ABOVE: **The Allison/Rolls-Royce Model 250 turboshaft has been used to power helicopters, including the Bo105 and Bell OH-58 Kiowa.**

ABOVE: **The Lycoming T55 turboshaft engine was first developed over 50 years ago, and was used on both helicopters and as a turboprop on fixed-wing aircraft.**

Boeing CH-47 Chinook

In the late 1950s, the Vertol Aircraft Corporation began development of the Model 107 (V-107) as a replacement for Piasecki H-21 Shawnee and Sikorsky H-34 Choctaw piston-engine helicopters. The US Army awarded a contract to Vertol in 1958 to produce the YHC-1A, but decided that the machine did not have an adequate performance for heavy-lift operations. Boeing acquired Vertol in 1960 and produced the larger Model 114 as the YHC-1B. On entering service the type was designated CH-47 and named Chinook. The US Army deployed the type to South Vietnam in February 1966, and it has remained in front-line service ever since.

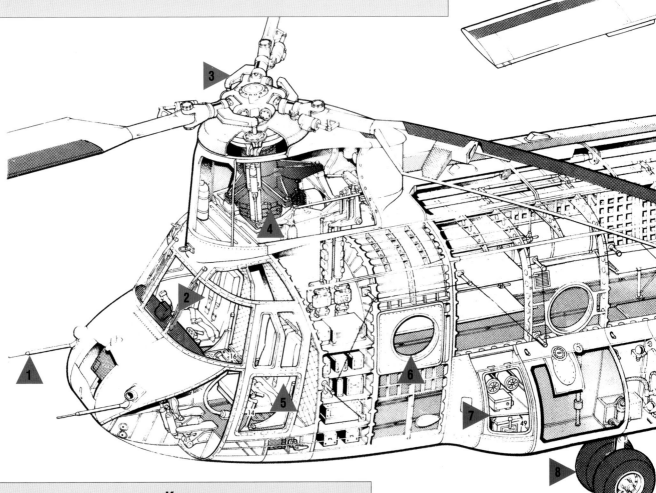

Key

1 Pitot head	11 Rear door
2 Pilot's seat	12 Vehicle loading ramps
3 Forward rotor hub	13 Solar T-62T-28 auxiliary power unit
4 Forward transmission gearbox	14 Rear rotor hub
5 Co-pilot/observer's seat	15 Rear rotor driveshaft
6 Emergency escape window	16 Avco Lycoming T-55-L-712 turboshaft engine
7 Electrical equipment bay	17 Transmission combining gearbox
8 Main landing wheels	18 Main transmission shaft
9 Main fuel tank	19 Engine intake dust screen
10 Rear landing wheel	20 Rotor blade

ABOVE: When this large and powerful twin-engine, tandem-rotor medium-lift transport was first flown, it proved to be faster than a number of contemporary smaller utility, and even attack, helicopters. Around 1,200 have been built, and new examples are still being produced.

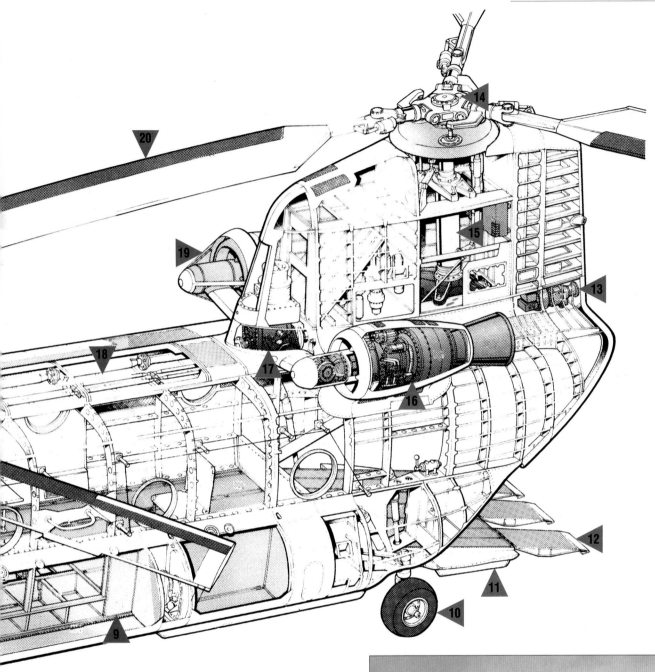

ABOVE: **The Chinook's powerful twin engines are mounted on the sides of the rear rotor mast, and drive both main rotors.**

ABOVE: **The CH-47 has proved itself to be a medium-lift workhorse in all environments, and will remain in service for many years to come.**

LEFT: **An image captured from a night vision device shows Sikorsky MH-53 Pave Low helicopters from the 20th Expeditionary Special Operations Squadron in Iraq departing on the last ever combat mission before the type retired from service.**

Night Vision Technology (NVT)

One of the technical innovations that gives many military helicopters a vital edge over opponents and allows surprise night-time attacks while operating unmolested under cover of darkness is Night Vision Technology (NVT). During Operation Desert Storm (the first Gulf War), night vision-equipped attack helicopters enabled Coalition forces to launch repeated and undetected stand-off (from a distance) attacks on Iraqi tanks and military installations to reduce the threat to ground troops involved in the ground war.

Night vision equipment can enhance any available light by a factor of 10,000, essentially turning night into day even on a cloudy moonless night. This is especially useful when landing a helicopter at night in unfamiliar surroundings, where there might be obstructions such as trees or power lines. It also means that a pilot can land more confidently and in the minimum amount of time, which reduces exposure to enemy fire in the hover.

Night vision can work in two very different ways, depending on the technology applied – image enhancement or thermal imaging. Night vision imagery tends to be green, because the human eye can differentiate more shades of green than any other colour in the spectrum.

Image enhancement works by collecting the miniscule amounts of ambient light, including the lower portion of the infra-red light spectrum, that are present but are imperceptible to the human eye, and amplifying it to the point that aircrew can easily observe the image through an eyepiece or goggles attached to a helmet.

Thermal imaging operates by capturing the upper portion of the infra-red light spectrum emitted as heat by objects. Hotter objects, such as troops or recently run vehicles, emit more of this light than cooler objects such as buildings or trees.

In the AH-64 Apache, both the pilot and the gunner use night vision equipment for operations after dark. The night vision sensors work on the Forward Looking Infrared (FLIR) system, which detects the infra-red light released by heated objects. The pilot's night vision sensor is linked to a rotating turret on top of the helicopter's nose, while the gunner's night vision sensor is attached to a separate turret on

LEFT: **Night vision equipment provides the user with a high-tech edge that could mean the difference between life or death in a combat environment.**

ABOVE: **Light-enhanced photography showing a US Air Force Sikorsky MH-53J Pave Low helicopter from the 6th Special Operations Wing during a mission over Afghanistan in support of Operation Enduring Freedom.** RIGHT: **Royal Marines of D Company, 40 Commando, are seen through Night Vision Goggles (NVG) as they depart HMS *Ark Royal* by Sea King HC4 helicopters, to take part in military operations on the Al Faw Peninsula in southern Iraq.**

the underside of the nose. The lower turret also houses a standard video camera and telescopic sight, which the gunner uses during daylight operations.

A computer transmits the night vision or video picture to a small display unit built into each crew member's flight helmet. The display unit then projects the image on to a monocular (single) lens in front of the pilot's right eye. Infra-red sensors built into the cockpit track how the pilot positions his helmet and where his line of sight is, and then relays this information to the turret control system – a technique known as "slaving". Each pilot can aim the sensors on an AH-64 Apache by simply moving his head, and the system is designed to have a high

rate of movement – 120 degrees per second – to accurately match head movement and ensure there is no time lag. The same technique is used for aiming the machine's devastating 30mm automatic cannon.

While first-generation NVT required the transition from looking through Night Vision Goggles (NVG) to looking down at the specially lit instrument panel with regular vision, the latest equipment offers a one-stop shop by superimposing all vital flight and instrument data in one view display on the flight helmet. This improves overall situational awareness and crew coordination, and speeds up reaction time for manoeuvring, targeting and for defensive actions, improving both crew and aircraft survivability.

LEFT: **A Sikorsky SH-60 Seahawk assigned to Helicopter Anti-Submarine Squadron 10 (HS-10), Expeditionary Sea Command Unit 1 (ESCU-1), preparing for a rescue mission to a stranded Taiwanese fishing vessel that has run aground on a reef near the Solomon Islands in the Pacific Ocean.**

LEFT: **The Boeing CH-47 Chinook twin-engine, tandem rotor helicopter has served with 17 nations since the 1970s. When the type first entered service, it was faster than many utility and attack helicopters.**

Military heavy-lift helicopters

Military transport helicopters are generally employed in preference to other forms of transport in situations where the cargo is required to be moved quickly, or because the destination is hard to access through other means, or the route over land or water to the destination presents threats to the cargo. Another reason is that the load to be carried might simply be an awkward shape or too heavy to transport easily by road or by fixed-wing aircraft. No other military asset can do what the helicopter, and especially the large helicopter, can do, as landing possibilities are almost limitless and in the situation where they cannot land, they can hover and set down underslung cargo or lower troops without even touching down.

When military forces have to be deployed quickly over any great distance to an area of operations, then large fixed-wing transport aircraft are used to get them to the area. Once there, it often falls to the large helicopter to move the troops and equipment to the fighting locations. Heavy-lift helicopters currently in service with military forces around the world include the Sikorsky CH-53 Sea Stallion and CH-53E Super Stallion, Boeing CH-47 Chinook, Mil Mi-26, and Aérospatiale Super Frélon. Capable of lifting up to 80 troops each and transporting small armoured vehicles (usually as slung loads but also internally in some cases), these helicopters have proved their worth in combat

RIGHT: **A Sikorsky CH-3C transporting a US Army Jeep-type vehicle mounted with a 106mm recoilless anti-tank rifle during Exercise Gold Fire in November, 1964.**

LEFT: **The Mil Mi-10 could normally carry 13,412kg/29,568lb internally, and up to 16,765Kg/36,960lb over a shorter distance. Alternatively, an underslung load of up to 8,941kg/19,712lb could be carried. The rear-facing gondola under the nose allowed a crewman to direct a lifting operation.**

numerous times. Mention should also be made of heavy-lift helicopters, including the Sikorsky CH-37 Mojave and the extraordinary Sikorsky CH-54 Tarhe, which can lift artillery pieces, trucks, medium tanks, other helicopters and boats, and be sent to recover downed aircraft.

The Boeing CH-47 Chinook has been operating around the world since it first flew in 1962. It has been regularly improved and has a cargo bay to accommodate loads well beyond the capacity of other helicopters, including heavy artillery weapons, light vehicles and even smaller helicopters. The heavy-lift use of one Royal Air Force Chinook helicopter illustrates how the type can help turn a battle. In 1982, during the Falklands War, a number of Special Air Service troops were dug in on a hill overlooking Port Stanley and were coming under artillery fire from Argentine forces. The only Chinook available at the time was tasked with delivering three 105mm howitzers to the troops at night. The three large guns were carried internally, and the ammunition was carried on pallets loaded in cargo nets slung under the helicopter.

The heavy-lift helicopter market has been dominated by companies in the USA and Russia by Mil, who specialized in developing large helicopters for the former Soviet Union. The Aérospatiale three-engine Super Frélon is, however, a notable exception, although it was developed with technical assistance from Sikorsky.

The closest that Britain came to developing a heavy-lift helicopter was the Westland Westminster, which was built and test-flown from 1958–60. The impressive machine could carry 6,359kg/14,000lb, and was described as the "largest twin-turbine mechanically driven single-rotor helicopter in the Western world". British helicopter industry mergers and government indifference led to the project being cancelled.

Mil has produced a number of large helicopters, but the largest was the Mil V-12, a twin-rotor helicopter that had a cabin more than 28m/92ft long that could carry a payload of 40,204kg/88,448lb. This machine was used to set many records that stand to this day. Mil chose to abandon further development, and focused on the Mi-26 for heavy-lift work.

In 2021 China and Russia signed a contract to jointly develop the AC332 AHL heavy lift helicopter with a maximum take-off weight of 38 tons, for use by the Chinese military. Russia will develop the transmission, tail rotor and anti-icing system while the Chinese, led by Avicopter, will design, test, and produce it.

ABOVE: **Heavy-lift helicopters can carry a variety of loads. Here, a reusable Ryan Firebee high-speed target drone is being carried by a Sikorsky HH-3.**

Anti-submarine helicopters

Fighting ships face numerous potential threats from an enemy in the form of submarine-launched torpedoes and missiles, and helicopters play a key role in detecting and neutralizing these threats. Helicopters and fixed-wing aircraft can use Magnetic Anomaly Detection (MAD) to locate submarines, and this involves the use of specialist equipment known as magnetometers. These have been developed from

ABOVE: **The Sikorsky SH-60 Seahawk is a development based on the UH-60 Black Hawk, and is used by many navies for anti-submarine and anti-shipping warfare, as well as Combat Search and Rescue (CSAR), Vertical Replenishment (VertRep) and MEDEVAC operations.**

scientific use in geological surveys; they sense changes in the Earth's magnetic field, which can indicate the presence of large metal items under the surface of the sea, i.e. submarines. The MAD equipment is either towed by a helicopter across the surface, but can also be installed in the tail boom of fixed-wing maritime patrol aircraft. Normally, the magnetic lines of the Earth are picked up as bands, and ferro-magnetic substances cause these bands to waver and distort. This distortion is detected by MAD sensors and sent to airborne or seaborne data centres for analysis. The complex system used for the analysis of these data already has readings of known objects preloaded, so can identify most anomalies swiftly and accurately as a specific class of submarine.

In an effort to reduce the anomalies created by magnetic disturbance and thereby avoid detection, defence manufacturers have constructed hulls from non-ferrous materials such as titanium, e.g. the Russian Alpha-Class nuclear-armed submarine. However, because of items such as steel rudder surfaces and nickel alloys in the interiors of these vessels, even these supposedly less detectable boats still produce some disturbance in the water and cannot evade the anti-submarine helicopters.

"Sonar" is the acronym for SOund Navigation And Ranging, a method of underwater detection, navigation and communication that has been used since before World War II. Dipping sonar

LEFT: **Two Kamov Ka-25 helicopters standing on the flight deck of a Russian Navy Moskva-class cruiser.**

LEFT: **A Sikorsky MH-60R Seahawk flying a mission to evaluate Airborne Low-Frequency Sonar (ALPS) equipment.**
BELOW: **A Mark 46 Mods lightweight anti-submarine torpedo. The braking parachute slows the weapon down before entry into the sea.**

was developed by the British for the Royal Navy, and then further developed for the US Navy during the Cold War, and is primarily used for anti-submarine detection.

The dipping or dunking sonar is an instrument operated by a hydraulically powered winch on board a helicopter, on which the automatic flight control system will include a cable hover mode control. The equipment known as the sonar transducer is then lowered into the water from the helicopter. Dipping sonar can be used in either an active (sound-producing) or a passive (echo-receiving) mode. If set to active, the dipping sonar will produce a sound that is broadcast through the water, and then it records the echo response of the sound wave as it hits other objects and reflects back to the instrument. The response time and strength can help indicate where and what type of object the sound has encountered.

As with MAD, by comparing these readings with known readings from a very broad database, it may then be possible to identify the specific class of submarine. For example, many vessels can be identified by the sonic emissions of the power to the engines – particularly what type of energy frequency they employ. Once the area has been declared "clear", then the dipping sonar is withdrawn and recovered to the helicopter.

If a helicopter is ordered to attack a submarine, it can use torpedoes or depth charges. "Torpedo" is the common name for an underwater self-propelled missile, and homing torpedoes can use the principles of passive and active sonar to identify the target. Again, like a dipping sonar, the torpedo can lock on to a target by focusing on either the active sound emission or the reflection of the sound emitted and reflected back the torpedo.

Semi-active homing focuses on the last known location of a target and, once in attack range, the torpedo will "ping" for reference and locate the target. Additionally, the homing torpedo can identify other acoustic signatures beyond a ship or object; it can also recognize energy movements, such as the wake of a ship, and track accordingly.

The simplest anti-submarine weapon is the depth charge, or depth bomb, which is a helicopter-dropped large canister filled with explosive set to explode at a predetermined depth. A Nuclear Depth Bomb (NDB) is the nuclear equivalent of the conventional depth charge, and these devastating weapons have been in service with the Royal Navy, Soviet Navy and US Navy. As a nuclear warhead has much greater explosive power than a conventional depth charge, the NDB significantly increases the likelihood of destroying a submerged submarine. It was because of this much greater destructive capacity that some NDBs were designed for a variable explosive yield – from a low setting for shallow water and areas where damage had to be limited, to maximum yield for deep-water attacks. Three types of Royal Navy helicopter were cleared to carry the 272kg/600lb WE.177A nuclear depth charge: the Westland Wasp, Westland Wessex HAS.3, and Wessex HUS.

From 1966, a total of 43 NDBs were deployed aboard Royal Navy surface vessels of frigate size and larger, for use by helicopters as an anti-submarine weapon.

Soviet helicopters in Afghanistan

One of the abiding images from the television news coverage of the war in Afghanistan from 1979–89 was of Soviet helicopters in action, inserting troops, firing on enemy forces, and indeed being increasingly fired upon as the war continued.

Helicopters were by far the main element of Soviet air power used in the conflict, and it is believed that a maximum of 650 machines were deployed. Soviet helicopters were used for every possible application, but up to 300 of the force are thought to have been the Mil Mi-24 (NATO identifier Hind) gunships. Armed with machine-guns, cannon and up to 200 rocket projectiles, the Mi-24 introduced a new dimension to helicopter warfare in Afghanistan. The Mi-24 was deployed for retaliatory strikes, armed reconnaissance missions, close

ABOVE: **The Mil Mi-8 (NATO identifier Hip) was widely used by the Soviet Army in Afghanistan for a number of roles, including ground attack. Some 40 were shot down by the Mujahideen during the conflict.**

support of ground troops, and to identify and attack any concentration of enemy fighters. The Mil Mi-24 was a gunship and an assault helicopter which could carry eight fully equipped armed troops, but a full load did limit manoeuvrability, especially at the high altitudes experienced in Afghanistan. To save weight, cabin armour was often removed, leaving those inside vulnerable. Instead, the Mil Mi-8 helicopters would be used to transport the troops, while the Mi-24 was flown in the armed-escort role.

RIGHT: **A Mil Mi-24 (NATO identifier Hind) of the Soviet Air Force on patrol over Afghan troops and vehicles on the Salang highway, north of Kabul, the capital of Afghanistan.**

LEFT: **Despite the variety of weaponry and troop numbers available, the invasion and ten-year occupation of Afghanistan was a Soviet failure.**

Mujahideen fighters began to use the Strela-2M heat-seeking surface-to-air missile against Soviet helicopters, and losses began to mount. The missiles were obtained from various sources, including Egypt and China, while the US Central Intelligence Agency (CIA) helped them source others. A total of 42 Soviet helicopters were shot down by various types of Strela-2 and, to overcome the problem, the Soviets began to fit exhaust shrouds to all helicopters to make them less vulnerable to the heat-seeking missile. Losses were, however, severe enough to cause a Soviet change of tactics which saw helicopters being operated at very low altitude, almost hugging the ground.

Nevertheless, for some time it was neither Soviet tanks nor ground forces that were taking the war to the Mujahideen. Mil Mi-24 helicopters were flown to attack enemy positions with guns and rockets, then insert combat troops to complete the assault on the ground. By 1986, technology was being harnessed more effectively, and the Soviet military went on the offensive against Mujahideen forces. One factor that contributed to the end of the Soviet presence in Afghanistan at that time was a US government decision to arm the Mujahideen with Stinger shoulder-fired anti-aircraft missiles. Although the guerrillas had enjoyed some success prior to the delivery of Stinger missiles using machine-guns or rocket-propelled grenades, the new missile increased the average shoot-down to one a day.

The CIA supplied at least 500 Stinger missiles to the Mujahideen from September 1986, and this enabled them to undermine a crucial Soviet advantage – the mobility and firepower provided by their helicopters. With losses mounting, the Soviet military were less inclined to risk helicopter gunships to escort the transport helicopter formations they were designated to protect, and so remained over safe territory.

On February 15, 1989, the last Soviet troops left Afghanistan as part of a general change in Soviet foreign policy.

LEFT: **With the support of the CIA, Mujahideen shoot-down successes increased, and at one point the Soviets were losing a helicopter a day. Here, rebel forces celebrate the capture of a Mil Mi-8.**

Gunships and attack helicopters

An attack helicopter can be defined as a military helicopter for which the primary role is optimized to provide close air support for troops on the ground and in the anti-tank role. The type can be armed for attacking enemy vehicles, both armoured and soft-skinned, troop concentrations, and military strongpoints such as a bunker or command post. Weapons carried can be varied, from machine-guns and cannon to unguided and guided rockets, and usually anti-tank missiles. Some of these fighting helicopters can also carry air-to-air missiles to attack or defend against enemy aircraft.

Attack helicopters evolved as a result of US Army helicopter experience from the Vietnam War, where it was realized that an agile, well-armed, purpose-designed

ABOVE: **Gunners in a Bell UH-1N Iroquois Huey armed with a 0.50in M213 (left) and a 7.62mm M134 Minigun (right).**

attack helicopter was needed to counter the increasingly intense attacks from forces of the Viet Cong (VC) and North Vietnamese Army (NVA). French forces had already experimented with armed helicopters by mounting rockets and machine-guns on Piasecki H-21 Shawnee helicopters during the Algeria campaign. Basic gunships were already in service with US forces in Vietnam in the form of the Bell UH-1A. The medical version of the Bell UH-IA, the famed "Huey", entered service in South Vietnam during June 1962, but the helicopters that arrived there in September that year were heavily armed. These Utility Tactical Transport Company (UTTC) helicopters were fitted with fixed, forward-firing 7.62mm machine-guns attached on each undercarriage skid, and 2.75in rockets that could be fired simultaneously from launching tubes. These first gunships were deployed to protect CH-21 Shawnees and other transport helicopters that were used to move troops in high-risk areas. The US Army believed that they needed heavier armament, and the UH-1B had a more powerful engine, could lift more and could be additionally armed with cabin-mounted machine-guns on flexible mounts. The similarly armed UH-1C was able to offer more effective protection to the troops carried, as it had improved performance and more fuel to allow the machine to provide cover for longer periods.

LEFT: **A crewman firing a Gatling-type rotary cannon mounted on the ramp of a Sikorsky HH-3E Jolly Green Giant.**

LEFT: **The Mi-24A (NATO identifier Hind) was the first version of the heavily armed helicopter gunship which served with many Warsaw Pact nations. The type was known as "The Flying Tank" by those who flew the machine.**

However, as the fighting grew more intense, the US Army developed a requirement for a dedicated attack helicopter – this was the Advanced Aerial Fire Support System (AAFFSS) project. The winning design was the Lockheed AH-56 Cheyenne, but the US military knew it would take time to develop such a specialized machine (it never entered service due to technical problems and being over budget), but still had a military challenge growing day by day in South-east Asia. An interim solution to this gap in their inventory was required, so they invited manufacturers to propose a combat helicopter that could be in service in Vietnam relatively quickly. Designs from Sikorsky and Kaman were submitted, but it was a Bell proposal, based on the UH-1s, that was successful, and led to a contract being issued in April 1966 for 110 AH-1 Cobra attack helicopters. With tandem cockpit seating (as opposed to the typical side-by-side), the Cobra (also known as the "HueyCobra") presented a significantly smaller frontal aspect as a target, had much improved armour and an impressive performance.

In 1967, the first were deployed to South Vietnam and opened a new chapter in the history of warfare – the type was the first helicopter designed from the outset to be armed for and optimized for combat. While the Cheyenne was slowly progressing through development, the AH-1 Cobra, armed with a formidable combination of nose-mounted 20mm cannon and multiple rocket launchers or Miniguns in pod mountings, delivered a new dimension to air warfare. Later in the Vietnam War, AH-1 Cobra helicopters were deployed against ANV tanks to great success. The Lockheed AH-56 Cheyenne project was cancelled in 1972, and within weeks a new requirement was issued by the US Army that incorporated lessons learned in the Vietnam War, applying them to the ever-present threat from Soviet armour

in Cold War Europe. This requirement led to the ultimate attack helicopter, the Hughes AH-64 Apache. The Soviet Union had also observed events in Vietnam, had learned from the war, and began to develop a dedicated attack helicopter.

ABOVE: **A 0.50in M213 Browning heavy machine gun mounted in the door of a Bell UH-1 Iroquois helicopter.**

Bravo November

The aircraft known by its call sign of Bravo November is one of the most historic operated by the Royal Air Force in the post-World War II era. It is not a high-performance jet fighter or strike aircraft, but a Boeing Vertol Chinook HC2 helicopter. The RAF has flown Bravo November on operations in Northern Ireland, the Falkland Islands, Lebanon, Germany, Kurdistan, Iraq, Afghanistan and the Balkans. Four of the pilots to have flown the machine have been awarded the Distinguished Flying Cross (DFC).

The helicopter was built as a Chinook HC1 and entered RAF service in 1982. It is the only survivor of the four deployed with the British Task Force sent later that year to the Falkland Islands following the Argentine invasion. The machines were transported to the Falklands on the MV *Atlantic Conveyor*, which was sunk by an Exocet missile on May 25, 1982. Bravo November was being flown on an air test at the time, so survived and was diverted to land on HMS *Hermes*. After this lucky escape, the helicopter was in action soon after the first British troops landed on the islands, being deployed to transport 105mm artillery to Special Air Service troops on Mount Kent, where they were under fire from Argentine artillery.

Later in the Falklands campaign, the aircraft was being flown over the sea at night through a heavy snow shower, and this caused the crew to lose horizon references. The aircraft hit the sea at 185kph/115mph, but in an almost upright attitude. The pilot, Sqd Ldr Langworthy, and co-pilot, Flt Lt Lawless, successfully lifted the aircraft from the water and were, remarkably, able to fly the machine and land safely. With damaged radio equipment, however, the crew was unable to communicate with British Forces, so when approaching San Carlos, they left the aircraft's lights on in the hope that they would not be fired upon.

ABOVE: **On the Falkland Islands in 1982, Bravo November was the only Chinook to be operated during the campaign.**

ABOVE: **Despite an unplanned impact with the sea, Bravo November continued to serve on vital troop and supply missions during the Falklands campaign.**

RIGHT: **Bravo November has seen service in Northern Ireland, the Falkland Islands, Lebanon, Germany, Kurdistan, Iraq, Afghanistan and the Balkans.**

British forces had in fact heard the distress calls from the crew, so did not open fire. The machine suffered surprisingly little damage – the radio antenna was ripped off, the fuselage damaged, and a cockpit door torn off by the violence of the impact. All spares, tools and servicing manuals had been lost aboard MV *Atlantic Conveyor*, and it was two weeks before spare parts and supplies would arrive, but the ground crews kept the machine flying.

On June 2, 1982, a force of 81 paratroopers, twice the normal troop load and a record for any troop carrying helicopter, were flown from Goose Green to retake the settlement of Fitzroy. After dropping the first group, the crew returned to Goose Green to pick up a further 75 to take part in the operation. By the end of the war, Bravo November had accumulated over 100 flying hours, transported some 1,500 personnel, 558,835kg/1,232,000lb of cargo, and moved 650 prisoners and some 95 casualties. Langworthy was awarded the DFC for his actions as the pilot of Bravo November during the Falklands War.

In 2003, over than 20 years after the Falklands campaign, Bravo November was deployed during the opening night operations of Operation Desert Storm for the assault on the Al Faw peninsula, the site of a major oil refinery. Piloting the machine, Sqdr Ldr Steve Carr led the five Chinooks that were to land Royal Marine commandos at the objective.

ABOVE: **By early 2011, four pilots who had flown Bravo November on operations had each been awarded the Distinguished Flying Cross (DFC).**

During the operation, Bravo November averaged 19 flight hours a day over a three-day period, delivering combat vehicles, troops and artillery. The mission was the largest helicopter assault in UK military history, and the first helicopter assault operation since the Suez Crisis in 1956. Carr was awarded the DFC for his bravery and leadership.

The helicopter continued to be operated in Iraq, but did not have to wait another 20 years to be flown in another war. On the night of June 11, 2006, Flt Lt Craig Wilson commanded the machine on a casualty recovery mission in Helmand Province, Afghanistan. In dangerous conditions and with little experience of night flying in Afghanistan, he flew at an altitude of 46m/150ft and made a perfect approach and landing to extract the casualty. Wilson flew a similar mission just a few hours later and ran low on fuel while waiting for enemy fire to be suppressed. On landing, despite having been on duty for over 22 hours, he then volunteered to take reinforcements to deal with a deteriorating ground situation. His gallantry and extreme and persistent courage that day ensured the recovery of two badly wounded soldiers. Wilson received the DFC for "exceptional courage and outstanding airmanship" while on operations in Helmand Province.

By 2010, Bravo November was a veteran of several operational tours in Afghanistan, and January that year saw it live up to the reputation of being a lucky aircraft. After picking up six wounded soldiers following a Taliban ambush, the machine, piloted by Flt Lt Ian Fortune, came under machine-gun fire from the ground. The helicopter received several hits which damaged some systems. Fortune was also hit by a Taliban bullet that entered through the cockpit windscreen, ricocheted and shattered the visor on his flying helmet, causing him some facial injuries. After calmly reporting what had happened to his fellow crew members, Fortune flew the helicopter back to Camp Bastion. He was awarded the DFC for his courage. Bravo November has been preserved for the nation and is displayed by the Royal Air Force Museum.

Operation Desert Storm

The Vietnam War had proved the military value of the helicopter gunship and, as that war came to an end, the US Army considered how it might apply this knowledge to the continuing Cold War situation in Europe. Attack helicopters such as the Bell AH-1Cobra were given the task of attacking, with missiles, Soviet command posts and armour behind enemy lines. Technology was also developed to help night operations and utilize superior Western technology against numerically superior Warsaw Pact forces. By the 1980s, the US had developed heavily armed helicopters as dedicated "tankbusters" to attack with guns and missiles. These tactics, although never tried in Europe, were put to the test during the first Gulf War in response to the Iraqi invasion of Kuwait, when many helicopter types saw action for the first time.

The international Coalition forces launched Operation Desert Storm on January 17, 1991, following the expiration of a deadline for Iraq to withdraw from Kuwait. Coalition naval assets operating from the Persian Gulf faced a modest but potent threat from the

ABOVE: **Helicopters operated by Coalition forces were used to patrol the Persian Gulf and the Straits of Hormuz.**

Iraqi Navy. Fast attack craft armed with missiles were of concern, so were attacked wherever possible. Helicopters such as the Sikorsky SH-60B Seahawk and Westland Lynx HAS Mk3, armed with Sea Skua anti-shipping missiles, together with other Coalition fixed-wing aircraft, damaged or destroyed most of the Iraqi fleet.

The Coalition had decided to try to bomb Iraqi forces into submission before any ground war began and, as part of this strategy, US helicopter gunships such as the Bell AH-1 Cobra and Hughes AH-64 Apache were roaming over enemy positions, often at night, destroying tanks, vehicles and anti-aircraft defences. On January 18, Iraq began Scud missile attacks on Saudi Arabia and Israel, which threatened to destabilize the Coalition. As part of an all-out effort to find and destroy the Scuds on mobile launchers, special forces units were inserted by helicopter under cover of darkness deep into Iraqi territory.

LEFT: **The heavy-lift capability available to Coalition forces included CH-47 Chinooks, which were able to rapidly move supplies and equipment forward in support of advancing troops.**

ABOVE: **Although first flown operationally in the Vietnam War, the Bell UH-1 Iroquois played a key role in Operation Desert Storm.**

ABOVE: **During the Gulf War, around half of all the Sikorsky UH-60 Black Hawk helicopters in US Army service were deployed, with only two lost in combat.**

Helicopters were a vital part of the prelude to the ground war, and were used to continue attacks on Iraqi assets, virtually unmolested. When the ground war began, Apache and Cobra gunships continued to destroy Iraqi armour, and vehicles as well as bunkers. The sheer numbers of US helicopters available to fight meant that these attacks were never-ending, as wave after wave of refuelled and rearmed helicopter gunships would take their place in the assault. Apaches were even taking the surrender of Iraqi troops, who were understandably in awe of the gunship.

Most attacks by Apache helicopters were carried out from a range of some 3km/2 miles and at a height of no more than 10m/33ft to minimize the risk of a successful surface-to-air missile strike. Armed with AGM-114 Hellfire anti-tank missiles,

30mm cannon and 70mm Hydra 70 unguided rockets, the machines halted and destroyed countless Iraqi vehicle columns. Any doubts regarding the military value of helicopter gunships disappeared, as large numbers of both types decimated Iraqi armour in the open desert.

Also under cover of darkness, large numbers of Coalition troops were ferried deep inside Iraqi territory, establishing facilities for supporting the attack helicopters as well as ground troops. The fighting helicopters were complemented by general-purpose helicopters moving troops and supplies to exactly where the Coalition needed them. These included the UH-60 Black Hawk, Bell UH-1, Lynx, Gazelle, CH-47 Chinook, CH-53 Super Stallion, Puma and Super Puma. After the fighting was over, many of these helicopters were used for humanitarian missions.

LEFT: **A Sikorsky UH-60 Black Hawk of the Saudi Arabia Air Force during Operation Desert Storm.**

LEFT: **A French Army Gazelle carrying HOT missiles to attack Iraqi armour. British Army Air Corps (AAC) Gazelles were flown on scouting and observation missions.**

LEFT: **The Boeing-Sikorsky RAH-66 Comanche was an advanced armed reconnaissance and attack helicopter designed with stealth features. The development programme was cancelled in 2004.**

The anti-tank helicopter

In the late 1950s, the French had experimented with mounting wire-guided Nord SS.11 anti-tank missiles on the Alouette II (lark) helicopter, but it took the US experience in Vietnam to force the development of what was to become the anti-tank helicopter. Having developed the helicopter into potent and effective ground attack aircraft in Vietnam, the US Army then sought to apply this new expertise and the associated technology to counter the growing threat from Soviet armour in Cold War Europe. If war had broken out, and NATO faced the prospect of large numbers of Soviet tanks sweeping through the Iron Curtain, dedicated anti-tank helicopters provided one solution to this daunting military problem. During the 1970s, a considerable amount of time and money was spent on research and development of a missile-armed attack helicopter which was evolving into a primary anti-tank weapon.

While the US military had the proven Bell AH-1 Cobra, other nations were developing or were keen to acquire an anti-tank helicopter. In common with most areas of Cold War military technology, both sides would strive to develop a means of equalling, surpassing or combating each new development. The Soviet Union also began developing the helicopter as an attack aircraft; the first attempt was a heavily armed version of the Mil-8 (NATO identifier Hip) mounted with four anti-tank missiles in addition to machine-guns and rocket launchers carried on stub wings. This was followed by the formidable Mil Mi-24 (NATO identifier Hind), which also had a troop transport capability.

RIGHT: **A dedicated anti-tank version of the MBB Bo105 armed with HOT missiles was procured by the German Army in the late 1970s, and a total of 212 were delivered.**

Helicopters are perfect for the anti-tank role because the type had been developed into a highly manoeuvrable machine that can be operated day or night to launch surprise attacks against enemy armour. A helicopter is an effective anti-tank aircraft because of the ability to be hovered behind cover, only to rise briefly and fire a missile. Early helicopter-launched missiles required a crew member to keep the target in sight and "fly" the wire-guided missile on to the target using a cockpit-mounted gun sight and a joystick controller. The development of the homing missile allowed targets to be designated by a laser so that the missile could then "home" in, although this still required the target to be kept in sight

TOP: **The Lockheed AH-56 Cheyenne was developed to be the US Army's first dedicated attack helicopter, but was cancelled in 1972.** ABOVE: **The AGM-114 Hellfire anti-tank missile and 70mm Hydra 70 unguided rockets.** ABOVE RIGHT: **An AGM-114 Hellfire being loaded on the weapons pylon of an AH-64 Apache.**

from the helicopter. Continued development of even more sophisticated sensors means that helicopters such as the AH-64 Apache have only the rotor head-mounted sensor high enough too see the enemy tank before the crew can launch a missile.

In combat situations, the endurance of these missile-armed helicopters would be supported by transport helicopters to carry ground crew and armourers to refuel and reload the combat machines, getting them back into action within minutes. Forward Arming and Refuelling Points (FARP) are set up at pre-arranged locations for the replenishment process, which can take place with engines running and rotors turning.

Helicopters have been used in anti-tank combat in many conflicts. During the 1973 Yom Kippur War, Israel had used fast fixed-wing jet aircraft against Syrian and Egyptian tanks and, although victorious, they were aware of the disadvantages compared to helicopters. As a result, Israel began procuring a force of anti-tank helicopters, opting for the Bell AH-1 Cobra armed with 20mm cannon and anti-tank weapons, and also the Hughes 500MD Defender fitted with a nose-mounted sight and the capability to carry

usually two Tube-launched Optically-tracked Wire-guided (TOW) missiles. In 1982 during the Lebanon War, these helicopters were used against Syrian armour, and destroyed many of the then modern, Soviet-designed T-72 tanks. This was of great interest to NATO strategists, who would hope to replicate the success if the Cold War in Europe ever became hot. The anti-tank helicopter was proved to be a vital element of any armed forces facing the potential threat of an attack by enemy armour.

BELOW: **The 9K11 Malyutka (NATO identifier AT-3 Sagger), a wire-guided anti-tank guided missile, was developed in the Soviet Union to be both man-portable and helicopter-fired.**

AgustaWestland AH-64W Apache Longbow

On November 15, 1972, the US Army issued a Request For Proposal (RFP) for an Advance Attack Helicopter (AAH), and specified a low-flying, highly manoeuvrable machine. Hughes produced the (Model 77) YHA-64A and Bell the (Model 409) YHA-63A. After evaluation, the US Army selected the Hughes machine. Bell used development data from the YHA-63A to produce the AH-1 Cobra gunship, and the AH-64A entered service in January 1984. Westland Helicopters built 67 of the type as the WAH-64A Apache for the British Army Air Corps (AAC), and it remains in service as the Apache Longbow.

RIGHT: **The Apache Longbow has a number of key features to aid its recognition: the deep disc-like radar scanner on top of the rotor head; the tandem cockpit; and the large 30mm cannon mounted externally beneath the cockpit.**

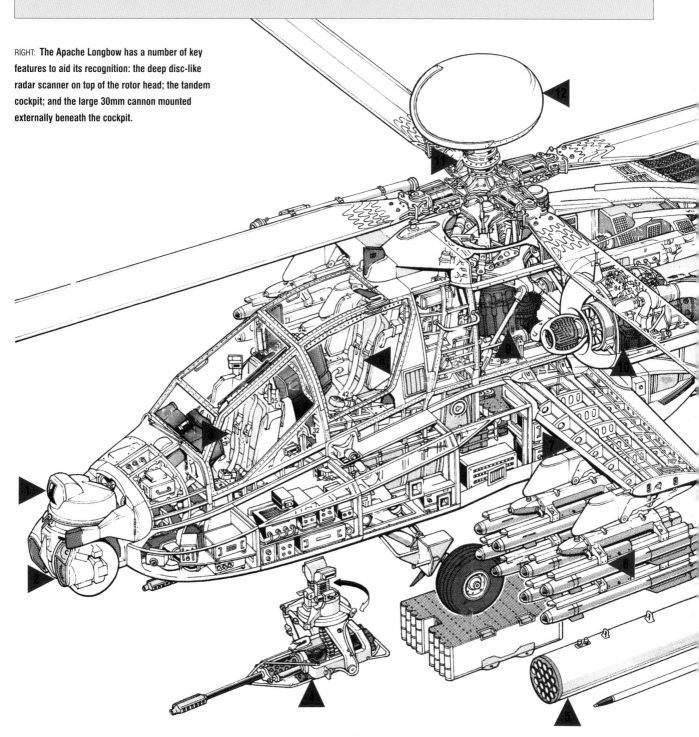

LEFT: **The Longbow mast-mounted fire-control radar detects, classifies, prioritizes (up to 128 in a minute) and engages targets in all conditions – whether those targets are stationary or mobile, multiple on the ground or airborne.**

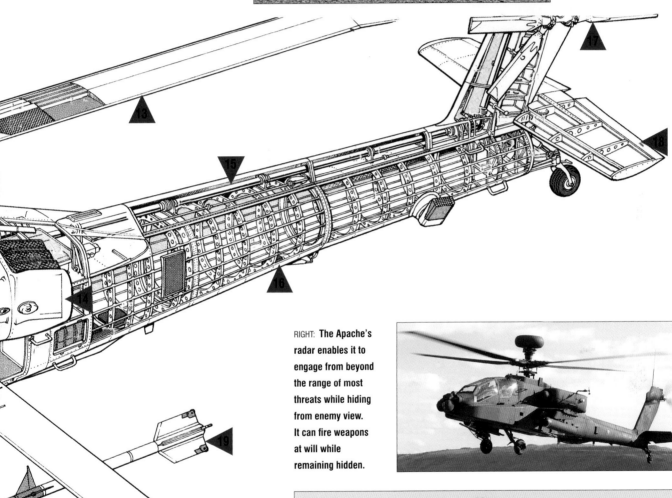

RIGHT: **The Apache's radar enables it to engage from beyond the range of most threats while hiding from enemy view. It can fire weapons at will while remaining hidden.**

Key

1	Pilot's Night Vision Sensor (PNVS)	10	Rolls-Royce/Turboméca RTM322 turboshaft engine
2	Target Acquisition and Designator Sight (TADS)	11	Main rotor head
3	Co-pilot/gunner's seat	12	Longbow radar
4	30mm M230 Chain Gun cannon and mounting	13	Rotor blade
5	70mm air to-ground rocket and pod	14	Infra-red suppressor duct
6	AGM-114 Hellfire missile	15	Tail rotor driveshaft
7	Stub wing	16	Tail boom structure
8	Pilot's seat	17	Tail rotor
9	Main gearbox	18	Tailplane
		19	AIM-9L Sidewinder missile
		20	AIM-92A Stinger missile

LEFT: The first type chosen for presidential service was the Bell H-13 Sioux, but this was soon replaced by a larger and more comfortable machine, the Sikorsky HUS-1 Seahorse, operated by the US Marine Corps. The type was later used by President John F. Kennedy. Note the machine is fitted with inflatable flotation bags on the main wheels for an emergency landing on water.

US presidential helicopters

In 1957, Dwight D. Eisenhower became the first serving US President to use a helicopter for his official duties. While the US military had been using helicopters since 1944, the cautious Secret Service had resisted their introduction as a presidential transport due to safety concerns over what was perceived to be new technology. However, in Cold War 1956, with the potential for Armageddon to be unleashed with just a few minutes' notice, it was clear that a quick means of evacuating the President was required. The need for a presidential helicopter was agreed, and the search for appropriate candidate types began. Safety and reliability were high on the list of deciding factors, and the first chosen was the Bell H-13 Sioux, proven in service during the Korean War. In addition to the pilot, the small helicopter could only carry the President and one other passenger, a Secret

Service protection agent. Bell modified an H-13J specifically for this usage, and it featured all-metal rotor blades, and special arm and foot rests for the right-hand seat, covered with custom upholstery. A frameless Plexiglas nose was tinted dark blue to reduce heat and glare. The H-13 was considered an odd choice by many, not least because of its size. It had a range of only 242km/150 miles, it was comparatively slow, and it had just one pilot, while larger machines had two in case one become incapacitated. The presidential H-13J, serial number 57-2729, also had a rotor-brake to reduce the shutdown time and allow the President a swift exit. Eisenhower's first flight left the South Lawn of the White House on July 12, 1957. In September 1957, he took a flight in a Sikorsky HUS-1 of the US Marine Corps, soon appreciated the shortcomings of the small Bell

LEFT: In 1961, the Sikorsky VS-34 was replaced in service with the Sikorsky H-3 Sea King, a larger and more comfortable machine operated by the USMC as the VH-3D. All presidential helicopters use the call sign "Marine One".

RIGHT: **The Sikorsky SH-3D Sea King was supplemented in service by the Sikorsky CH-53 Super Stallion. All presidential flights are operated by Marine Helicopter Squadron One (HMX-1).**

machine, and requested that the Sikorsky machine became the presidential helicopter. Until then, the President had always been flown by the US Air Force, but as the Sikorsky was not in USAF service, the honour now fell to both the United States Marine Corps and the US Army, who took it in turns to transport the Commander-in-Chief. This split responsibility remained, albeit with different helicopters, right through to 1976, when the administration of Gerald Ford removed presidential helicopter obligations from the US Army for economic reasons.

Most people are familiar with "Air Force One", the Presidential Boeing 747 operated by the USAF. However, the President's journey to Air Force One often begins with a flight from the White House lawn in a helicopter always known as "Marine One", the call sign of any one of the fleet of USMC machines available to carry the President. When the Army operated presidential helicopters, the call sign was, logically, "Army One". In 1961, the HUS-1 was replaced by

another Sikorsky machine, the VH-3A VIP version of the Sea King. The VH-3D replaced some VH-3As in 1978. The Sikorsky VH-60 was added to the Marine One fleet of helicopters from 1989, in both VH-60D Nighthawk and VH-60N Whitehawk variants. Marine One is typically operated by the USMC HMX-1 Nighthawks squadron, and is currently either the VH-3D Sea King or the VH-60N Whitehawk, which are both due to be replaced by the Sikorsky/Lockheed Martin VH-92, a militarized variant of the Sikorsky S-92.

Over 800 USMC ground crew and pilots are involved in the operation of the Marine One fleet, which is based in Quantico, Virginia. It is notable that marine aviators flying Marine One do not wear regular flight suits during presidential flights, but wear dress uniform. As a security measure, Marine One always flies in a group of up to five identical helicopters. One of these carries the President, while the others are decoys to confuse any potential attacker on the ground, and change formation to add to the confusion.

LEFT: **The Sikorsky VH-60D Nighthawk version of the SH-60 Seahawk entered service with HMX-1 in 1989. The Sikorsky VH-60N Whitehawk variant is also in Marine One service. Along with all the VH-3D helicopters, the type is due for replacement within the next decade.**

LEFT: **US Marine Corps troops being flown to the beachhead in Boeing Vertol CH-46 Sea Knight helicopters. A Landing Craft, Air Cushion (LCAC) is approaching the beach.**

Helicopter assault ships

The development of the military helicopter significantly increased the options open to naval planners in terms of how they could conduct operations. The Allies' and particularly the US experience in World War II in the Pacific demonstrated how air power could turn battles, provide vital top cover for seaborne assaults, and attack defensive strongpoints as the first part of a seaborne assault. Nevertheless, there were still many restrictions on the type of coastline that could be considered for amphibious assault, including tides and the steepness of the beach, which could rule out the use of landing craft. These factors limited military options but the arrival of the helicopter made it possible, in theory, to land troops anywhere, regardless of tides or beach topography, and pose a threat that is hard to defend against.

Today's assault ships are designed to support amphibious warfare – the landing and support of troops on to or near enemy territory by an amphibious assault. They have their origins in the ships of the 1950s that were used by some navies in early airborne assaults, such as by the Royal Navy in Suez. Ships were then converted to carry more, or perhaps only, helicopters, and this evolution led to purpose-designed assault ships that can not only accommodate helicopters but also amphibious landing craft, by the inclusion of a well deck. These ships are quite different from a fixed-wing aircraft carrier, but do also have the ability to operate V/STOL aircraft.

ABOVE: **HMS *Ocean* (L12), a Royal Navy Landing Ship, Personnel, Helicopter (LPH) carrying Westland Sea King helicopters and a Boeing CH-47 Chinook.**
RIGHT: **HMS *Albion* was built as a Centaur-class aircraft carrier in 1947, and converted to a Commando Carrier in 1962.**

LEFT: **USS *Boxer* (LHD-4) is a Wasp-class amphibious assault ship. The vessel can carry up to 42 aircraft, including the Sikorsky CH-53 Super Stallion and the Bell-Boeing MV-22 Osprey.**

The US Navy operates the largest fleet of this type of ship, including the Wasp class introduced in 1989 and the America class which joined the US fleet in 2014.

The Wasp class can carry a variety of helicopters including twelve Sikorsky CH-53E Super Stallions and four MV-22B Ospreys, four AH-1W/Z Super Cobra/Viper attack helicopters for attack and support, as well as six Harriers or six F-35B Lightning IIs. A US Marine Corps Battalion of up to 1,900 troops can be embarked as well as trucks, assault vehicles and tanks.

The first Royal Navy ship to be built specifically for the amphibious assault role was HMS *Ocean* (L12), which entered service in 1998. It could carry up to 12 Sea King or four Merlin helicopters, six Lynx or AH-64 Apache helicopters. and a full battalion of troops, as well as light vehicles and equipment. A large flooding dock allowed the ship to carry and deploy landing craft and large assault hovercraft. *Ocean* left Royal Navy service in 2018.

By way of comparison, France's Mistral-class amphibious assault ships can transport and deploy 16 NI Industries NH90 or Eurocopter E665/Airbus HAD Tiger helicopters, four landing craft, up to 70 vehicles, including 13 tanks, or an entire 40-strong tank battalion and 450 troops. The flight deck has six helicopter landing spots, one of which is capable of supporting a heavy helicopter. The hangar deck can hold 16 helicopters, and has an overhead crane – two aircraft lifts connect the hangar to the flight deck. Every helicopter operated by the French military is capable of flying from Mistral-class ships.

BELOW: **A US Navy SH-60F Seahawk, assigned to Helicopter Anti-Submarine Squadron 14 (HS-14), flying over the Republic of Korea (RoK) Dokdo-class amphibious assault ship *Dokdo* during joint exercises in 2010.**

Tilt-wing and tilt-rotor

The path that led to the Bell-Boeing V-22 Osprey in service today with the US Air Force and US Marine Corps was beaten by a relatively small number (in aerospace industry terms) of gifted, forward-thinking and stubborn designers who refused to accept that a viable tilt-rotor or tilt-wing aircraft could not be designed. The benefit of both designs is that they combine the take-off, landing and hover capability of a helicopter with the range and performance of a fixed-wing aircraft, achieved through tilting the wing with engines and rotors attached (tilt-wing) or just the rotors (there were usually more than one) through around 90 degrees (tilt-rotor).

The dream of lifting off from a city centre helipad and then flying at high speeds was of great interest to the airline industry. Some individuals among the military, having realized the limitations inherent in a helicopter, could also see the remarkable versatility and capability this type of machine could give the armed forces – landing and taking off virtually anywhere, and transiting between locations at high speed. There were, however, enormous technical problems to overcome, as well as numerous design failures and mishaps. A number of the designs that added to an understanding of the capability warrant examination.

Credit for creating the first working tilt-rotor aircraft goes to the team at the splendidly named Transcendental Aircraft Corporation of Pennsylvania. In 1954 and 1955, their experimental aircraft were routinely achieving up to 70 degrees of tilt, with the wings supporting over 90 per cent of the aircraft's weight.

RIGHT: The Canadair CL-84 Dynavert was a V/STOL turbine-powered tilt-wing aircraft, four examples of which were manufactured by Canadair between 1964 and 1972. Although two CL-84s crashed due to mechanical failure, the type was considered a successful experimental type.

ABOVE: The Vertol VZ-2 was built in 1957 to investigate tilt-wing technology for Vertical Take-Off and Landing (VTOL). The T-tail incorporated small ducted fans to act as thrusters for greater control at low speeds. On July 23, 1958, the aircraft made a full transition from vertical to horizontal flight. This groundbreaking research aircraft is now preserved by the National Air and Space Museum.

Bell had been working on the tilt-rotor concept since the late 1940s, and built the XV-3. A slender metal wing was mounted mid-fuselage, and a large 7.63m/25ft helicopter-type rotor was mounted on each wing tip. The machine was powered by a single Pratt & Whitney R-985-AN-1 Wasp Junior radial piston engine. Power to the rotors was transmitted via gearboxes and drive shafts. Wind-tunnel testing showed positive results, but what did not exist at this point in aerospace history was the ability to predict in advance the impact of what is known as aeroelasticity – the effect that the large, slow-turning rotors would have on the wing structure and other flexible components of the aircraft, which can be both destabilizing and damaging to the structure. The XV-3 was plagued by the resulting instabilities, which ultimately caused the first prototype to crash. The second prototype which, like the

LEFT: **The Ling-Temco-Vought (LTV) XC-142 was designed to investigate the operation of V/STOL transports. The first conventional flight took place on September 29, 1964, and the first transitional flight on January 11, 1965.**

first prototype, was modified and refined after each series of testing, finally achieved a full 90-degree conversion to forward flight in December 1958, three years after the first hover flight. Although the XV-3 also successfully demonstrated the feasibility of the tilt-rotor concept, it was not taken any further, but provided a wealth of data for subsequent related research programmes.

Meanwhile, Vertol were working on tilt-wing concepts, and produced the VZ-2A. A single Lycoming turboshaft engine was mounted above the fuselage, driving two wing-mounted propellers for lift as well as two ducted fans, one in the fin and the other in the horizontal stabilizer. These fans were used for pitch and yaw control of the craft during hovering and transition flight. The VZ-2A was flown vertically in April 1957. On July 15, 1958, the first complete transition took place, demonstrating vertical take-off to forward flight and then back to a vertical landing, proving the tilt-wing concept.

Hiller's large (for a test vehicle) X-18 of 1959 mated the fuselage of a Chase transport aircraft with a high-set tilting wing, but the design for the US Air Force did not progress beyond 20 test flights. In 1962, Kaman developed a tilt-wing aircraft for the US Navy which had a Grumman Goose fuselage mated to an all-new Kaman-designed tilting wing. This exotic design did not progress beyond the wind-tunnel testing.

The Vought/Hiller/Ryan XC-142 tilt-wing aircraft was developed with US Government backing to create a design that, unlike most preceding tilt-wing experiments, really could have tri-service military applications for the US Army, USN and USAF. Proposed as a transport aircraft, the XC-142 was 18m/59ft long and had an all-up weight of 16,900kg/37,258lb. It was powered by four General Electric T64-GE-1 turboprop engines mounted on the wings, cross-linked to drive four-bladed propellers. The engines also drove a fifth propeller – a three-bladed unit in the tail, which rotated in the horizontal plane. Despite great promise, shortcomings and a number of accidents halted progress but, again, much useful data was gathered for later programmes.

ABOVE: **The Bell XV-15 tilt-rotor aircraft, which first flew in May 1977, was the first of its kind to demonstrate the high-speed performance of the type compared to that of a conventional helicopter. It had a top speed of 557kph/345mph.** BELOW: **The Bell XV-15 undergoing a test flight programme at Ames Research Centre (ARC), located at Moffett Field in Silicon Valley, California.**

LEFT: **A Northrop Grumman RQ-8A Fire Scout approaching for the first autonomous landing aboard USS** *Nashville* **(LPD-13) during sea trials in 2006.**

Vertical Unmanned Aircraft Systems (VUAS)

Unmanned rotary aircraft have been in military service since the early 1960s but development in the early 2000s has led to a number of highly advanced examples entering front line service with the US military in particular.

The Gyrodyne QH-50 DASH (Drone Anti-Submarine Helicopter) was a small, coaxial rotor helicopter built as a long-range anti-submarine weapon to be deployed on US Navy warships too small to operate a full-sized ASW helicopter. In the late 1950s, the US had to urgently increase anti-submarine capability to counter the threat of the growing numbers of Soviet submarines, and the QH-50 gave an anti-submarine capability to existing ships that were outdated for other duties. The machine was powered by a Boeing T50-4 turboshaft engine and could carry two Mk 44 torpedoes or a nuclear depth charge. A total of 378 were produced before production ended in January 1966. The QH-50 DASH required two controllers – one on the flightdeck and another in the Combat Information Centre (CIC). The flight-deck controller would handle take-off and landing, while the CIC controller flew the drone to the target and attacked using semi-automated controls and radar. The type had a range of up to 35km/ 22 miles, so the submarine would have no warning of the attack until a torpedo had entered the water. The CIC controller could not see the aircraft and occasionally lost control, so to improve this far-from-ideal situation, television cameras were installed experimentally late in the programme. The DASH programme was cancelled in 1969, but some modified

machines were operated in a number of roles during the Vietnam War. The Japanese Maritime Self-Defense Force (JMSDF) also operated a fleet of 20 of the type until 1977.

The Northrop Grumman Corporation Fire Scout, a Vertical Unmanned Aircraft System (VUAS), is under development to provide unprecedented situational awareness and precision targeting support for the US military. The MQ-8B Fire Scout is based on the Schweizer Model 333 helicopter, a proven design. The machine can take off and land autonomously on any air-capable warship or at unprepared landing zones in proximity to the edge of the forward battle area.

With vehicle endurance greater than eight hours, the MQ-8B Fire Scout will be capable of operating to provide coverage some 161km/100 miles from the launch site. The type is equipped with electro-optical/infra-red sensors and a laser pointer/laser rangefinder to enable the machine to locate, track and designate targets.

In January 2006, two Fire Scout VUAS drones completed nine autonomous ship-board landings on USS *Nashville* (LPD-13), the first time a VUAS in USN service performed vertical landings on a moving ship without a pilot controlling the aircraft.

Lockheed Martin and the Kaman Aerospace Corporation have successfully transformed the proven Kaman-built K-MAX power-lift helicopter into an unmanned aircraft for autonomous or remote-controlled cargo delivery. This unmanned helicopter can routinely be used to undertake

ABOVE: **The Bell/Textron Eagle Eye in service with the US Coast Guard can fly at over 370kph/230mph, has a range of 1,481km/920 miles, and can fly at up to 6,096m/20,000ft for some six hours.** RIGHT: **In April 2011, US Navy Fire Scouts were despatched to support US Army and Coalition forces in Afghanistan. Fire Scout is a small helicopter able to stay aloft for more than eight hours at altitudes up to 5,182m/17,000ft.**

battlefield cargo resupply missions in hazardous conditions, and drew considerable interest from the US Marine Corps who deployed the type in Afghanistan. On 17 December 2011, the USMC conducted the first unmanned aerial system cargo delivery in a combat zone using the unmanned K-MAX, moving about 1,600kg/3,500lb. The aircraft can fly at higher altitudes with a larger payload than any other rotary-wing unmanned vehicle, and is fitted with a four-hook carousel. The K-MAX drone can also deliver more cargo to more locations in one flight. The machine can lift 2,725kg/6,000lb at sea level, and more than 1,817kg/4,000lb at an altitude of 4,575m/15,000ft.

Meanwhile, Northrop Grumman developed the MQ-8C Fire Scout (known as Fire-X in development) for use by the United States Navy. The MQ-8C has autonomous take-off and landing capability and is designed to provide reconnaissance, situational awareness, aerial fire support and precision targeting support for ground, air and sea forces.

The MQ-8C airframe is based on the proven civilian Bell 407 helicopter, while the avionics and other systems are developed from those used on the MQ-8B Fire Scout. It first flew in October 2013 and was declared operational in June 2019. The type has an endurance of up to 14 hours and can lift up to 1,363kg/ 3,000lb in total, of which 1,181kg/2,600lb is carried externally.

Unmanned helicopters are offering the military an increased, cost-effective capability and are expected to become, like fixed-wing drones, a major part of the air assets available to military commanders in the field.

LEFT: **Northrop Grumman state that "The transformational Fire Scout Vertical Take-off and Landing Tactical Unmanned Aerial Vehicle system provides unprecedented situation awareness and precision targeting support for US armed forces of the future."**

Directory of Military Helicopters

At the end of World War II, Germany's aircraft industry was in ruins, leaving the Sikorsky Aircraft Corporation in the USA as the sole established manufacturer of helicopters. However, other US-based companies, including Bell, Hiller, Piasecki and Vertol, began to develop the type, and were soon producing helicopters for the US military.

The British companies Bristol and Saunders-Roe began to design and build helicopters, whereas Westland chose to negotiate a licence with Sikorsky to manufacture and later develop the US-designed machines. In France, the manufacturers Sud-Est and Sud-Ouest began to produce a series of experimental machines. The companies merged as Sud Aviation and later became Aérospatiale, the manufacturer of the highly successful Alouette turbine-powered helicopter. The Italian company Agusta designed and built a number of machines, then decided to concentrate on producing US-designed aircraft under licence.

In the post-war Soviet Union, Kamov established the first helicopter design and manufacturing bureau, followed a little later by Mil. Both produced helicopters for all Soviet services, Warsaw Pact countries and other friendly nations around the world.

In 2012, the People's Republic of China announced their decision to fund the design, development and production of a series of military helicopters, in order to cease reliance on foreign suppliers.

LEFT: **A search and rescue swimmer plunges into the sea from a Sikorsky SH-60F Seahawk during a training exercise.**

LEFT: **The Fuerza Aerea Argentina (Argentine Air Force) began operating the Alouette II in 1973.**

Aérospatiale SE 3130 Alouette II

The French-built Aérospatiale Alouette II (lark) secured a place in aviation history by being the first production helicopter to be powered by a gas turbine (turboshaft) engine. Originally manufactured by Sud Aviation and later Aérospatiale, the Alouette II was a sound and successful design that was supplied to the armed forces of 47 nations around the world. It was used for an impressive range of military purposes including observation, photo-reconnaissance, rescue and anti-tank missions. For naval operations, homing torpedoes were carried. When production ended in 1975, over 1,500 had been built, including those under licence in Brazil, Sweden, India and the USA.

The SE 3130 was first flown on March 12,1955, and was soon being used to set altitude records. In July 1956, the type achieved widespread publicity for the first helicopter mountain-rescue. The machine's impressive altitude performance made it ideal for this specialized role. The first delivery to the Armée de l'Air (French Air Force) was on May 1, 1956, and 19 were used in action in Algeria by 1958.

The military version was the first helicopter in the world to be armed with anti-tank missiles (Nord SS11). Aircrews thought the Alouette II was pleasant to fly and easy to manoeuvre, and the bubble-type cockpit made the type ideal for the observation role. The open-frame fuselage contributed to performance by keeping empty weight low. The distinctively shaped tail bumper was fitted to protect the tail rotor from damage during take-off and landings.

The turboshaft-powered Alouette II represented a great advance in performance, serviceability and reliability. The West German armed forces purchased 267 examples and the type also served with the Army Air Corps (AAC) in the UK. After years of military service, many of the type were sold on the civilian market.

ABOVE AND LEFT: **The Army Air Corps (AAC) first trialled the type in 1958 due to technical problems with the development of the Westland Scout. Eventually a total of 17 were purchased and designated Alouette AH Mk2.**

Aérospatiale SE 3130 Alouette II

First flight: March 12, 1955
Power: 1 x Turboméca Artouste IIC6 turboshaft
Armament: None
Size: Rotor diameter – 10.2m/33ft 5in
Length – 9.66m/31ft 9in
Height – 2.75m/9ft
Weights: Empty – 895kg/1,973lb
Take-off – 1,699kg/3,746lb (maximum)
Performance: Speed – 185kph/115mph (maximum)
Service ceiling – 3,300m/10,824ft
Range – 565km/350 miles

Aérospatiale SE 316 Alouette III

The single-engined Alouette III, developed as a successor to the Alouette II, was larger and could carry up to seven passengers and weapons. In addition to production in France, it was also built under licence by Hindustan Aeronautics Limited as the Chetak (horse) in India and Industria Aeronautic in Romania. Assembly was also carried out in Switzerland and the Netherlands.

The SE 3160 prototype was first flown on February 28, 1959, with full-scale production of the SA 316 (later 316A) starting in 1961. The SA 316B, first flown on June 27, 1968, was fitted with an improved transmission driven by the more powerful Turboméca Artouste IIIB, which allowed an increase in maximum take-off weight. Both were produced simultaneously for a time, but the B model was the main production version. Over 1,400 examples of both versions were built before the main production line closed in 1979, although limited production continued in France until 1985. An early demonstration of high-altitude performance came in 1960 when an Alouette III carrying a 250kg/551lb payload was operated in the Himalayas at altitudes of 6,004m/19,698ft.

French Army experience in Algeria indentified the requirement for a fast, well-armed helicopter. The Alouette fitted this criterion by carrying four wire-guided anti-tank missiles. The helicopter was also used in the counter-insurgency role by the Portuguese military during their

ABOVE: **The Alouette III was a larger machine than the SE 3130 and was built with an all-metal monocoque fuselage.** RIGHT: **In 1964, Aérospatiale produced a single prototype of the SE 3164 Alouette-Canon as an experimental gunship armed with a 20mm MG 151 cannon and fitted with hardpoints to carry the Matra SS 10 anti-tank missile.**

colonial conflicts in the 1960s and 1970s, and were the first of the type to be armed with a 20mm cannon.

Pakistan deployed the Alouette III in the Indo-Pakistan War of 1971, mainly for liaison and VIP transport. Two were shot down by Indian forces. The crew of a Rhodesian Air Force Alouette III, armed with 20mm cannon and four 0.50in machine-guns, were credited with shooting down a Britten-Norman Islander of the Botswana Defence Force (BDF) on August 9, 1979.

The Venezuelan Air Force retired the Alouette III in the late 1990s. In June 2004, the type was retired from the Armée de l'Air after 32 years of service. Long-time operator the Irish Air Corps retired the Alouette III in 2007 after 44 years of service, during which over 77,000 flying hours were amassed, including 2,882 air ambulance flights and 1,717 search and rescue missions which

saved 542 lives. Argentina purchased 14 for naval operations, and one was used during the invasion of South Georgia, the prelude to the Falklands War of 1982. The last of these was retired at the end of 2010. The Alouette III remains in service with a number of military and civilian operators.

Aérospatiale SE 316 Alouette III

First flight: June 27, 1968 (SA 316B)
Power: 1 x Turboméca Artouste IIIB turboshaft
Armament: Various – anti-tank missiles, 20mm cannon or machine-guns
Size: Rotor diameter – 11.02m/36ft 2in
Length – 12.84m/42ft 2in
Height – 3m/9ft 10in
Weights: Empty – 1,143kg/2,440lb
Take-off – 2,250kg/4,960lb (maximum)
Performance: Speed – 210kph/130mph (maximum)
Service ceiling – 3,200m/10,500ft
Range – 480km/298 miles

Aérospatiale SA 315B Lama

This special "hot and high" helicopter developed from the Alouette family was originally designed by Aérospatiale in response to a 1968 Indian military requirement for a helicopter that could be operated in inaccessible and demanding conditions. To create the five-seat (including pilot) SA 315B Lama, Aérospatiale strengthened the airframe of the Alouette II and fitted it with the Artouste IIIB turboshaft and the rotor

system from the Alouette III. The first flight of the SA 315 prototype was on March 17, 1969, but it was to be two years before the Lama name was officially adopted by the manufacturers.

The Lama is used in a variety of military roles, including transport, liaison, photography, reconnaissance, observation, ambulance (two stretchers and an attendant can be carried) and air sea rescue, for which a 160kg/352lb

hoist is fitted. External loads of up to 1,135kg/ 2,502lb can also be carried. The skid landing gear is of the universal type and can be fitted with castoring wheels for ground handling and floats for water operations.

The aircraft has an impressive performance, not least the ability to lift loads to high altitudes. In 1969, a Lama landed and took off in the Himalayas at an altitude of 7,500m/24,605ft – the highest ever recorded for any aircraft.

The high-profile record-breaking flights and the type's performance led to orders from the Indian military. In 1971, negotiations were completed for Hindustan Aircraft Limited (HAL) to produce the Lama under licence in India, and were designated Cheetah. The first Indian-assembled SA 315B flew on October 6, 1972, with deliveries to the military beginning at the end of the following year. In 1978, Aérospatiale agreed a contract with Helibras for the assembly of the type in Brazil. Given the name Gavião (hawk), this version was also exported to Bolivia.

LEFT: **Two Indian-built HAL Cheetals of No.114 Helicopter Squadron (Siachen Pioneers), Indian Air Force.**

LEFT: **An HAL Cheetal from No.114 Squadron, Indian Air Force, at a forward high-altitude helipad in the remote Ladakh region in northern India.**

Aérospatiale built 407 Lamas in France before production ceased in 1989. An upgraded variant was developed by HAL in 2006–07 using the Turboméca TM 333-2M2. Known as the Cheetal, the version, in contrast to the conditions for which the original Lama was designed, was developed for Indian Army operations in the Siachen Glacier region in the eastern Karakoram Range of the Himalayas. The territory is the highest battle-ground on earth, and India and Pakistan have been fighting there intermittently since April 1984. At a height of over 6,000m/20,000ft, it is site of the highest helipad in the world, built by Indian forces to support a base for troops. An order for 20 Cheetals was placed the Indian Army in early 2010.

LEFT: **The space frame-type fuselage on the Cheetal allows ground crew easy access for servicing or routine maintenance. Note the position of the main fuel tank.** BELOW: **Two HAL-built Cheetal helicopters of the Indian Air Force (IAF) operating from a base at Leh in the eastern Karakoram Range, high in the Himalayas.**

Operators of the Lama and licence-built versions have included the People's Air Defence Force of Angola, Argentine Air Force and Army, Bolivian Air Force, Chilean Army, Chilean Air Force, Ecuadorian Army, Namibian Air Force, Nepal Army, Pakistan Army and Togolese Air Force.

On June 21, 1972, Aérospatiale test pilot Jean Boulet flew a Lama to a height of 12,442m/40,820ft, setting an altitude record for helicopters that stands to the present day.

Aérospatiale SA 315B Lama

First flight: March 17, 1969
Power: 1 x Turboméca Artouste IIIB turboshaft
Armament: None
Size: Rotor diameter – 11.02m/36ft 2in
  Length – 12.92m/42ft 5in
  Height – 3.09m/10ft 2in
Weights: Empty – 1,021kg/2,251lb
  Take-off – 2,300kg/5,070lb (maximum)
Performance: Speed – 192kph/119mph (maximum)
  Service ceiling – 5,400m/17,715ft
  Range – 515km/320 miles

Aérospatiale SA 321 Super Frélon

In the 1960s the Super Frélon (hornet) was the largest helicopter produced in Western Europe, and had to compete for sales with US and Soviet manufacturers. The design comes from a requirement by the French military for a multi-role, medium helicopter. Three military variants were proposed: transport, anti-submarine and anti-shipping. Civil versions were also built.

The first version by Sud Aviation was flown on June 10, 1959, but was abandoned so that the design team could work on a larger, more useful aircraft. The US manufacturer Sikorsky

became involved, developing the main and tail rotor systems and the final design. The larger SA 321, later named Super Frélon, was first flown on December 7, 1962. In Italy, the Fiat company worked on the design of the gearbox and transmission, and later manufactured these items for the production helicopter.

The Super Frélon differed from the first design by being built with a watertight hull and outrigger floats for amphibious operation. The prototype aircraft, completed as a troop transport to carry 38 equipped troops or 15 stretcher cases, was used in

ABOVE: **An SA 321L on display at the South African Air Force Museum, Zwartkop, near Johannesburg. Note the aircraft is not fitted with outrigger floats.**

July 1963 to set a number of world speed records for large helicopters. The second prototype was completed for naval service and flown on May 28, 1963. This version was the first to enter production. When production ended in France during 1983, a total of 99 had been built.

The SA 321D was first delivered to the Aéronavale (French Navy) in 1966. Some of these were later modified to carry AM 39 Exocet missiles and fitted with a large thimble-shaped nose cone housing the attack radar scanner. The missiles were carried on mountings on both sides of the fuselage. The alternative weapons load of four torpedoes was twice the number carried by a Sikorsky S-61 Sea King. The SA 321G was a dedicated Anti-Submarine Warfare (ASW) version equipped with dipping sonar and search radar.

When the SA 321G was withdrawn from service, those remaining in Aéronavale service were used for transport, search and rescue, and vertical replenishment of ships in the

LEFT: **A Super Frélon on display at the Israeli Air Force Museum. Note the outrigger floats for waterborne operations.**

LEFT: **The People's Republic of China negotiated an agreement with Aérospatiale to build the Super Frélon under licence in China. The aircraft, designated Z-8, is operated by the air force for search and rescue. The navy operates the type in the same role and for anti-submarine warfare. The thimble-shaped nose cone houses a search radar scanner. The Z-8 remains in production.**

French Navy. The last Super Frélon in French military service was retired in 2010.

Sixteen export aircraft, designated SA 321H, were supplied to the Iraqi Air Force from 1977, complete with radar and Exocet missiles. These helicopters were used in the Iran–Iraq war to attack Iranian shipping. The Super Frélon was also sold to the Israeli Air Force (IAF) in the late 1960s, and the type was used extensively in action as a troop and heavy lift transport. The type was retired from IAF service in 1991.

The People's Republic of China ordered 16 of the SA 321Ja, an improved version of the SA 321J built for the civil market. Deliveries began in 1975 and were completed by 1977. These aircraft were used in naval service for rescue and ASW operations. Later Chinese licence-built machines, designated Changhe Z-8, were supplied and deployed in the rescue and ASW role. The ASW version was equipped with search radar, dipping sonar and armed with anti-submarine torpedoes. From 2007, the air force acquired a number to operate in the search and rescue role. The Z-8 remains in front-line service and has been upgraded with the latest glass cockpit technology.

Other military operators have included the Imperial Iranian Air Force/Islamic Republic of Iran Air Force, Libyan Air Force, Libyan Navy, South African Air Force and Zairian Air Force.

LEFT: **The Super Frélon, like the Sikorsky S-61 Sea King, was designed with a watertight lower fuselage and fitted with outrigger floats for stability to allow the aircraft to be landed on calm water during a rescue operation.**

Aérospatiale SA 321 Super Frélon

First flight: December 7, 1962
Power: 3 x Turboméca Turmo IIIc turboshaft
Armament: Torpedoes, AM 39 Exocet missile
Size: Rotor diameter – 18.9m/62ft
   Length – 23.03m/75ft 7in
   Height – 6.66m/21ft 10in
Weights: Empty – 6,700kg/14,775lb
   Take-off – 13,000kg/28,660lb (maximum)
Performance: Speed – 237kph/147mph
   (maximum)
   Service ceiling – 3,150m/10,325ft
   Range – 632km/1,020 miles

Aérospatiale SA 330 Puma

The Aérospatiale SA 330 Puma was first developed in response to a French Army requirement for an all-weather, day or night tactical helicopter. The type is a twin-engined, medium transport/utility helicopter originally manufactured in France by Sud Aviation. It was the first all-weather helicopter to enter service with the military forces of Western Europe.

The first of two Puma prototypes was flown on April 15, 1965. Six pre-production machines were then built, the last of which was flown in July 1968. The first production Puma flew two months later, and the deliveries to the Armeé de Terre (French Army) began in early 1969.

In 1967, the Puma was chosen for Royal Air Force service, and this led to a joint production arrangement between Aérospatiale and Westland Helicopters Limited to produce components for the Puma and assemble the type for the RAF. Production continued until 1987,

with a total of 697 having been built. The type was widely exported and is still in service around the world. Civil variants were also produced.

The two Turboméca Turmo 3-64 turboshaft engines are mounted on top of the fuselage and forward of the rotor assembly, which is then driven through a main gearbox that transmits engine power via a single main driveshaft. Originally, the main rotor blades were made of light alloy, but after 1976 they were gradually replaced with those of composite construction. The tricycle landing gear is of the semi-retracting type, with provision for emergency flotation gear.

Argentinian forces deployed the Puma during the Falklands War of 1982. Those in Romanian military service (licence-built by IAR) have been armed with anti-tank missiles. In 2022 the type remained in service with the forces of Brazil, Chile, Democratic Republic of the Congo, Ecuador, Gabon, Guinea,

ABOVE: **The Westland-built Puma HC Mk1 entered service with the Royal Air Force in 1971.**

Indonesia, Kenya, Kuwait, Lebanon, Malawi, Morocco, Pakistan and Romania. French Air and Space Force and French Army machines will be gradually phased out in favour of the NH Industries NH90.

The Puma HC Mk1 first entered RAF service in 1971 and, thanks to upgrades, the type has continued in Royal Air Force service for over half a century. In 1991, during the first Gulf War, the HC Mk1 was widely used by the RAF on the battlefront. The type can be optimized for both desert and arctic warfare by the fitting of specialist equipment. The Puma is used on the battlefield to facilitate tactical troop and load movement by day or by night. It can carry up to 12 fully equipped troops or 2,000kg/4,400lb of freight carried either internally or as an under slung load. In the casualty (CASEVAC) or medical evacuation

LEFT: **In 1969, the Royal Air Force ordered 40 SA330 Puma helicopters which were to be built under licence by Westland Helicopters Limited. The first production machine was flown on November 25, 1970. A further eight were procured in 1979. In 2009, the RAF announced that 24 of the type were to be upgraded to HC Mk2 standard, which involved the fitting of the more powerful Turboméca Makila engine, revised cockpit displays and improved avionics.**

(MEDEVAC) support role, six stretcher cases can be carried internally.

Each aircraft is equipped with GPS and an Instrument Landing System (ILS) to enable the aircraft to be navigated accurately and landed at suitably equipped airfields in poor weather conditions. The aircraft is crewed by two pilots, or a pilot and a weapons systems officer, plus a crewman. The pilots are equipped with Night Vision Goggles (NVG) for low-flying missions at night. The Puma defensive equipment includes an integrated radar warning receiver, missile-approach warning system, an infra-red jammer and automatic chaff and flare dispensers. Additionally, two cabin-mounted 7.62mm General Purpose Machine Guns (GPMG) can be fitted.

In 2009, as a result of operational experience in Afghanistan, a significant upgrade of 24 RAF machines was announced. Changes included installation of the Turbomeca Makila 1A1 turboshaft (as used in the Super Puma) offering 35 per cent more power and 25 per cent improvement in fuel efficiency, increased fuel capacity and advanced digital avionics among other major changes. The RAF trialled the new version in 2013 and the HC Mk 2 was in service from 2015, offering crews radically improved performance and enhanced situational awareness provided by new avionics.

ABOVE: **The RAF operates the Puma primarily as a troop and logistics transport. Note the engine air intakes protected by debris filters which project forwards over the top of the cockpit.**

Aérospatiale SA 330 Puma

First flight: April 15, 1965
Power: 2 x Turboméca Turmo 3-64 turboshaft
Armament: 7.62mm General Purpose Machine Gun (GPMG)
Size: Rotor diameter – 15.09m/49ft 7in
Length – 18.15m/59ft 7in
Height – 4.54m/14ft 11in
Weights: Empty – 3,615kg/7,970lb
Take-off – 7,400kg/16,280lb (maximum)
Performance: Speed – 274kph/170mph (maximum)
Service ceiling – 5,185m/17,000ft
Range – 572km/355 miles

LEFT: **A Eurocopter AS 332L2 Super Puma, operated by the Hong Kong Governmental Flight Service (HKGFS), alighting on the landing pad of USS *Mobile Bay* (CG-53), a Ticonderoga-class missile cruiser, during an exercise in the western Pacific.**

Eurocopter AS 332 Super Puma/AS 532 Cougar

The Super Puma first flown September 1978 was essentially a Puma fitted with more powerful engines, composite rotor blades, new avionics, a modified tail and improved landing gear. These were the AS 332B versions, whereas the AS 332M first flown on October 10, 1980, was a stretched and, from 1986, re-engined version.

In 1990, the military Super Puma (the type has also been very successful on the civil market) were designated as AS 532 Cougar Mk I. Suffix letters denote the version: U – Unarmed; A – Armed; C – Short fuselage; and L – Stretched fuselage. The Cougar Mk II series, launched in 1993, are larger and have had an additional fuselage stretch to

allow extra seats to be fitted. The Cougar was designed to provide high performance, low operating cost and high mission readiness through ease of maintenance. Rotors blades are constructed from composite materials giving excellent serviceability, low vulnerability, an unlimited useful life and resistance to salt-water corrosion. Other improvements include a simplified main rotor hub, a modular main gearbox and a high energy-absorption undercarriage.

As a multi-role helicopter, the Cougar can be armed with machine-guns, cannon, rockets and various missiles. The type is in service with many air forces around the world in numerous military configurations, including transport, Combat Search and Rescue (CSAR), anti-shipping armed with the Exocet missile, and attack helicopter.

An experimental surveillance version served with the French military during Operation Desert Storm in the first Gulf War. A Cougar, equipped with specialized radar, was flown on 24 missions and proved the capability of this remarkable configuration. The helicopter, fitted with Thomson-CSF

ABOVE: **An AS 332 Super Puma operated by the Singapore Air Force landing on the deck of USS *Harpers Ferry* (LSD-49) to refuel during a cross-operating exercise.**

Target radar, was operated behind the front line at an altitude of up to 4,000m/ 13,123ft to survey the battlefield. This radar is designed to scan 20,000sq km in just ten seconds, and is able to monitor the movements of up to 4,000 vehicles at distances of up to 200km/124 miles. The surveillance version (AS 532UL/Horizon) remains in service with the French Army.

Naval versions of the Cougar include the AS 532SC, which can be armed with two Exocet anti-shipping missiles. The ASW version can be identified by the black nose cone housing for the powerful Varan maritime surveillance radar. The aircraft is also equipped with HS312 dipping sonar completing a potent ASW weapons system.

Operational experience gained with Puma, Super Puma and Cougar helicopters led to the development of the EC725 Caracal, unofficially known as the "Super Cougar" before being officially designated the Eurocopter EC725 Caracal and ultimately the Airbus Helicopters H225M. The type was introduced into the French Air Force service in 2005 and is designed for the most demanding missions. A combat-proven multi-role helicopter, the type has been deployed on many battle-fronts around the world, including in Afghanistan.

The H225M is powered by two of the latest generation Turboméca Makila 2A1 turboshaft engines driving a five-bladed main rotor, allowing a high level

ABOVE: **An AS 532 Cougar in service with the Ecuadorian military. Note the aircraft is not fitted with side pods.**

of manoeuvrability. The type is fitted with the latest glass cockpit technology and mission-dedicated avionics. The manufacturer claims to have equipped the aircraft with the most advanced autopilot in the world.

The H225M is suitable for a full range of military missions, including Combat Search and Rescue, tactical transport, and also casualty/medical evacuation operations. The type has operated in combat and crisis areas including Lebanon, Afghanistan, Chad, Ivory Coast, Central African Republic, Somalia, Mali, and Libya. Operators include France, Brazil, Mexico, Malaysia, Indonesia, Kuwait, Singapore and Thailand.

ABOVE: **An EC725R2 Caracal in service with the French Air Force. The aircraft is equipped for inflight refuelling, and is fitted with a 20mm GIAT cannon in each side pod.**

Eurocopter AS 532UL Cougar

First flight: September, 1978 (Super Puma)
Power: 2 x Turboméca Makila 1A1 turboshaft
Armament: 7.62mm machine-gun, two 20mm GIAT cannon
Size: Rotor diameter – 15.6m/51ft 2in
Length – 15.53m/50ft 11in
Height – 4.92m/16ft 2in
Weights: Empty – 4,350kg/10,250lb
Take-off – 9,000kg/19,840lb (maximum)
Performance: Speed – 249kph/155mph (maximum)
Service ceiling – 3,450m/11,319ft
Range – 573km/357 miles

Aérospatiale SA 341 Gazelle

The design that became the Gazelle was developed by Sud Aviation (later Aérospatiale) in the mid-1960s from a requirement by the French Army for a light multi-role helicopter to replace the Alouette. The design was ultimately refined, bore a resemblance to the Alouette II and used some common components. The new all-metal machine was streamlined and had a fully enclosed cockpit with side-by-side seating for two pilots. The type also featured an anti-torque ducted fan in place of a tail rotor. Known as the Fenestron, the fan is less prone to damage or a tail strike during take-off or landing.

The British military expressed an early interest in the type, and this led to a development and production agreement between Aérospatiale and Westland

ABOVE: **The SA 341B was ordered by the British Army Air Corps (AAC) and built under licence by Westland Helicopters. The first of 158 procured was flown on January 31, 1972, and the type entered service as the AH 1 on July 6, 1974.**

being signed in February 1967. This covered aircraft for the French military as well as those for the RAF, Royal Navy and the Army Air Corps.

LEFT: **The HT2 (SA 341C), fitted with a stability augmentation system and a rescue winch, was ordered by the Royal Navy as a training helicopter. The type entered service with the Fleet Air Arm on December 10, 1974.**

fire from Argentine forces, while another was shot down by an Argentine Pucara ground attack aircraft. British Army Gazelles have seen service in Kuwait and Kosovo, and in Iraq as scouts for other attack aircraft.

In the Light Aviation division of the French Army, the Gazelle (SA 342M) has been used primarily in the anti-tank role and armed with four HOT missiles. The French have deployed the Gazelle to combat areas on many occasions, including Chad, the former Yugoslavia, Djibouti, Somalia, the Cote d'Ivoire (Ivory Coast), and Afghanistan. During the first Gulf War in 1991, French machines were used in action carrying HOT anti-tank missiles in attacks against Iraqi armour. Few Gazelle sorties were flown by the Iraqi forces due to Allied dominance of air space in the region. Kuwaiti Gazelle crews claimed some kills against Iraqi vehicles during the 1990 invasion. Ironically, Iraq had been one of the major export customers for the HOT-capable Gazelle, and made extensive use of this weapons system in the Iran–Iraq war.

In 1982, Syrian forces used the Gazelle in action against Israeli armour and claimed to have destroyed 30 tanks. The type has also been used in action by Lebanese and Moroccan forces.

The prototype SA 340.001 was first flown on April 7, 1967, followed by four pre-production SA 341 aircraft in August 1968. The Westland-built prototype of the AH1 for the British Army was first flown on April 28, 1970. Within a few weeks, an Aérospatiale-built pre-production machine had been used to set three world speed records for helicopters. The Gazelle continued to be used to set and break records, which gave this fast, light helicopter a very high profile, and this ultimately led to export sales for both military and civil versions.

The first production AH 1 was flown on January 31, 1972, and a total of 174 were built. The aircraft was fitted with a powerful Nightsun searchlight and radar when it entered service with the British Army in July 1974. Fondly referred to as the "Whistling Chicken Leg" by some British soldiers, the Gazelle has proved an incredibly reliable helicopter for many years. It has been used as an Air Observation Post and for Forward Air Controller, casualty evacuation, liaison, command and control roles. An upgrade enables crew voice control of avionics equipment using standard helmet microphones and intercom. This allows the pilot to control the aircraft's systems without lifting his hands from the flight controls or having to look ahead or at the ground below.

The Gazelle can be flown by one pilot who relies on the speed and agility of the aircraft to evade detection and enemy fire. However, the type is lightly armoured and vulnerable to ground fire – during the Falklands War in 1982, two AAC Gazelles were lost to small arms

Aérospatiale Gazelle SA 343M

First flight: April 7, 1967
Power: 1 x Turboméca Astazou XIVM turboshaft
Armament: HOT anti-tank missile, 7.26mm machine-gun or 20mm cannon
Size: Rotor diameter – 10.5m/34ft 5in
Length – 11.97m/39ft 3in
Height – 3.19m/10ft 6in
Weights: Empty – 991kg/2,184lb
Take-off – 1,900kg/4,188lb (maximum)
Performance: Speed – 260kph/161mph (maximum)
Service ceiling – 4,100m/13,450ft
Range – 710km/440 miles

LEFT: **An Aéronavale (French Navy) AS 565 Panther landing on the deck pad of USS *Decatur* (DDG-73), a guided-missile destroyer.**

Eurocopter AS 565 Panther

The single-engined Aérospatiale SA 360 Dauphin (dolphin) was developed by Eurocopter to become the twin-engined AS 365 Dauphin 2. The type is one of the most successful helicopter designs and has achieved excellent sales worldwide. The military version is the Eurocopter AS 565 Panther, which has been sold to a number of air arms around the world.

The Panther is a multi-role light helicopter suitable for troop transport, logistic support and medical evacuation. The type is supplied in two main versions – AS 565UB (Army) and AS 565MB (Navy). The Panther was first flown on February 29, 1984, and entered production in 1986. The airframe is of light alloy construction similar to that of the Dauphin, but with a greater use

of composite materials, including extensive use of glass reinforced plastic and Nomex. This allows a stronger, lighter-weight airframe to be built. The infra-red signature of the AS 565 has also been greatly reduced by finishing

BELOW: **The Z-9C is a version of the AS 565 developed and built under licence in China by the Harbin Aircraft Corporation.**

the airframe with a coating of special infra-red-absorbing paint. The airframe has a high crash tolerance, and the helicopter at maximum take-off weight of 4,300kg/9,480lb has been tested to withstand a vertical impact from 7m/23ft. The fuel system, fitted with self-sealing fuel tanks, is designed to withstand a 14m/46ft impact.

The AS 565MB naval version is designed for anti-surface vessel warfare, anti-submarine warfare, search and rescue, troop/logistic transport and casualty evacuation. This type is fitted with an ingenious seaborne-landing system to secure the aircraft to a deck

in the roughest of sea conditions. The so-called "harpoon" is a retractable probe mounted on the underside of the helicopter. On landing, it is lowered to engage in a grid on the deck, which automatically secures the head of the harpoon and stabilizes the aircraft.

The AS 565M can be armed with a cabin-mounted 20mm cannon, the AS 15 TT anti-shipping missile or the Mk 46 anti-submarine torpedo, and for shallow water attack the Whitehead A244/S torpedo. The aircraft can be equipped for over-the-horizon laser-designated targeting to allow an attack on an enemy vessel from beyond visual range.

In 1979, the Dauphin was selected by the US Coast Guard to replace the ageing Sikorsky (S-62) HH-52A Sea Guard air sea rescue helicopter. An order for 99 was placed, and was designated HH-65A Dolphin to be used for the Short-Range Recovery (SRR) role. The HH-65A cannot be landed on water, so a rescue swimmer is carried as part of the four-man crew. The aircraft were manufactured in the US by the Aérospatiale Helicopter Corporation, a division of Eurocopter.

In USCG service, the HH-65 is equipped with pre-programmable autopilot capable of guiding the aircraft on an automatic approach to an exact point in the ocean, then establishing it in a stable 15m/49ft hover. The autopilot can also be programmed to fly the aircraft in a precise search pattern. The system greatly reduces crew fatigue during a rescue mission.

In February 2003, following the terror attacks on the US, an Air Defense Identification Zone (ADIZ) was instigated around Washington, DC. Seven new-build HH-65Cs were acquired by the USCG for an "airborne use of force" mission to intercept unidentified light aircraft operating within the restricted air space.

The AS 565 is built under licence in Brazil by Helibras as the HM-1 Pantera (panther), and in the People's Republic of China by the Harbin Aircraft Manufacturing Corporation as the Z-9C.

LEFT: **A marine abseiling down from an AS 565 Panther of the Mexican Navy during a multi-national maritime military exercise.**

Eurocopter AS 565 Panther

First flight: February 29, 1984
Power: 2 x Turboméca Arriel 2C turboshaft
Armament: Various
Size: Rotor diameter – 11.94m/39ft 2in
    Length – 13.68m/44ft 10in
    Height – 4.06m/13ft 4in
Weights: Empty – 2,380kg/5,247lb
    Take-off – 4,300kg/9,480lb (maximum)
Performance: Speed – 296kph/183mph (maximum)
    Service ceiling – 2,500m/8,500ft
    Range – 875km/540 miles

LEFT: **At one stage the South African Air Force (SAAF) operated 27 AgustaWestland A109LUH helicopters in a light transport role. The machine is painted in standard SAAF camouflage with low-visibility markings.**

AgustaWestland AW109E Power

The manufacturer describes the AW109 as "the world's most versatile light twin helicopter". Originally conceived as a single-engined machine for civilian use, the design was the result of extensive market research.

In 1969, the aircraft was redesigned and fitted with two Allison 250 turboshaft engines, and the prototype was first flown on August 4, 1971. Production deliveries of the eight-seat civil version (named Hirundo, but this was later dropped), began in 1975, the same year that the military potential of the design was being assessed. Agusta worked with Hughes to equip the A109 with the Tube–launched Optically-tracked Wire-guided (TOW) missile. Trials proved to

RIGHT: **The A109LUH is the military version of the AgustaWestland AW109 Power. The type is operated by the Swedish Armed Forces for Search and Rescue (SAR) duties but has also taken part in anti-piracy operations.**

be very successful and led to the Italian military placing firm orders for two versions – one for the army, the other for the navy.

Belgium ordered scout and anti-tank versions armed with the TOW missile. Argentina was an early export customer, but two of four machines purchased were lost to British military forces when the Falkland Islands were re-taken in 1982. The two captured helicopters continued to be operated by 8 Flight, Army Air Corps in support of Special Air Service (SAS) units until 2008.

The A109K version developed for operations in mountainous regions had more powerful engines, fitted with dust filters to prevent sand and other material being ingested, which could affect performance or mechanical damage.

More than half a century after the type first flew, Agusta (as the company is now known) continues to support and market versions for military service.

The AW109E Power is a cost-effective, high-performance and

versatile aircraft allowing a wide range of military missions to be performed. The pilot's workload is reduced by the use of an advanced digital glass cockpit fitted with six liquid-crystal displays and a four-axis digital Automatic Flight Control System auto-coupled to GPS and ILS. Among the operators of the AW109E Power is the Royal Air Force, which operates three of the type, acquired in 2006, for VIP transport and communications flights with No. 32 (The Royal) Squadron based at RAF Northolt in West London.

The AW109 LUH is established as one of the world's best-selling military light-twin helicopter and is suitable for a wide range of military requirements. The LUH is fitted with duplicated hydraulic and mechanical systems, and the robust airframe has excellent ballistic tolerance for maximum safety and survivability in combat conditions. The availability of a wide range of mission equipment makes the LUH a true multi-role

ABOVE: **The Royal Air Force operates the AW109E Power for VIP flights.**

helicopter for all light helicopter roles, including training, transport, MEDEVAC, SAR, maritime patrol, observation and anti-tank. In addition, the LUH can be armed with machine-guns, rocket pods, machine-gun pods, anti-tank and air-to-air missiles.

AgustaWestland AW109E Power

First flight: August 4, 1971
Power: 2 x Pratt & Whitney Canada PW206C turboshaft or 2 x Turboméca Arrius 2K1 turboshaft
Armament: None
Size: Rotor diameter – 11m/36ft 2in
Length – 13.03m/42ft 9in
Height – 3.5m/11ft 6in
Weights: Empty – 2,000kg/3,461lb
Take-off – 3,000kg/6,608lb (maximum)
Performance: Speed – 285kph/177mph (maximum)
Service ceiling – 6,000m/19,600ft
Range – 964km/599 miles

LEFT: The production
version of the Agusta
A129 Mangusta
(mongoose) was
powered by two
Rolls-Royce 2-1004D
turboshaft engines.
An improved version
A129CBT (ComBaT) was
built and armed with a
20mm M197 Gatling-
type cannon. The type
was ordered by the
Italian Army. Deliveries
of the 60 machines
began in 1990.

Agusta A129 Mangusta/AgustaWestland AW129

The concept that led to the first attack helicopter to be designed and produced in Western Europe was initially based on the highly successful Agusta A109 but evolved into an all-new aircraft. The initial design studies were undertaken with (then) West German helicopter manufacturer MBB, as both the Italian Army and the German Army were considering the options for a light observation and anti-tank helicopter. When the research and preliminary design work was complete, MBB withdrew and Agusta carried on alone.

Detailed design work began in 1978, and the A129 prototype was first flown on September 11, 1983. The Italian Army then placed an order for 60 aircraft. Although Spain, the Netherlands and the UK all expressed interest in an improved A129, all decided to purchase either the Eurocopter Tigre or Hughes AH-64 Apache.

RIGHT: The AgustaWestland T129 is the latest
version of the A129 Mangusta, a battle-proven
multi-role attack helicopter.

The machine is fitted with stub wings and can carry an impressive array of weapons. Both cockpits are equipped with multi-function displays to present information from the integrated aircraft management system, and provide navigation data, weapon status, weapon selection and communications. The helicopter is equipped with an automatic terrain-following flight control system

which provides the level of stability essential for precise weapon aiming.

The A129 can be used in the anti-tank, armed reconnaissance, ground attack, and anti-aircraft role. In the anti-tank role, the AGM-114 Hellfire, BGM-71 TOW and Spike-ER missile can be carried. The A129 can also be equipped with 81mm or 70mm Hydra 70 unguided rockets. A three-barrel 20mm

RIGHT: The AgustaWestland T129 is powered by two LHTEC-T800 turboshaft engines. The type is being produced in association with Tusa Aerospace Industries (TAI) in Turkey, and is equipped with avionics designed and manufactured in that country.

M197 Gatling-type cannon is mounted in a turret under the nose. For the anti-aircraft role, the AIM-92 Stinger or Mistral missile can be carried. The type is also equipped with systems which allow it to be operated day or night in all weather conditions.

Deliveries to the Italian Army began in 1990, and the A129 has been successfully deployed to back UN missions to Macedonia, Somalia and Angola. Three helicopters were flown in Iraq until Italian forces were withdrawn.

In January 2002, AgustaWestland was awarded a contract to upgrade the first 45 aircraft built to the improved multi-role A129 CBT (ComBaT) standard, and the first of these were delivered to the Italian Army in 2002. The work included fitting a five-blade main rotor, advanced avionics equipment and improved transmission. A new type of counter-measures suite, including missile launch detector and also a new Global Positioning/Inertial Navigation System (GPS/INS), was part of the A129 CBT upgrade. The work was completed in July 2008.

In June 2007, five A129 CBTs were deployed by the Italian Army to Afghanistan as part of Italy's commitment to the NATO-led International Security Assistance Force (ISAF) in the eastern province of Herat against increased threats from Taliban forces. The helicopters were fitted with the SIAP self-protection package that automatically detects and fires flares to defend against attack from a man-portable anti-aircraft missile.

In 2007, it was announced that Turkey had ordered 51 of the type, designated T129, under the attack and tactical reconnaissance helicopter programme.

Tusas Aerospace Industries (TAI) is the prime contractor and is responsible for final assembly. AgustaWestland is the prime airframe subcontractor, and the Turkish company Aselsan is responsible for the electronics equipment. The T129 is powered by LHTEC-T800 turboshaft engines manufactured by Tusas Engine Industries (TEI) under licence from the Light Helicopter Turbine Engine Company (LHTEC), a joint venture between Rolls-Royce and Honeywell. The first T129 was flown on September 28, 2009, and deliveries began in 2012.

The T129 is a powerful all-weather, day or night multi-role attack helicopter with a formidable weapons payload, excellent performance for hot and high conditions, long range, and an endurance of up to three hours.

ABOVE: The fuselage of the T129 is constructed as a semi-monocoque with an aluminium frame. Some 50 per cent of the airframe assembly is fabricated from composite materials, and is designed to withstand hits from 12.7mm armour-piercing ammunition. The engines are also protected to the same standard.

AgustaWestland T129

First flight: September 11, 1983
Power: 2 x LHTEC-CTS800-4N turboshaft
Armament: 20mm M179 Gatling-type, BGM-71 TOW missile, 70mm Hydra 70 rocket, AGM-114 Hellfire missile, AIM-92 Stinger or Mistral missile
Size: Rotor diameter – 11.9m/39ft
Length – 12.5m/41ft
Height – 3.4m/11ft 2in
Weights: Empty – 2,529kg/5,564lb
Take-off – 5,000kg/11,023lb (maximum)
Performance: Speed – 278kph/170mph (maximum)
Service ceiling – 4,725m/15,500ft
Range – 510km/320 miles

AgustaWestland AW101 Merlin

The Merlin, as it is known in British, Danish and Portuguese service, is one of the world's most capable medium helicopters. It resulted from a 1977 UK Naval Staff Requirement seeking a new ASW helicopter needed to replace the Westland Sea King in Royal Navy service. By late 1977, Westland started work on design studies to meet this requirement. At the same time in Italy, the Italian Navy and Italian helicopter company Agusta were considering the

replacement of the Agusta-built Sea Kings then in service. Inter-company discussions led to a joint venture agreement between both companies and countries. A joint company, European Helicopter Industries (EHI), was set up to manage the project, by now designated the EH101 – this was changed to AW101 in 2007.

Manufacture began in March 1985 in both Britain and Italy. The first prototype, PP1 (British military serial ZF641), was rolled out at Yeovil on

ABOVE: The AgustaWestland AW101 Merlin has a range of over 1,300km/808 miles and can accommodate 38 passengers or 26 fully equipped troops. The type can also be configured to carry 16 casualties on stretchers. In the logistical transport role, the machine can lift up to 5,080kg/11,200lb of cargo.

April 7, 1987, and after exhaustive ground testing, first flew on October 9 that year. The second pre-production example, PP2, flew in Italy on November 26, 1987. Assembly of the Merlin began in early 1995, and the first production example flew on December 6, 1995.

Powered by three Rolls-Royce/ Turboméca gas turbines, the rugged, crashworthy airframe is of modular construction and is composed mainly of conventional aluminium alloy construction with some composite materials in the rear fuselage and tail section. The naval version has powered main rotor blade folding and tail rotor pylon folding. All versions can fly in severe icing conditions, and incorporate triple hydraulic systems, three independent alternators and a gas turbine auxiliary power unit.

LEFT: The AW101 Merlin saw extensive front-line service with the Royal Air Force in Afghanistan until 2013. Note the 7.62mm General Purpose Machine Gun (GPMG) mounted in a cabin window.

LEFT: **A Royal Air Force aircrewman leaving an RAF Merlin helicopter at Camp Bastion in Helmand Province, Afghanistan, following a mission.**

The aircraft and its mission system are managed by two computers, linked by dual data buses. All crew stations can access the management computers and can operate the tactical displays, fed by the Blue Kestrel radar. Navigation is state of the art, with ring laser gyros, inertial reference systems GPS, Doppler and radar altimeters. The avionics include a digital flight control system, a glass cockpit with colour Multi-Function Displays and a comprehensive navigation suite for all-weather navigation and automatic flight.

The Royal Navy received its first fully operational Merlin HM.1 in May 1997 for trials, and the type entered service in June 2000. Although the Merlins are primarily employed as anti-submarine helicopters, the Merlin can also participate in surface warfare. It is designed to operate from both large

and small ship flight decks, in severe weather and high sea states, by day or night. Overall dimensions are less than those of a Sea King, and when embarked at sea, British examples can operate from any ship with a capable flight deck.

The type entered RAF service, designated Merlin HC.3, in January 2001. It shares the same RTM322 engines as the Royal Navy examples, but the RAF Merlin has two 7.62mm General Purpose Machine Guns (GPMG) converted for the air role, long-range fuel tanks, air-to-air refuelling capability and has double-wheel main landing gear compared to the Navy version with its single wheel main gear.

The Merlin's operational debut came in early 2003, when four Royal Navy aircraft from No. 814 NAS embarked aboard RFA *Fort Victoria* were deployed into the northern Gulf as part of the UK Amphibious Task Group for Operation

Iraqi Freedom. With no submarine threat, the helicopters were used in an anti-surface warfare role, protecting against swarm attacks by small, fast inshore attack craft. With no ASW requirement, the aircraft's active dipping sonar (ADS) was removed to free up space in the cabin for an extra eight seats plus racks for four stretchers. A 7.62mm GPMG was also fitted in the forward starboard window, and a semi-automatic cargo release unit for loading and vertical replenishment or air drops.

The first operational RAF deployment of the type was to the Balkans in early 2003, and Merlins also served in Iraq as part of Operation Telic until July 2009, when British Forces withdrew from Iraq.

Other operators include the Italian Navy, Royal Danish Air Force, Portuguese Air Force and Japanese Maritime Self-Defense Force.

RIGHT: **The AgustaWestland AW101 is a versatile helicopter, and is combat-proven. The Royal Danish Air Force is one of a number of export customers, and operates the type in the transport and Air Sea Rescue (ASR) role.**

AgustaWestland Merlin HM.1

First flight: October 9, 1987 (PP1)
Power: 3 x Rolls-Royce/Turboméca RTM322-01 turboshaft
Armament: Torpedoes, sonobuoy or anti-shipping missiles
Size: Rotor diameter – 18.59m/61ft
    Length – 22.81m/74ft 10in
    Height – 6.65m/21ft 10in
Weights: Empty – 10,500kg/23,149lb
    Take-off – 14,600kg/32,188lb (maximum)
Performance: Speed – 309kph/192mph
    (maximum)
    Service ceiling – 4,575m/15,000ft
    Range – 925km/574 miles

AgustaWestland/Leonardo AW159 Wildcat

In June 2006, the UK Ministry of Defence awarded AgustaWestland a contract to deliver to the Royal Navy and Army Air Corps the latest twin-engine multi-role utility aircraft developed from the extremely successful Lynx family of helicopters. The AW159 Lynx Wildcat, now designated just Wildcat, was designed to meet the requirement for the British Army's Battlefield Reconnaissance Helicopter (BRH), formerly the Battlefield Light Utility Helicopter (BLUH), and the RN's Surface Combatant Maritime Rotorcraft (SCMR).

Described as a major development of the existing Lynx design, incorporating advanced technology and providing increased capability, the Wildcat has a high level of commonality in airframe, cockpit displays and avionics between the Army and Navy versions. It has more powerful engines, offering increased

power, endurance and economy over existing Lynx powerplants. The most notable changes in appearance are a new tail rotor, low-set tailplane and a redesigned larger nose and rear fuselage. The Army version will meet land utility and reconnaissance requirements, including designation of targets, particularly for the Apache, by using a laser target designator and rangefinder. The RN version will be built for naval warfare. The original contract called for 70 helicopters – 40 for the Army and 30 for the Royal Navy. This was reduced to 62 in December 2008 – 34 for the Army and 28 for the Navy.

The manufacturer's designation for the Wildcat is the AW159, and this is how the helicopter is marketed for export sales. The AW159 provides a unique, significant upgrade in terms of operational capability when compared to other aircraft in its class. The helicopter

ABOVE: **The AW159 is designed to be operated from destroyers, frigates and offshore patrol vessels or corvettes, and can operate in all environments. The navigation suite is based on an integrated Global Positioning System (GPS) inertial system.**

is equipped with a comprehensive, integrated avionics suite, enabling advanced navigation, communication, weapon management and integration.

Mission sensor options offered to customers include the latest technology radar, active dipping sonar for the naval warfare variant, electro-optical imaging and electronic surveillance measures, and also an integrated self-defence suite. The AW159 is built for at-sea operations, and is designed for all environments, including the harshest sea conditions associated with ship-borne operations. The type is equipped

The standard Lynx composite main rotor blades are used, but a new type of four-blade tail rotor is fitted to give improved yaw control. The AW159 Wildcat will have an endurance of approximately 3 hours with standard fuel, and 4½ hours with auxiliary tanks. The machine is armed with two British-built Sting Ray acoustic lightweight homing torpedoes.

with modern systems designed to minimize crew workload, increase reliability and for ease of maintenance. The Wildcat delivers an advanced day/night, all-weather, network-enabled capability to find, fix and strike maritime targets. The aircraft has the ability to detect autonomously, identify and engage surface, land and sub-surface targets. Armament options include air to surface missiles, torpedoes, depth charges, air to ground rockets, cannon and heavy machine-guns.

The utility or multi-purpose version of the Wildcat, in common with the naval version, has a fully marinized airframe and provisions for a range of mission and utility equipment, which enable a true multi-role capability. The helicopter has a spacious cabin with large doors for easy exit and unloading, and is capable of carrying and deploying a wide range of troop, equipment or weapon payloads. Exceptional agility and the proven LHTEC CTS800 turboshaft engines give the AW159 unrivalled "hot and high" performance.

Construction of the first AW159 began in October 2007, and on November 12, 2009, the first machine completed its maiden flight at the AgustaWestland facility in Yeovil.

The most notable changes in appearance compared to earlier Lynx are the new tail rotor and low-set tailplane with fins to improve flying qualities. The redesigned nose and rear fuselage give more space and easier access to avionic units for servicing and removal, so that aircraft down-time is kept to a minimum. Larger cockpit doors have been designed to give improved crew access and, most importantly, easier exit from the aircraft in an emergency.

The Wildcat is in service with the British Army (Wildcat Mk1), The Royal Navy (HMA2), the Philippine Navy and the Republic of South Korea Navy.

ABOVE: **The Wildcat was designed to carry up to 20 of the lightweight Martlet anti-surface guided weapon developed by Thales as the Lightweight Multi-Role Missile (LMM).**

AgustaWestland/ Leonardo AW159 Wildcat

First flight: November 12, 2009
Power: 2 x LHTEC CTS800-4N turboshaft
Armament: Torpedoes, anti-shipping missiles, 7.62mm machine-gun, 0.50in heavy machine-gun, CRV7 rockets
Size: Rotor diameter – 12.8m/42ft
  Length – 15.24m/50ft
  Height – 3.73m/12ft 2in
Weights: Empty – Unknown
  Take-off – 6,000kg/13,228lb (maximum)
Performance: Speed – 291kph/181mph (maximum)
  Service ceiling – 3,050m/10,000ft
  Range – 963km/598 miles

Bell 47 H-13 Sioux

The Bell 47 is acknowledged to be one of the earliest practical helicopter designs to be used for both military and civil operations around the world. The Royal New Zealand Air Force (RNZAF) still had five in their active inventory at the time of writing, 66 years after the prototype was first flown on December 8, 1945.

Originating from an experimental project evaluated by the US Army during World War II, the Bell 47 was

designed by the brilliant Arthur Young. Having experimented with helicopter design alone for 12 years, Young identified and addressed many of the challenges facing designers of the type, but specifically control and stability. Numerous manufacturers turned down the opportunity to see Young and his designs. In 1941, Bell agreed to allow him to build full-scale versions of what had only been produced as models. The resulting Bell Model 30

ABOVE: **The Bell 47 was built under licence by Westland Aircraft Limited for the Army Air Corps (AAC) and entered service as the AH 1 Sioux. The type was also produced by Kawasaki in Japan and by Agusta in Italy. Note the skid-mounted wheels in the down position as an aid to ground handling.**

BELOW: **A Bell H-13B Sioux in US Army service. The machine is painted bright orange, the standard colour for a training helicopter.**

LEFT: **Licence-built in the UK by Westland Aircraft Limited, XT151 was one of the first AH 1 Sioux helicopters to enter service with the Army Air Corps. The machine has been preserved and is displayed at The Museum of Army Flying, Middle Wallop, Hampshire, in the south of England.**

was evaluated by the US Army and this experimental design led to the Bell 47. In March 1946, the Civil Aeronautics Administration (CAA) issued the Bell 47 with Helicopter Type Certificate H-1.

In 1947, the United States Army Air Force ordered 28 for evaluation, some of which were also delivered to the US Navy for evaluation. US Army production orders followed under the designation Bell H-13B, later named Sioux; this was the first of many helicopters to enter US Army service to be named after a Native American Indian tribe.

The H-13 saw widespread use with the US Army during the Korean War, being used for observation, transport and, most importantly, for casualty evacuation fitted with a stretcher – carrying panniers mounted on each skid. During this conflict, the H-13 was one of the types that proved the military usefulness of the helicopter. Early in the Vietnam War, the H-13 was used for observation duties.

The Bell 47 had a 27-year manufacturing history. Over 5,000 military and commercial machines were

built in 20 versions in the US, and under licence by Kawasaki in Japan, and by Agusta in Italy. In the UK, Westland Aircraft Limited built the type for the British military as the AH 1 Sioux and HT 2. The first of these was flown on March 9, 1965. However, the first 50 machines delivered to the British Army were, for contractual reasons, built by Agusta in Italy. The Royal Air Force also operated some as training aircraft with the Central Flying School (CFS).

NASA used a number of the type to allow Apollo astronauts to train for piloting the Lunar Lander spacecraft in preparation for landing on the surface of the moon.

The type was used to set a number of records, including the helicopter altitude record of 5,650m/18,550ft in May 1949. A year later, a Bell 47 was the first helicopter to be flown over the Alps.

BELOW: **The Bell H-13B was used for a multiplicity of roles by many military services around the world. Although simple in design, the machine was nevertheless strong and reliable.**

Bell 47 H-13 Sioux

First flight: December 8, 1945
Power: 1 x Lycoming TVO-435-A1A piston engine
Armament: Usually none
Size: Rotor diameter – 11.32m/37ft 2in
Length – 13.2m/43ft 5in
Height – 2.83m/9ft 4in
Weights: Empty – 825kg/1,819lb
Take-off – 1,340kg/2,950lb (maximum)
Performance: Speed – 169kph/105mph (maximum)
Service ceiling – 3,200m/10,500ft
Range – 412km/256 miles

Bell UH-1 Iroquois

The Bell UH-1 can rightly be considered as one of the greatest military aircraft of all time. Numerous variants, too many to detail here, were produced, and they served all four arms of the US military, as well as numerous military services around the world.

In 1952, Bell Helicopters responded to a US Army requirement for a medical utility helicopter. Fighting in the Korean

BELOW: **Since the Bell UH-I Iroquois was first flown on October 20, 1956, a total of over 16,000 have been built.**

War was intensifying at this time, and the helicopters deployed there were effectively writing the rule book about the best use of rotary craft in war. Early helicopters, including the Bell H-13 Sioux, were being used, saving countless lives, and by using a larger, higher performance helicopter, even more lives could be saved. It was not obvious to military planners that while the helicopter could move wounded troops away from the front line, the machine could also be used to move fresh troops forward.

ABOVE: **Troops of the 2nd Battalion, 14th Infantry Regiment, 25th Infantry Division boarding a US Army Bell UH-1 Iroquois after an operation in South Vietnam. The UH-1 was known to all service personnel as the "Huey". The name comes from the pronunciation of the original HU-1 (Helicopter Utility) designation, which remains in use today and is the most usual name by which the type is known.**

The Bell-designed Model 204 (first flown on October 20, 1956) had a semi-monocoque metal fuselage and was powered by a single turboshaft engine driving a two-blade main

rotor. On February 23, 1955, the US Army announced its decision, and contracted Bell to build three Model 204 helicopters for evaluation under the designation XH-40.

The US Army finally ordered the helicopter into production (100 aircraft) in March 1960 as the HU-1A Iroquois, which was the first series-built turbine-powered helicopter for the US military. Since that first order, more than 16,000 have been produced worldwide, placing the type among the most commercially successful military aircraft since the World War II. Although the UH-1 offered huge improvements over previous piston-powered helicopters, after flight testing it was concluded that the UH-1A was underpowered. The UH-1B had a more powerful engine and a longer cabin for more passengers or four stretchers, and successful Army trials led to an order for the improved version. This process was to be repeated throughout the service life of this versatile helicopter as improved performance or military requirements drove development.

The US Marine Corps required an assault helicopter to replace fixed-wing and other aircraft, and selected the UH-1B. The machine was navalized by treating the airframe against corrosion. For carrier deck operation,

a brake was fitted to the rotor hub to stop rotation quickly on engine shutdown. A rescue hoist was also fitted. This variant of the helicopter was designated UH-1E.

The very capable UH-1A was deployed to Vietnam, and the first arrived in April 1962 for the CASEVAC role. The transport version arrived in September that year. During the course of the war, the UH-1 went through several upgrades. The short fuselage UH-1A, B and C variants each had

improvements in performance and load-carrying capability. The UH-1B and C served in the gunship role in the early years of the Vietnam War. From 1967, the UH-1B and C gunships were replaced by the new Bell AH-1 Cobra attack helicopter. At the height of the Vietnam War, it was estimated that there could be some 2,000 in the air at the same time. A total of 7,013 were deployed to the South-east Asian conflict and, of these, some 3,305 were destroyed.

LEFT: **The UH-1 Huey will always remain an iconic image of the war in South-east Asia. Since then, the type has been used in many military operations on various battlefronts around the world.**

Bell UH-1B Iroquois

First flight: October 20, 1956
Power: 1 x Avco Lycoming T53-13B turboshaft
Armament: Guns, missiles, grenades and rockets projectiles
Size: Rotor diameter – 14.64m/48ft
   Length – 16.15m/53ft
   Height – 3.77m/12ft 5in
Weights: Empty – 2,177kg/4,789lb
   Take-off – 3,856kg/8,483lb (maximum)
Performance: Speed – 204kph/126mph (maximum)
   Service ceiling – 5,790m/19,000ft
   Range – 383km/237 miles

LEFT: **The Bell UH-1H Iroquois was used by the US Air Force for the advanced training of helicopter pilots at the 23rd Flying Training Squadron (FTS), Fort Rucker, Alabama.**

Bell UH-1D/H Iroquois

Bell responded to a US Army requirement for a helicopter to carry more troops into battle by stretching the UH-1 already in US Army service. The manufacturer lengthened the fuselage of a UH-1B model by 1.04m/41in, which was enough space for four more seats, allowing up to 15 troops to be carried. Larger, easy to remove doors were fitted to provide easier access – when troops are being inserted into a hostile location and under fire, the speed with which they can egress an aircraft is vital. Designated the Model 205 by Bell (first flight August 16, 1961), after extensive testing the US Army ordered this new version into production as the UH-1D. Front-line US Army units began to receive the new type in August 1963 and some 2,008 had been delivered by 1966. A total of 2,561 D models were built, including 352 built by Dornier for the then West German armed forces.

As more and more was demanded of the aircraft serving in South-east Asia, in terms of both level of usage and the need for increased carrying capacity, Bell considered how to get more from the design. In 1966, the company

LEFT: **The Fuerza Aerea Boliviana (Bolivian Air Force) was one of the many military forces to operate the Bell UH-1H Iroquois. The aircraft is operating during Fuerzas Unidas (United Forces), a joint military exercise with US forces.**

trialled the installation of a Lycoming T53-L-13 turboshaft to increase the helicopter's lifting capacity. The US Army approved the design for production, and designated it the UH-1H. This was the version to be produced in the greatest numbers. Deliveries to the US Army began in September 1967, and they received a total of 3,573.

Fuel on the UH-1H was stored in five interconnected self-sealing fuel tanks – two under the cabin floor and three under the engine to the rear of the cabin. These helicopters did not leave the Bell factory with armour and none was fitted, although armoured pilot seats could be installed.

The large, semi-rigid rotor design used on the UH-1 was a development of that used on earlier Bell helicopters. The two-blade configuration is the reason for the distinctive noise that the type makes in flight, especially when descending to land or turning. The rotor

ABOVE: **A Dornier-assembled UH-1D, one of 325 ordered by the West German government for service with the Luftwaffe.**

blades were fabricated from glass fibre (GRP) but had a metal leading edge. In an emergency, this was strong enough to cut through vegetation while descending into a jungle location.

The final UH-1H built by Bell left the factory in 1986. The type was also built under licence by AIDC in Taiwan and by Agusta in Italy as the AB 205. In Japan, Fuji carried on producing the improved UH-1J into the 1990s. In 2009, the US National Guard (USNG) finally retired the last UH-1 from its inventory.

With more than 16,000 built, the UH-1D/H was produced in greater numbers than any other helicopter in history, and served with some 60 armed forces.

BELOW: **The HH-1H Iroquois was equipped for search and rescue operation. This machine was operated in that role by Detachment 1, 37th Aerospace Rescue and Recovery Squadron (ARRS) from their base at Davis-Monthan, Arizona.**

Bell UH-1D/H Iroquois

First flight: August 16, 1961
Power: 1 x Avco Lycoming T53-L-13 turboshaft
Armament: Guns, missiles, grenades and rockets projectiles
Size: Rotor diameter – 14.63m/48ft
　　　Length – 17.62m/57ft 10in
　　　Height – 4.41m/14ft 6in
Weights: Empty – 2,363kg/5,210lb
　　　Take-off – 4,309kg/9,500lb (maximum)
Performance: Speed – 204kph/126mph (maximum)
　　　Service ceiling – 3,840m/12,600ft
　　　Range – 512km/318 miles

Bell OH-58 Kiowa/TH-67 SeaRanger

The Bell YOH-4 was built to meet a US Navy requirement for an all-metal, four-seat light observation helicopter, and was first flown on December 8, 1962. It was not selected for production. However, Bell went on to develop the design into the widely produced Model 206 JetRanger, the world's most successful turbine-powered light helicopter.

Four years later, this design was chosen by the US Army for observation, scout, and command and control duties to serve alongside the Hughes OH-6 Cayuse. The Bell Model 206A was designated as the OH-58 Kiowa, and over 2,200 were to be built for the US Army. The two-blade, semi-rigid,

all-metal main rotor on the Kiowa differed from the JetRanger by having longer blades. The type was deployed to serve in South-east Asia as soon as it was available in May 1969. In Vietnam, the OH-58A Kiowa operated with air cavalry, attack helicopter and field artillery units, but this versatile helicopter could also be configured for troop transport, MEDEVAC or for supply missions.

The OH-58A Kiowa was frequently operated with a Bell AH-1G Cobra and would be used to draw enemy ground fire, enabling the crew of the AH-1G to locate the source and attack. The OH-58A was for a time armed with a 7.62mm M134 Minigun mounted

ABOVE: **The Bell OH-58A Kiowa was sold to the Canadian military as the COH-58A (CH-139), and the OH-58B was exported to Austria. A number were assembled in Australia for military service as the 20B-1.**

on the left-hand side of the fuselage, but the resulting vibration when it was fired was too severe for the airframe. Grenade launchers could also be fitted.

Canada also ordered 72 of the type, designated COH-58A Kiowa, later CH-139. The type designated OH-58B was also exported to Austria, and a number were assembled in Australia, as the 20B-1 Kiowa.

The OH-58C was an improved version fitted with a more powerful engine. In 1978, all existing OH-58A machines began to be converted to the same engine and mechanical specification as the OH-58C.

As well as the engine, the OH-58C was equipped with a unique infra-red suppression system mounted on the turbine exhaust to reduce the heat signature, making it difficult for a heat-seeking missile to lock on. This OH-58C was also was equipped for Night Vision Goggles (NVG) capability. Also, it was the first US Army scout helicopter equipped with the AN/APR-39 radar to alert the crew when

LEFT: **A US Army Bell OH-58A Kiowa on an observation mission over South Vietnam. The type was first deployed to South-east Asia in 1969.**

an anti-aircraft radar system locked on to the aircraft. The C-model was also the first to be trial-fitted with an air-to-air missile installation for two AIM-92 Stingers.

From 1998, the US Army began to replace the OH-58C with the more capable OH-58D Kiowa Warrior. In the early 1990s, US Congress decided that the considerable assets of the

ABOVE: **A Bell OH-58C Kiowa and a Bell AH-1 Cobra on an artillery spotting and suppression mission. Both were operated by the 19th Air Cavalry of the Hawaii National Guard.**

ABOVE: **A Bell TH-57 Sea Ranger about to land on Helicopter Landing Trainer (HLT) USS *Bay Lander* (IX-514).** BELOW: **This Bell TH-57 Sea Ranger was flown at NAS Whiting Field-South, Milton, Florida, to provide Advanced Helicopter Training (AHT) for USN, USMC and USCG pilots.**

Army National Guard (ANG) should be deployed in the war on illegal drugs. In 1992, a total of 76 Bell OH-58As were modified with an engine upgrade, a thermal imaging system, a compatible communications package and improved navigation equipment as part of the Counter Drug Program (CDP).

The US Navy ordered a version of the Kiowa, the TH-57 SeaRanger, as a dual-control, training helicopter. The type was also operated by the US Marine Corps.

In 1993, some 25 years after first ordering the OH-58A Kiowa, the US Army began to take delivery of the TH-67 Creek, a training version of the helicopter.

Bell OH-58 Kiowa

First flight: January 10, 1966 (Bell 206A)
Power: 1 x Allison T63-A-700 turboshaft
Armament: 7.62mm M134 Minigun or 40mm M129 grenade launcher
Size: Rotor diameter – 10.77m/35ft 4in
Length – 12.49m/40ft 11in
Height – 2.91m/9ft 7in
Weights: Empty – 718kg/1,583lb
Take-off – 1,361kg/3,000lb (maximum)
Performance: Speed – 222kph/138mph (maximum)
Service ceiling – 5,800m/19,000ft
Range – 481km/299 miles

Bell OH-58D Kiowa Warrior

This version of the proven and long-serving OH-58 came about as a result of Bell winning the US Army Helicopter Improvement Program (HIP) to produce a comparatively low-cost scout and observation helicopter to support the Hughes AH-64 Apache in combat. Bell's winning design was the OH-58D Kiowa, which was first flown on October 6, 1983.

An upgraded transmission and Allison turboshaft engine housed in an enlarged engine fairing gave the two-seat aircraft the power required for low-level terrain following flight operations. A four-blade main rotor allowed improved performance and reduced noise levels. The distinctive Mast-Mounted Sight (MMS) located on top of the rotor head has TV and infra-red sensors for better target acquisition. The MMS enables the helicopter to be operated in both day and night conditions at the maximum range of the weapons systems and with minimum exposure to an enemy. The helicopter

ABOVE: An OH-58 Kiowa Warrior (bottom) and an AH-64 Apache (top) from the 3rd Armored Cavalry Regiment (ACR) on a Combat Air Patrol (CAP) over Tal Afar, Iraq.

remains concealed during all but a few seconds of an engagement, then rises to deliver the attack weapons.

A mixed-glass cockpit is a standard fit – computer screens carry all essential flight information but are backed up by analogue flight instruments for emergency use.

The D was conceived as an unarmed scout, but all aircraft were gradually upgraded to Kiowa Warrior status and fitted with offensive weaponry that turned the machine into an attack helicopter. The main difference that distinguishes the Kiowa Warrior from the original D-model is a universal-type weapons pylon to carry AGM-114 Hellfire anti-tank missiles, Stinger air-to-air missiles, 2.75in rockets and a 0.50in M296 heavy machine-gun. The Kiowa Warrior upgrade also featured an improvement in engine power, navigation, communication and survivability (including all-composite rotor blades capable of absorbing direct hits from 0.50in ammunition). Other modifications were made so that

LEFT: The D model has a distinctive Mast-Mounted Sight (MMS) assembly above the rotor system, housing TV and infra-red sensors for target acquisition.

LEFT: **A US Army OH-58D Kiowa Warrior in service with the 4th Squadron, 7th Cavalry Regiment, flying below the tree line during an exercise with armoured forces.**

the aircraft, after being off-loaded from a Lockheed C-130 Hercules, could be assembled, fuelled and armed ready for battle in less than 10 minutes.

Designed to be operated autonomously at stand-off ranges, the Kiowa Warrior is deployed for armed reconnaissance, command and control, day/night target acquisition and designation under all weather conditions. The type can be used to designate targets for precision-guided munitions carried by attack helicopters and other aircraft. Using the Airborne Target Handover System (ATHS), the crew of an OH-58D is capable of rapidly providing ranging information to land artillery or designating targets to other airborne weapons platforms equipped with digital receiving equipment.

The first OH-58D Kiowa Warrior

was delivered to the US Army in May 1991, replacing the Bell AH-1 Cobra attack helicopter serving with air cavalry troops and light attack companies. The type also replaced all OH-58A and OH-58C Kiowas in air cavalry units.

The Bell 406CS Combat Scout was based on the OH-58D, and 15 were supplied to Saudi Arabia fitted with a roof-mounted sighting system manufactured by Saab and detachable weapon mountings on each side of the fuselage.

In early 1988, armed OH-58D helicopters were deployed in Operation Prime Chance, to escort oil tankers during the Iran–Iraq War. These operations were primarily reconnaissance flights conducted at night. The US Army used the OH-58D extensively during Operation Iraqi Freedom and Operation Enduring Freedom in Afghanistan.

The OH-58D is considered by some to have the most demanding cockpit workload for the crew of any helicopter in the US Army inventory. The scout/attack role requires much of the flight to involve long periods in the hover at very low altitudes. While the pilot in the right-hand seat flies the aircraft, the crew member in the left-hand seat operates the sighting and other aircraft systems.

The OH-58F was the designation for an upgrade confirmed in January 2011 to extend service life into the 2020s, more than 50 years after the type first entered service. The changes included cockpit and sensor upgrades and a nose-mounted targeting and surveillance system replacing the MMS.

LEFT: **An OH-58D from 1st Battalion, 25th Aviation Regiment, on patrol over the city of Baghdad, Iraq.**

Bell OH-58D Kiowa Warrior

First flight: October 6, 1983
Power: 1 x Allison T703-AD-700 turboshaft
Armament: AGM-114 Hellfire missile, Stinger air-to-air missile, 70mm Hydra 70 rockets, 0.50in M296 heavy machine-gun
Size: Rotor diameter – 10.67m/35ft
Length – 12.85m/42ft 2in
Height – 3.93m/12ft 11in
Weights: Empty – 1,492kg/3,829lb
Take-off – 2,495kg/5,000lb (maximum)
Performance: Speed – 237kph/147mph (maximum)
Service ceiling – 4,575m/15,000ft
Range – 555km/345 miles

Bell 209 AH-1 Cobra

Early US military experience in Vietnam identified the urgent requirement for gunship and attack helicopters. Bell had been investigating attack helicopter designs since 1958, and the early design concepts appeared to be very similar to the

BELOW: **The tandem cockpit arrangement was developed to give the AH-1 the narrowest practical frontal aspect, thereby presenting the smallest possible target when approaching the enemy head-on.**

modern perception of an attack helicopter – a stepped, two-seat tandem cockpit in a slim fuselage to reduce frontal area. The US Army instructed Bell to produce a prototype for evaluation, and the Model 207 Sioux Scout was completed in August 1963. While the US Army was impressed by the concept, the 207 was never going to be a fighting aircraft, so they carried on with the search for an attack helicopter. The project was defined as the Advanced Aerial Fire Support System

ABOVE: **The AH-1 Cobra was the world's first operational purpose-designed helicopter gunship.**

(AAFSS) and was eventually won by the Lockheed AH-56 Cheyenne. Although Bell had lost the main attack helicopter project, the design they proposed for the interim combat helicopter was accepted. The Cheyenne project was eventually cancelled in 1972. The very first operational purpose-designed helicopter gunship, the Bell AH-1 Cobra, remains in production.

RIGHT **AH-1G Cobra gunship of the 334th Helicopter Company, 145th Aviation Battalion, flying over Vietnam in 1969.**

Bell rolled out the prototype of the AH-1 on September 3, 1965, and it was first flown on September 7, only six months after being given the go-ahead by the US Army. Bell appreciated the urgency of the requirement as the US military was building an ever-greater presence in South-east Asia and that many US helicopters were being lost to ground fire. The design team chose to use proven mechanical components from the UH-1 Iroquois to save production time, but the slender fuselage was a completely new design. The US Army issued a production contract for a first batch of 110 aircraft given the designation AH-1 (A – Attack; H – Helicopter), and named it Cobra.

The aircraft were produced in record time and were deployed to Vietnam in 1967. Production versions incorporated a number of changes to the prototype. The landing skids, originally designed to be retractable, were removed to save production time and cost, and also to reduce the number of parts that could require servicing or repair.

The AH-1 was the first helicopter designed from the outset to be armed and optimized for combat. Armed with a nose-mounted 20mm cannon and a combination of multiple rocket launchers or 7.62mm Miniguns, the Cobra brought a new dimension to air warfare. Later, in South-east Asia the type was used to attack North Vietnamese armour, and did so with great success while continuing the main role of providing fire support to ground forces and escorting transport helicopters.

Between 1967 and 1973, Bell built 1,110 of the type for the US military, and these accumulated over 1,000,000 operational hours on combat operations, during which some 300 were lost in combat and accidents.

After Vietnam, the Bell AH-1 Cobra remained in service with the US Army as its prime attack helicopter. It was the main weapon to oppose the Soviet tank threat in Europe until replaced in service by the Hughes AH-64 Apache.

The Bell AH-1 Cobra has been exported to the military forces of a number of nations around the world.

BELOW: **A Kawasaki-built AH-1S Cobra in service with the Japanese Self-Defense Force (JSDF).**

Bell AH-1G Cobra

First flight: September 7, 1965
Power: 1 x Lycoming 1 T53-L-13 turboshaft
Armament: 20mm cannon, 7.62mm Minigun pods or 70mm Hydra 70 rockets
Size: Rotor diameter – 13.41m/44ft
  Length – 16.26m/53ft 4in
  Height – 4.17m/13ft 8in
Weights: Empty – 2,754kg/6,071lb
  Take-off – 4,309kg/9,500lb (maximum)
Performance: Speed – 277kph/172mph (maximum)
  Service ceiling – 3,530m/11,600ft
  Range – 574km/357 miles

Bell AH-1W SuperCobra

The aviation units of the US Marine Corps (USMC) have always had very specific requirements for the type of aircraft in their service. Having seen the impact the helicopter had made during action in Vietnam, the USMC then evaluated the AH-1G which was in US Army service. In May 1968, the USMC ordered an improved, twin-engine version designated AH-1J and

LEFT: **An AH-1W SuperCobra armed with eight AGM-114 Hellfire anti-tank missiles, two LAU 68D/A pods each carrying seven 70mm Hydra 70 Folding-Fin Aerial Rockets (FFAR), and two chaff/flare dispenser pods. Two AIM-9 Sidewinder air-to-air missiles can also be carried.**

ABOVE: **The AH-1Z Viper is a significantly upgraded version of the AH-1W, fitted with the four-blade rotor system from the Bell Model 609.**

named Sea Cobra. Two engines were required for improved safety for over-water operations and for improvements in performance, including lift capacity. The power unit chosen was the military version of the Pratt & Whitney Canada T400-CP-400 turboshaft, with the same transmission as used in the Bell UH-1N Iroquois. The USMC also requested an increase in firepower, and specified a 20mm M197 Vulcan-type cannon to be fitted in the nose turret.

In 1971, Iran became the first export customer for the type, and purchased 202 of the AH-1J International model with the more powerful T400-WV-402 engine. Some 70 of these were built to be armed with the Tube-launched, Optically-sighted, Wire-guided (TOW) anti-tank missile. These helicopters were active during the Iran–Iraq war, and reportedly were involved in numerous air combat engagements with Iraqi Mil Mi-8 and Mi-24 attack helicopters. The type remains in

BELOW: **The main armament on an AH-1W SuperCobra is a 20mm M197 three-barrel Gatling-type cannon mounted in a General Electric A/A49E-7 electrically operated turret.**

ABOVE: **An AH-1W SuperCobra from Marine Medium Helicopter Squadron 264 firing against a target during an exercise with ground forces. The machine is carrying an extended-range fuel tank mounted under each wing.**

service today, having had been updated with a series of locally manufactured and installed upgrades.

In 1974, the AH-1T was ordered by the USMC as there was a requirement for improved load-carrying capability in high temperatures. This was achieved by installing a more powerful T400-WV-402 engine, driving a new rotor assembly similar to that used on the Bell Model 214 medium transport helicopter.

The AH-1T was fully compatible with the TOW anti-tank missile, as the targeting system and associated sensors were fitted as standard. An improved version known as the AH-1T+ fitted with the T700-GE-700 engines was initially offered to Iran, but negotiation ceased when the Shah of Iran was deposed.

In 1981, when funding was refused to buy a navalized version of the Hughes AH-64 Apache, the USMC instead looked for a more powerful and improved version of the AH-1T. This led to an order for the AH-1W SuperCobra, equipped to carry AIM-9 Sidewinder air-to-air missiles and AGM-114 Hellfire anti-tank missiles. The USMC acquired 179 new-build aircraft and 43 upgraded from existing AH-1T airframes.

By 1996, the USMC were looking for a more capable aircraft but were again refused funding to purchase the

AH-64 Apache. Bell proposed the AH-1Z Viper, a significant upgrade to the AH-1W in service.

On the AH-1Z the stub wings are longer, and each has three mounting points for 70mm Hydra rocket pods, AGM-114 Hellfire anti-tank missile launchers or AIM-9 Sidewinder air-to-air missiles. A Longbow targeting radar pod can be carried on a wingtip mounting.

The AH-1Z Viper is fitted with a composite four-blade main rotor based on that from the Bell 609. This provides improvements in flight characteristics, including an increase in maximum speed, better rate of climb and reduced rotor vibration levels. The AH-1Z was first flown on December 8, 2000, and in 2010 it was confirmed that of the 189 aircraft on order, 58 will be new airframes with

deliveries continuing until 2019. During September 2010, the AH-1Z Viper was declared combat-ready by the US Marine Corps.

Bell AH-1W SuperCobra

First flight: May 8, 1969 (AH-1S)
Power: 2 x General Electric T700-401 turboshaft
Armament: 20mm M197 cannon, 70mm Hydra 70 rockets, 5in Zuni rockets, TOW anti-tank missiles, AGM-114 Hellfire anti-tank missiles, AIM-9 Sidewinder air-to-air missiles
Size: Rotor diameter – 14.6m/48ft
Length – 17.7m/58ft
Height – 4.19m/13ft 9in
Weights: Empty – 4,630kg/10,200lb
Take-off – 6,690kg/14,750lb (maximum)
Performance: Speed – 352kph/218mph (maximum)
Service ceiling – 3,720m/12,200ft
Range – 587km/365 miles

Bell CH-135/UH-1N/UH-1Y

The Bell UH-1 series of military helicopters had been so successful that it was just a matter of time before the type was further and dramatically improved. This came in mid-1968 when the Canadian military, who had recently taken delivery of some UH-1H models, proposed a new version with two turboshaft powerplants instead of the single engine. The resulting

development aircraft, funded by Bell, the Canadian Government and Pratt & Whitney Canada, was the Bell Model 212 which was designed, at this stage, for military use. Pratt & Whitney Canada produced the innovative PT6T Twin-Pac, two turboshaft engines mounted side-by-side driving through a common gearbox to power the rotor. The safety dividend of this arrangement was

ABOVE: **A Bell Model 212 in Philippine Army service. The type, developed from the Bell Model 205, was the basis for the twin-engined CH-135 (UH-1Y) series of helicopters.**

ABOVE: **The UH-1Y Twin Huey was built due to a request from the Canadian military for a twin-engined utility helicopter. The machine was powered by the Pratt & Whitney Canada Twin-Pac, two PT6T/T400 turboshaft engines driving through a common gearbox.**

considerable. In the event of one engine failing, a gearbox sensor would signal the working engine to increase output to ensure the continued safe operation of the rotor.

The Canadian Armed Forces (CAF) purchased 50 machines and designated them as the CH-135 after delivery began in May 1971. Bell proposed the type to the US military as the UH-1N Iroquois, and it was procured by the US Air Force. Officially, the UH-1N is known as the Iroquois; inevitably the machine became known as the "Twin Huey". Other early export customers included the air forces of Bangladesh and Argentina. The latter deployed two to the Falkland Islands during the war in 1982, but both were later captured by the British forces.

The Bell Model 212 was sold widely to civilian customers, who were impressed by the performance. Apart from the innovative powerplant

ABOVE: **Swimmers from the 20th Special Operations Squadron dropping from a distinctively camouflaged Bell UH-1N Iroquois during an open-water training exercise.**

arrangement, the helicopter was very similar to the military UH-1H, and retained the two-blade system.

Agusta built the type under licence in Italy as the AB 212, and developed a unique anti-submarine warfare version armed with torpedoes and missiles for the Italian Navy.

The US Navy and US Marines were the largest operators in the US military. During the invasion of Iraq in 2003, the USMC deployed the UH-1N to provide reconnaissance and communications support to ground troops. These helicopters were also assigned to provide close air support to USMC ground forces during heavy fighting around Nasiriyah in March 2003.

In the late 1990s, the USMC requested Bell to upgrade the UH-1N, and the result is far from a remodelling of the original 1960s design. The Bell UH-1Y Venom, also known as the "Super Huey", is a thoroughly 21st-century fighting helicopter, and is described by the manufacturer as "the legendary Bell UH made better".

The Venom was produced by either upgrading existing machines or was built as new. It has all the effectiveness, safety and reliability of the original UH-1N and, like its predecessor, can operate in the most extreme environments. The UH-1Y is powered by two General Electric T700-GE-401C turboshaft engines which allow a 125 per cent higher payload to be carried, almost 50 per cent increase in range and a higher maximum cruising speed than the UH-1N. The UH-1Y is equipped with a Target Sighting System (TSS), manufactured by Lockheed Martin, to provide target identification in all weather conditions. The UH-1Y is also fitted with an advanced electronic warfare self-protection system which has missile, laser and radar warning receivers, and an automatic countermeasures dispenser.

ABOVE: **A salvo of 70mm Hydra 70 unguided rockets being fired from a pre-production Bell UH-1Y Venom during weapons trials at Fort A. P. Hill, Virginia, USA.**

Bell UH-1Y

First flight: December 20, 2001
Power: 2 x General Electric T700-GE-401C turboshaft
Armament: 7.62mm M134 Minigun, 0.50in heavy machine-gun, 70mm Hydra 70 rockets
Size: Rotor diameter – 14.88m/48ft 10in
Length – 17.78m/58ft 4in
Height – 4.5m/14ft 7in
Weights: Empty – 5,370kg/11,840lb
Take-off – 8,390kg/18,500lb (maximum)
Performance: Speed – 304kph/189mph (maximum)
Service ceiling – 6,100m/20,013ft
Range – 482km/299 miles

LEFT: **A Canadian CH-146 Griffon helicopter from the 430th Helicopter Squadron flying over Wisconsin during a military exercise. The Griffon is equipped with a hoist that enables it to extract people and cargo from almost any terrain. It can also be equipped with a Forward Looking Infra-Red (FLIR) system and a powerful searchlight.**

Bell CH-146 Griffon

The Bell Model 412 is described by the manufacturer as "the most rugged and reliable medium twin-engine civil helicopter, designed to perform brilliantly in everything, to extreme cold and heat". This versatility and toughness to operate in extremes attracted the attention of the Canadian military when they were considering a replacement for CH-135, OH-58 Kiowa, UH-1 Iroquois and CH-47 Chinook helicopters in the army tactical, observation, rescue and heavy lift roles respectively.

The CH-146 Griffon is the utility helicopter version of the Bell 412 and has the manufacturer's designation of Bell 412CF (CF – Canadian Forces). The Griffon is used for tactical airlift of troops and equipment, logistics, reconnaissance,

casualty evacuation (CASEVAC), search and rescue (SAR) missions, and artillery command and control.

The Griffon has served with the Canadian military since 1995, and has played a key role in many national and international humanitarian relief operations, including the 1997 Manitoba Red River flood (Operation Assistance) and the 1988 ice storm (Operation Recuperation) in Canada. In 2004, the type was deployed to Haiti (Operation Halo) to be used in the United Nations relief operations.

The Canadian Army CH-146 Griffon helicopters became part of the Joint Task Force Afghanistan Air Wing (JTFAAW) deployed on Operation Athena. They helped to reduce the risk to ground forces of ambush, land mines

and improvised explosive devices (IUD) by providing increased protection to movement of troops by road transport. For air transportation the machine can be partly and quickly disassembled to fit into the Lockheed CC-130 Hercules or Boeing CC-177 Globemaster transport aircraft operated by the Royal Canadian Air Force.

The Griffon has a crew of two pilots (in armoured positions) and a crewman. The cabin has an armoured floor as protection against ground fire, and can accommodate up to ten passengers, eight fully equipped troops or six stretchers.

Although the CH-146 has a maximum gross weight of 5,397kg/11,898lb, the machine has a top speed of 260kph/162mph. Other dedicated military equipment includes missile warning receivers and military radios. The Dillon Aero M134D Minigun was first fitted to eight of the type operating in Afghanistan from late 2008, and these were deployed in a defensive and support role to act as armed escorts for Boeing Vertol CH-47 Chinook helicopters.

The CH-146 Griffon was assembled at the Bell Canada plant at Mirabel, Montreal. The Pratt & Whitney

LEFT: **A Canadian Forces CH-146 Griffon operating in the search and rescue (SAR) role.**

LEFT: **The Bell 412EP Griffin HAR2 is used as a multi-role helicopter by No. 84 Squadron based at RAF Akrotiri, Cyprus. The squadron operates three aircraft, supplied and maintained by a civilian company, but operated by experienced military aircrew.**

PT6T-3D turboshaft engines were also manufactured in Canada. The aircraft was fitted with 30 different mission kits, including a winch for search and rescue, a searchlight or Forward Looking Infra-Red (FLIR) that can be fitted to make the multi-purpose helicopter mission-specific. The Canadian military procured 100 machines, and the majority serve with tactical helicopter squadrons in the Utility Transport Tactical Helicopter (UTTH) role around Canada and overseas. Others are operated as dedicated search and rescue (SAR) helicopters in Combat Support Squadrons (CSS). The last of the type was delivered to the Canadian Forces in mid-1998. In 2005, nine aircraft were sold to a private company contracted to train future helicopter pilots at the Canadian Forces Flying Training School (CFFTS) in Manitoba. As well as military service in Afghanistan, the CH-146 has been deployed to Haiti, Bosnia and Kosovo. Through a radical upgrade programme, the type is expected to remain in Canadian service into the 2030s.

The AB 412 Grifone was a version of the Bell 412 built in Italy under licence by Agusta for the Italian Army as a tactical transport.

BELOW: **A CH-146 helicopter providing close air support to Coalition forces on the ground during a clearing operation involving Afghan National Army Commandos and troops of Special Operations Task Force, Kandahar Province, Afghanistan.**

Bell CH-146 Griffon

First flight: 1992
Power: 2 x Pratt and Whitney Canada PT6T-3D Twin-Pac turboshaft
Armament: 7.62mm M134D Minigun or 7.62mm C6 General Purpose Machine Gun (GPMG), 0.50in GAU-21 heavy machine-gun
Size: Rotor diameter – 14m/45ft 11in
Length – 17.1m/56ft 1in
Height – 4.6m/15ft 1in
Weights: Empty – 3,065kg/6,760lb
Take-off – 5,397kg/11,898lb (maximum)
Performance: Speed – 260kph/162mph (maximum)
Service ceiling – 3,111m/10,200ft
Range – 656km/405 miles

LEFT: **An MV-22 Osprey from USMC squadron VMM-263 approaching to land on USS *Nassau* (LHA-4), a Tarawa-class amphibious assault ship. For forward flight, the proprotor power nacelles take 12 seconds to rotate to the horizontal position. When the aircraft is operated in the Short Take-Off and Landing (STOL) role, the nacelles are tilted forwards at an angle of 45 degrees.**

Bell Boeing V-22 Osprey

The Bell Boeing V-22 Osprey is unique for a number of reasons, but not least because it is the first aircraft designed from the outset to meet the requirements of all four US military services, although to date only the USAF, US Navy and USMC have taken delivery due to cuts in the US defence budget.

The Osprey is a tiltrotor aircraft which can take off, land and hover like a helicopter. Once airborne, the two propulsion nacelles are rotated forward to convert the machine into a fuel-efficient turboprop fixed-wing aircraft capable of high-speed, high-altitude flight. While offering the Vertical Take-off and Landing (VTOL) advantages

of a helicopter, as an aircraft it can fly twice as fast as a helicopter and has a much greater range, resulting in greater mission versatility.

This aircraft's novelty factor is enhanced by a true multi-mission capability for a variety of roles, including amphibious assault, combat support, long-range special operations, transport, MEDEVAC and SAR. The V-22 can be refuelled in flight so can self-deploy (it does not need to be flown in a transport aircraft) and can carry 24 fully equipped combat troops, 9,084kg/20,000lb of internal cargo or up to 6,813kg/15,000lb of external cargo.

The V-22 was first flown in March 1989, and after extensive testing and

development which showed that the aircraft met or exceeded required performance parameters, the US Department of Defense approved the Osprey for production in September 2005.

The US Marine Corps, the lead service in type development, has procured the MV-22B version to perform combat assault and assault support missions. The first Osprey-equipped squadron, VMM-263, was also first of three USMC units to deploy the Osprey in a combat zone in Iraq, October 2007. During May 2009, the type was embarked with the 22nd Marine Expeditionary Unit (MEU), marking the inaugural ship-based deployment of the aircraft. In

RIGHT: **An MV-22 Osprey being refuelled during a night mission. In November 2009, the USMC deployed the type on offensive operations in Afghanistan.**

LEFT: **Two MV-22 Ospreys from USMC squadron VMM-162 preparing to lift off from USS *Nassau* (LHA-4). For stowage aboard ship, the wings are rotated to align with the fuselage. The blades of the proprotors are also folded to reduce space.**

November of the same year, the USMC deployed the type to Afghanistan for the first time. The first offensive combat mission involved the machine being used to deploy 1,000 US Marines and 150 Afghan troops into the Now Zad Valley in Helmand Province, southern Afghanistan, to disrupt Taliban communication and supply lines.

The US Air Force procured the CV-22, a long-range special operations version, configured for terrain-following, low-level,

high-speed flight. Special Operations Command (SOC) received the first operational CV-22 in March 2006, and the first operational unit, the 8th Special Operations Squadron (SOS), was activated at Hurlburt Field in 2007. The type was declared fully operational in March 2009, and by the end of that year the USAF confirmed that the CV-22 was being used on special operations. A CV-22 in USAF service is known to have crashed during a mission in Afghanistan during April 2010.

The US Navy procured the CMV-22B variant of the MV-22B as the replacement for the C-2A Greyhound for the Carrier Onboard Delivery (COD) mission, as well as SAR and delivery and retrieval of special warfare teams.

Production of this complex aircraft is divided between Boeing Rotorcraft Systems and partner Bell Helicopter Textron. Boeing is responsible for the fuselage, landing gear, tail, digital avionics and fly-by-wire flight-control systems. Bell is responsible for the wing, transmissions, rotor systems and engine installation. Final assembly is by Bell at the company's facility in Amarillo, Texas. The 100th aircraft was delivered to the US military in March 2008.

ABOVE AND LEFT: **With twin tail fins and oversized proprotors for an aircraft of its size, the Osprey is very easy to identify in forward flight.**

Bell Boeing CV-22 Osprey

First flight: March 19, 1989
Power: 2 x Rolls-Royce Allison T406/AE1107C turboshaft
Armament: 7.62mm M240G machine-gun, 0.50in M2 heavy machine-gun, 7.62mm GAU-17 Minigun
Size: Rotor diameter – 11.6m/38ft
Wingspan – 25.8m/84ft 7in
Length – 17.4m/57ft 4in
Height – 6.73m/22ft 1in
Weights: Empty – 15,032kg/33,140lb
Take-off – 23,982kg/52,870lb (maximum VTOL);
27,443kg/60,500lb (maximum STOL)
Performance: Speed – 446kph/277mph (maximum)
Service ceiling – 7,620m/25,000ft
Range – 3,890km/2,417 miles

Boeing Vertol CH-46 Sea Knight

In 1960, when Boeing purchased the Philadelphia-based helicopter manufacturer, the Vertol Aircraft Corporation, the company had three types of tandem-rotor helicopter under development. The Vertol CH-46 Sea Knight was in production for the US Navy and US Marine Corps. The aircraft was first flown on April 22, 1958. The first production version was flown on October 16, 1962, and the type has remained in front-line service for over 40 years due

to a series of upgrades. Some 200 of the CH-46E variant will remain in front-line USMC service for the foreseeable future, until a suitable replacement is found. Between 1964 and 1990, over 600 Sea Knight helicopters had been delivered to the USMC and USN.

The USN acquired the HH-46 Sea Knight to lift stores from supply ships to replenish warships of the US Fleet at sea. Equipped with a winch, the machine is also used for SAR duties.

ABOVE: **The CH-46E was a re-engined version of the earlier CH-46A and D models – the upgrade also included self-sealing fuel tanks, protected crew seats and improved avionics. The D model was an A model with improved rotor blades and better engines. In USMC service, the Sea Knight provided all-weather, day or night, assault transport of combat troops, supplies and equipment during amphibious and subsequent operations ashore.**

In contrast, the USMC wanted the Sea Knight as an assault helicopter, to airlift fully equipped troops to and from the battlefront. The fuselage is large enough to accommodate a jeep-type vehicle loaded via a ramp.

The first USMC machine was delivered in 1964 and entered operational service in Vietnam a year later, where the type began to replace the Sikorsky H-34 Choctaw on troop and cargo-carrying duties from US Navy ships in the China Sea. By 1968, the Sea Knight fleet had flown 75,000 hours on 180,000 operations (including

LEFT: **During the US invasion of Grenada, a USMC CH-46 was shot down. Like many helicopters, the type can be vulnerable to small arms fire, but is equipped to deploy flares to confuse heat-seeking missiles.**

ABOVE: **A Canadian Forces CH-113 Labrador landing on the top of Bell Island, a rocky sea stack.**

LEFT: **The CH-113 Labrador was used by the Canadian Forces from 1963 until 2004. This machine is preserved at the Canadian Aviation Museum in Ottawa.**

8,700 missions to rescue wounded USMC personnel) and had carried 500,000 troops.

Known in the USMC as the "Phrog", the Sea Knight has been used in all USMC combat and peacetime deployments. In the first Gulf War (Operation Desert Storm), some 60 US Navy machines were engaged in vertical replenishment (VertRep), supply and CASEVAC duties. During the invasion of Iraq in 2003, CH-46Es of the USMC transported personnel and supplies, including ammunition, to Forward Arming and Refuelling Points (FARP).

The USN retired the HH-46 Sea Knight on September 24, 2004, and replaced it in service with the Sikorsky MH-60S Seahawk. However, the USMC kept the MH-46E in frontline service until 2014 when it was replaced by the Bell Boeing MV-22 Osprey.

The Model 107 was also built under licence in Japan by Kawasaki. The first production aircraft was the airliner version, which pre-dated the delivery of the military type by two years. On July 1, 1962, New York Airways put the Model 107-II into service, operating between midtown Manhattan and Idlewild (later Kennedy), La Guardia and Newark airports. When the service was abandoned in the late 1970s, the helicopters were sold to Columbia Helicopters of Aurora, Oregon, for heavy lift and logging operations. One of these machines, built in 1962, was flown for a record 50,000 hours.

Other versions of the CH-46 included the CH-113 Labrador and CH-113A Voyageur, built for the Royal Canadian Air Force and Canadian Army respectively – the Labrador was primarily for search and rescue, while the Voyageur was for the transport of troops and supplies. When the Canadian forces became integrated, both versions were upgraded to a common SAR standard. When the type was retired from Canadian military service, all were purchased by Columbia Helicopters.

Kawasaki-built versions were also exported to Sweden and Saudi Arabia. The US Army evaluated the CH-46 but chose not to procure the type.

ABOVE: **The Boeing Vertol CH-46 Sea Knight has a non-retractable undercarriage.**

Boeing Vertol CH-46 Sea Knight

First flight: April 22, 1958
Power: 2 x General Electric T58-GE-16 turboshaft
Armament: None
Size: Rotor diameter – 15.24m/50ft
Length – 25.7m/84ft 4in
Height – 5.09m/16ft 9in
Weights: Empty – 5,255kg/11,585lb
Take-off – 11,022kg/24,300lb (maximum)
Performance: Speed – 265kph/165mph (maximum)
Service ceiling – 4,300m/14,000ft
Range – 296km/184 miles

Boeing CH-47 Chinook

The Boeing CH-47 Chinook is a twin-engine, tandem rotor transport helicopter that has served with the military forces of 17 nations, some for over 60 years. The US Army and Royal Air Force are the largest operators of the type.

When this large helicopter first appeared, it was faster than many smaller utility, and even attack, helicopters. With almost 1200 examples built to date, new versions are still in production. Primary roles include troop movement, artillery emplacement and battlefield resupply, and its wide rear loading ramp and three

external-cargo hooks means it can carry a lot of cargo or personnel. Despite its age, the Chinook is still among the western world's heaviest lifting helicopters. The wide rear loading ramp and three external-cargo hooks allow heavy payloads to be carried.

The Chinook story began in late 1956 when the US Army announced plans to procure a turbine-powered helicopter to replace the Sikorsky CH-37 Mojave. After much debate, a decision was made to order the Vertol Model 114 under the designation YHC-1B.

ABOVE: **The Royal Air Force operated the second largest fleet of Boeing Vertol CH-47 Chinooks and the type saw extensive service with the RAF in Afghanistan and Iraq.**

The machine was first flown on September 21, 1961. In the following year it was designated the Boeing CH-47A (Boeing had purchased Vertol in 1962) under the Tri-Service Aircraft Designation System (TSADS).

The Boeing CH-47A Chinook entered US Army service in August 1962, and had a gross weight of 14,969kg/33,000lb. Boeing was keen to increase lifting capacity, and introduced the CH-47B in 1966. The much improved aircraft was fitted with more powerful Honeywell T55-l-7C engines, which allowed an increase in gross weight to 18,144kg/40,000lb. A year later the CH-47C was developed because the US Army had identified a requirement to move a 6,804kg/15,000lb slung load over a distance

LEFT: **The Boeing Vertol YHC-1B (CH-47A) was developed from the Vertol Model 114, and was flown for the first time in 1961.**

RIGHT: **The US Army operated the Boeing Vertol H-1B (CH-47B) in the transport and heavy-lift role. This machine is being used to recover a damaged North American T-2 Buckeye naval training aircraft.**

of 56km/35 miles. Then powered by T55-I-11 engines, the C model had a gross weight of 20,865kg/46,000lb.

The CH-47 Chinook had first been used on combat operations over South-east Asia in 1965. By 1968, US Army Chinooks had accumulated 161,000 hours of flying time. During the last days of the war, one Chinook is reported to have carried 147 refugees in a single lift.

After the war, Boeing and the US Army began to plan a major fleet upgrade, which led to development of the CH-47D. Some 500 early model Chinooks were extensively modernized by Boeing, and the result was essentially a new aircraft. Boeing completed the first D-model in 1982 and concluded the work in 1994. Only two CH-47Ds were new aircraft which were built to replace US Army losses during Operation Desert Storm.

The CH-47D is a multi-mission aircraft, and is probably the most recognizable transport helicopter in the world. The distinctive twin-rotor configuration allows exceptional handling qualities, enabling the CH-47 to be operated in climatic, altitude and crosswind conditions that typically keep other helicopters on the ground. The CH-47D can be flown at more than 241kph/150mph over

distances in excess of 610km/380 miles when fitted with long-range fuel tanks.

With a flight crew of three, the CH-47D can transport 44 seated troops or 24 stretcher cases. The cabin, which is 9m/30ft 6in in length, can accommodate palletized cargo internally, or a sling load such as a 155mm M198 howitzer externally using a triple-hook system.

The CH-47 Chinooks in RAF service are used primarily for troop and logistical transport, and can carry up to 54 troops or 10,000kg/22,047lb of freight. The cabin is large enough to accommodate two Land

Rover vehicles, while the three external load hooks allow flexibility in the type and number of loads that can be carried. The British Chinook is also used in secondary roles, including SAR and CASEVAC (a total of 24 stretchers can be carried). The aircraft is crewed by either two pilots, or a pilot and navigator and two loadmasters. The aircraft can be armed with up to three M-134 Miniguns or machine-guns.

The Boeing CH-47 Chinook has been in military service with many nations around the world, including Argentina, Australia, Egypt, Iran, Greece, Italy and Japan, as well as with the military forces of Libya, Morocco, the Netherlands, Singapore, Spain, South Korea, Taiwan and Thailand.

ABOVE: **In 1965, the Boeing Vertol CH-47B was deployed to South Vietnam with the 1st Cavalry Division to replace Piasecki H-21 Shawnee helicopters. The type was particularly useful for Pipe Smoke missions to recover downed aircraft.**

Boeing Vertol CH-47D Chinook (US Army)

First flight: September 21, 1961
Power: 2 x Lycoming T-55-GA-712 turboshaft
Armament: 7.62mm Minigun, machine-guns
Size: Rotor diameter – 18.29m/60ft
Length – 30.18m/99ft
Height – 5.77m/18ft 11in
Weights: Empty – 10,615kg/24,000lb
Take-off –22,680kg/50,000lb (maximum)
Performance: Speed – 269kph/167mph (maximum)
Service ceiling – 2,575m/8,450ft
Range – 1,207km/748 miles

LEFT: **Crewmen of a US Navy Special Warfare Combatant-Craft (SWCC) attaching their rigid-hull inflatable boat to a CH-47 Chinook during a maritime air transportation system training exercise. Special Forces can increase their range of operation by being transported complete with a boat.**

Boeing CH-47F Chinook

It was inevitable, given the remarkable success of the Chinook, that the manufacturer would seek to develop the type to meet the changing demands of military customers, and extend the life of the design. In July 2007, Boeing announced that it was to begin full-scale production of a new Chinook for the US Army, the CH-47F, all to be remanufactured from existing CH-47D machines.

Developed under the Improved Cargo Helicopter Program (ICHP), the CH-47F completed US Army operational testing in April 2007. The F model is fitted with Honeywell T55-GA-714A turboshaft engines, which allow a top speed of over 315kph/196mph to be attained and an improvement in payload capacity to 9,538kg/21,000lb.

The Chinook fleet is ageing, and the first CH-47Ds reached their designed service life of 20 years in 2002 – it is worth remembering that the D model was remanufactured from earlier A, B, and C models. An ageing helicopter

requires more maintenance per flight hour, and a "new" helicopter was required to keep pace with increases in operational requirements, including cargo capacity and a longer range.

The US Army required their helicopters to link up as part of a battlefield network, and equipped the aircraft with a significantly improved digital communications and situational awareness capability. The primary mission of CH-47F, however, remains

the day or night transportation of troops, supplies and equipment in adverse weather, wherever operations are being conducted by US forces.

The CH-47F is intended to restore the ageing CH-47D to new condition and extend airframe life by another 20 years for the type to remain in service until 2025–30. Fuselage stiffening to reduce vibration, stress and metal fatigue are being applied to the F model to give an improvement in

RIGHT: **A US Army CH-47F being prepared to lift a 155mm M198 Howitzer of the 101st Airborne Division in training at Fort Benning, Georgia, USA.**

reliability and therefore lower maintenance and operating costs. The new airframe is manufactured using advanced techniques in which large single-piece components replace conventional sheet metal assemblies and light-alloy honeycomb formers, improving the structural integrity of the aircraft.

The 1970s analogue technology in the cockpit of the CH-47D is replaced with the latest controls and digital displays, including multi-function Liquid Crystal Display (LCD) screens to provide situation awareness for the flight crew through a moving map display with force symbol overlays and electronic messaging. The new systems will also ease cockpit workload and mission planning with the addition of a Data Transfer System (DTS) that allows for the preflight loading and storage of mission data. In addition to making the aircraft a cost-effective and capable digitized tactical platform, the upgrade will cut operation and support costs due to the use of reliable solid-state systems.

Improved air-transportability is an important feature of the CH-47F. Modifications to the aft rotor pylon and internal systems allow for quick removal in preparation for loading into large USAF transport aircraft.

The upgrade has been conceived as what Boeing call "an open architecture system", which allows for future growth and technology upgrades,

including advanced aircraft survivability equipment. Coupled with displays projected in Night Vision Goggles (NVG), the avionics upgrade will greatly improve flight safety at night, especially for challenging external load operations. The new vital avionics is designed to withstand electromagnetic interference and electronic warfare measures. More reliable components that are easier to maintain and repair have been used to improve at-sea compatibility for operations with the US Navy.

The Boeing CH-47F Chinook prototype, the sixth Chinook model designed for the US Army, was first flown at the company's Philadelphia plant on June 25, 2001. Flying the test aircraft from location to location around the US not only proved the aircraft's range capability, but also provided the US Army with an opportunity to conduct trials and assess various operational missions, including desert and mountain conditions.

The US Army agreed to procure 55 new-build CH-47F models and will have 61 remanufactured to CH-47G standard for use by US Special Forces units. Boeing began CH-47F production in October 2005, and the type was declared combat-ready by July 2007.

By April 2010, a force of 20 of CH-47Fs had been operating for a year in Afghanistan, often flying up to eight missions per day, every day. This sustained use in a combat

environment was used to identify and rectify any technical or maintenance problems with the type.

All Boeing CH-47D Chinooks in US Army service are to be remanufactured as CH-47F models. In Royal Air Force service the Chinook Mk 6 is a UK-specific CH-47F variant with a Digital Automatic Flight Control System to improve safety and handling especially in recirculating show or dust conditions.

Boeing CH-47F Chinook

First flight: June 25, 2001
Power: 2 x Honeywell T55-GA-714A turboshaft
Armament: Various
Size: Rotor diameter – 18.29m/60ft
Length – 30.18m/99ft
Height – 5.77m/18ft 11in
Weights: Empty – 10,615kg/23.402lb
Take-off – 22,668kg/50,000lb (maximum)
Performance: Speed – 315kph/196mph (maximum)
Service ceiling – 6,100m/20,000ft
Range – 370km/230 miles

LEFT: **A US Army MH-47G assigned to the 160th Special Operations Aviation Regiment departing from the flight deck of USS *Wasp* (LHD-1), an amphibious assault ship, during a deck-landing qualification operation.**

Boeing Vertol MH-47E/G

The MH-47 is the US Army's 160th Special Operations Aviation Regiment (Airborne) (SOAR[A]) long-range, heavy-lift helicopter. Fitted with a probe for air-to-air refuelling, a fast-rope rappelling system and other operation-specific equipment, the MH-47 is used to operate on overt and covert infiltrations, exfiltrations, air assault and resupply missions operations over a wide range of operational conditions. The aircraft can be used for a variety of other missions, including VertRep,

CASEVAC and CSAR. With the use of special mission and night vision equipment, a crew can operate over hostile territory at low altitude, and any terrain in low visibility, with pinpoint navigation accuracy.

Eight CH-47Cs fitted with Night Vision Goggles (NVG) equipment were used by the 160th SOAR(A) from 1981 in the long-range transport role. A further 16 of the CH-47E version equipped with improved navigation, satellite communications and electronic

warfare systems entered service in 1984. The MH-47D, built from the airframe of the CH-47D, entered service in the mid-1980s, but lacked much of the specialized equipment fitted in the MH-47E.

In December 1987, Boeing was contracted to develop and flight-test an MH-47E prototype and then build 25 production aircraft all converted from earlier-model CH-47 airframes. Delivery of the final MH-47E to the 160th SOAR(A) took place in May 1995, having received the first of the type in 1993. The MH-47E Chinook is a modified CH-47D equipped with an integrated cockpit, upgraded Textron Lycoming T55L-714 engines, air-to-air refuelling capability, Terrain Following/Avoidance (TF/TA) radar and upgraded Navigation/Communication (NAVCOM) systems.

Among other modifications is a much greater fuel capacity due to a 3,637-litre/800-gallon auxiliary fuel tank located in the cabin. Boeing-designed sponson-type fuel tanks of honeycomb shell construction are also fitted. The tanks are self-sealing against 12.7mm/0.50in ammunition but can withstand direct hits from larger non-explosive ordnance, even when multiple hits are sustained.

LEFT: **The first Boeing MH-47G Chinook being rolled out of the company's factory. After an extensive flight testing and development programme, the type entered service with the US Army, and was deployed to Afghanistan in March 2007 for front-line operations.**

LEFT: **A US Army MH-47G Chinook departing from the USS *Wasp* (LHD-1). Note the size of the starboard fuel tank that runs the length of the fuselage.**
BELOW: **The MH-47E special operations aircraft is a long-range, heavy-lift helicopter, which is equipped with aerial refuelling capability, a fast-rope rappelling system and other upgrades of operations-specific equipment.**

The MH-47E has a glass cockpit in which display screens have replaced the many instruments. Flying a helicopter on special operations over hostile territory in darkness and poor weather is a high workload occupation, and digital displays are proven to present key information in the most accessible way. An Integrated Avionics System (IAS) permits global communications and navigation, and is the most advanced system of its kind ever installed in a US military helicopter. The IAS includes Forward Looking Infra-Red (FLIR) and Multi-Mode Radar (MMR).

A key US Army operational requirement was that the avionics systems on MH-47E Chinook and MH-60K Pave Hawk helicopters were interchangeable. Crucial equipment such as radios, mission computers and multifunction displays could be exchanged between the types in a few minutes.

In 1991, the type was deployed to Iraq during Operation Desert Storm. Missions included providing ground refuelling for a force of Sikorsky MH-53 Pave Low and Hughes AH-64A Apache helicopters deployed for CSAR duties.

In the first six months, CH-47Es of the US Army flew some 2,000 hours on 200 combat missions. Over 70 of these involved the infiltration or extraction of forces from enemy territory. These missions of up to 15 hours duration were flown at altitudes of up to 4,880m/16,000ft, and crews had to use oxygen. The MH-47 is the only helicopter in the US Army inventory capable of supporting special operations in such a difficult and challenging environment.

Boeing delivered an upgrade to the MH-47E Chinook, which led to the MH-47G. This included a new cockpit with improved displays and a range of avionics upgrades. The MMR in the MH-47G provides terrain avoidance data to a moving map display, and an improved

missile-warning receiver has also been fitted. All existing aircraft will be or have been upgraded to this standard. The US Army deployed the MH-47G to Afghanistan from March 2007.

Boeing MH-47E Chinook

First flight: September 21, 1961 (prototype)
Power: 2 x Textron Lycoming T55-GA-714 turboshaft
Armament: 7.62mm Minigun, 7.62mm machine-gun
Size: Rotor diameter – 18.29m/60ft
Length – 30.18m/99ft
Height – 5.59m/18ft 4in
Weights: Empty – 12,210kg/26,918lb
Take-off – 24,494kg/54,000lb (maximum)
Performance: Speed – 259kph/161mph (maximum)
Service ceiling – 3,094m/10,150ft
Range – 1136km/705 miles

Boeing AH-64D/E Apache Longbow/Guardian

The AH-64D Apache Longbow, which was first flown as a prototype on May 14, 1992, is a significant improvement on what was already a formidable weapons system. With enhanced performance and new avionics, the new Apache was developed as a result of experience gained in Operation Desert Storm, the first Gulf War. The Longbow name attached to the D-model refers to the advanced AN/APG-78 Longbow millimetre-wave mast-mounted Fire Control Radar (FCR) in a housing mounted above the rotor head. The radar rapidly detects, classifies, prioritizes (up to 128 per minute) and locks on to multiple stationary, mobile or aerial targets in adverse weather, fog, dust and smoke. The unique system enables an attack to be made from beyond enemy range, thereby significantly increasing the helicopter's survivability. An integrated Radio Frequency Interferometer (RFI) passively gives identification of, and precise bearing to, threat emitters at long range.

The D-model can be concealed from enemy view, using terrain, trees or buildings for cover, and hover with only the Longbow radar scanner "looking" over the top. Weapons can be launched from this position. The Pilot Night Vision Sensor (PNVS) and Integrated Helmet And Display Sighting System (IHADSS) provide a visually integrated, night and adverse weather piloting system. Flying and weapon aiming information is presented "head-up" to the pilot. The terrain picture from the FCR may also be selected on the IHADSS.

A radio modem integrated with the sensor suite enables the crew of an AH-64D to share targeting data with other D-model crews. This allows the Apache Longbow to be used as a group to attack targets detected by the FCR of a single helicopter.

The aircraft is powered by two General Electric T700-GE-701C turbo-shaft engines, which provide better performance during combat. The forward fuselage of the aircraft was revised and the cockpit protected by ballistic armour. Airbags are also fitted, to reduce the risk of injury in the event of a crash landing.

RIGHT: **The Apache's permanent weapon is an underslung M230 30mm cannon, which is directed either manually or slaved to the helmet of the gunner, who sits in the front crew seat.**

Defensive equipment includes chaff and flare dispensers, as well as laser and radar warning sensors.

Deliveries to the US Army began in 1997, and publicity material from Boeing summed up the capabilities of the AH-64D Apache Longbow by highlighting the statement, "the potential for one attack helicopter regiment to destroy up to 256 targets in less than 5 minutes".

LEFT: **An Army Air Corps (AAC) AgustaWestland AH-64D Apache lifting off from the deck of HMS *Ocean*, a Royal Navy amphibious assault helicopter carrier.**

The US Army ordered 501 original AH-64A aircraft to be upgraded to AH-64D standard to be delivered by August 2006. A total of 42 new-build machines were also ordered and the first were delivered in 2007, followed by an order for a further 96 remanufactured machines.

Export customers acquiring new or remanufactured machines have included Egypt, Greece, Israel, Japan, Kuwait, the Netherlands, Taiwan, Saudi Arabia, Singapore and the UAE.

In July 1995, a licence was agreed to allow AgustaWestland to produce the machine in the UK as the WAH-64 Apache Longbow for the Army Air Corps (AAC), where it is designated Apache AH Mk1. A total of 67 were built between 2000 and 2004.The WAH-64D is powered by two Rolls-Royce/Turboméca RTM322 Mk 250 turboshaft engines, a version of which is used to power the AgustaWestland Merlin. The British Army considers the Apache Longbow to be the most significant battlefield weapon to

enter service since the introduction of the tank in 1916.

The improved AH-64E Apache Guardian has improved digital connectivity, more powerful T700-GE-701D engines, the capability to control unmanned aerial vehicles, virtually all-weather capability, improved landing gear and can be operated in maritime conditions. New composite rotor blades increase cruise speed, climb rate, and payload capacity. 634 US Army AH-64Ds will be upgraded to AH-64E standard.

ABOVE: **An early AH-64 Apache without the Longbow radar scanner flying over a battery of Royal Artillery 155mm AS90 self-propelled guns. The aircraft is operating as part of the NATO-led Stabilization Force (SFOR) in Bosnia and Herzegovina.**

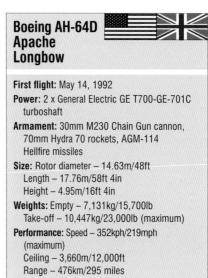

Boeing AH-64D Apache Longbow

First flight: May 14, 1992
Power: 2 x General Electric GE T700-GE-701C turboshaft
Armament: 30mm M230 Chain Gun cannon, 70mm Hydra 70 rockets, AGM-114 Hellfire missiles
Size: Rotor diameter – 14.63m/48ft
  Length – 17.76m/58ft 4in
  Height – 4.95m/16ft 4in
Weights: Empty – 7,131kg/15,700lb
  Take-off – 10,447kg/23,000lb (maximum)
Performance: Speed – 352kph/219mph (maximum)
  Ceiling – 3,660m/12,000ft
  Range – 476km/295 miles

Bristol Type 171 Sycamore

When the Bristol Sycamore entered Royal Air Force service in April 1953, it became the first British-designed helicopter in British military use. The prototype of the Type 171 was first flown on July 24, 1947, ground running trials having begun earlier in May. In April 1949, the type became the first British-built helicopter to be issued with a certificate of airworthiness, granted so the prototype could be flown to France to be demonstrated at the Paris Salon (Paris Air Show).

The design team for the Type 171 was led by Raoul Hafner, who had been involved in the development and the building of autogyros and gyroplanes in the 1930s. During World War II, he worked at the Airborne Forces Experimental Establishment (AFEE) before joining the helicopter department of the Bristol Aeroplane Company, Filton, near Bristol in 1944.

The Type 171 was very much a helicopter of the time, having a light alloy fuselage. The rotor blades were constructed from spruce and ply ribs fitted to a metal spar and covered with thin plywood. The rotor was to fail dramatically on the second test flight.

The Bristol machine was considerably more streamlined than any Sikorsky helicopter of the period. The Ministry of Supply (MoS) ordered two prototypes which were powered by the US-built Pratt & Whitney Wasp Junior radial engine due to the unavailability of the British-built Alvis Leonides, a sleeve-valve radial piston engine, which was under development. The Leonides engine was fitted in the third prototype, designated Type 171, Mk 2, and first flown on September 3, 1949.

Bristol then built 15 machines (Type 171, Mk 3) with a shorter but wider cabin for evaluation by the British

ABOVE: **One of four Sycamore HC II (Mk 3) aircraft built by Bristol for evaluation by the Royal Air Force for the air sea rescue role. The type entered RAF service in April 1953 as the Sycamore HR.14.**

military. Only the RAF ordered the type in quantity, and took delivery of some 90 machines primarily for SAR and light transport duties. The primary RAF version was the Sycamore HR14, modified to position the pilot on the right-hand side of the cockpit.

The Type 171, now named Sycamore, first entered RAF squadron service with Fighter Command. This was because the RAF had numerous fighter squadrons flying from airfields located around Britain, and the prompt rescue of downed aircrew had always

BELOW: **The Federal German government procured 50 Bristol Sycamore Mk52 helicopters for service with the army and navy.**

LEFT: **The Royal Australian Navy obtained three Sycamore Mk50 helicopters and a further seven HC51s for air sea rescue duties from RAN aircraft carriers. All were powered by the Alvis Leonides sleeve-valve radial piston engine.**

been a problem. The Sycamore was optimized for SAR, meaning that a pilot could be located and rescued from the sea or a mountainside very quickly. The first dedicated SAR squadron was No. 275, based at Linton-on-Ouse, North Yorkshire.

The Sycamore was also deployed overseas for combat in the light assault role, first in Malaya with No.194 Squadron (where the type was to replace the Westland S-51 Dragonfly) and later in Cyprus with No.284 Squadron. It was the latter unit that worked to develop two key aspects of military helicopter operations – landing troops in difficult-to-reach locations and night flying. In early 1958, a force of some 40 British soldiers were landed from five Sycamores to attack a terrorist position 915m/3,000ft up a mountain south of Nicosia, Cyprus; the British achieved complete surprise due to the use of helicopters. In late 1962, the type was operated in Borneo by No.110 Squadron to transport British troops.

ABOVE: **The Royal Air Force ordered 85 of the Sycamore HR.14 for the air sea rescue role. Early rescue helicopters in RAF service were equipped with a net to lift a survivor. Later, the rescue strop (sling) was developed, and this is the current method used for recovery operations.**

The RAF continued to operate the Sycamore as a front-line helicopter until October 1964, but retained the type for communications duties until mid-1972.

Bristol received export orders for the Type 171 from the military services of Australia, Belgium and West Germany.

As a footnote, British European Airways (BEA) was keen to investigate the commercial opportunities for civil operations, and leased two Type 171s from Bristol. The two machines, designated Mk 3a, had a baggage compartment at the rear of the engine bay. In 1954, BEA operated an experimental passenger service between Southampton, London and Northolt airports. Then, in 1955, a service was inaugurated between Birmingham, Heathrow and Gatwick airports.

Bristol Sycamore HR.14

First flight: July 24, 1947
Power: 1 x Alvis Leonides piston radial engine
Armament: None
Size: Rotor diameter – 14.81m/48ft 7in
Length – 18.63m/61ft 2in
Height – 3.71m/12ft 2in
Weights: Empty – 1,728kg/3,810lb
Take-off – 2,540kg/5,600lb (maximum)
Performance: Speed – 204kph/127mph (maximum)
Range – 531km/330 miles

Bristol Type 192 Belvedere

The Bristol Type 192 Belvedere was a tandem-rotor, twin-engine helicopter operated by the Royal Air Force from 1961 to 1969 for troop transport, supply dropping and CASEVAC. It was the first twin-rotor, twin-engine helicopter and first turbine-powered helicopter to enter service with the RAF.

The Belvedere was developed from the radial-engined Bristol Type 173, first flown on January 3, 1952, which had been designed for the civil market. When this version was cancelled, Bristol focused on developing the military version, having had interest from the Royal Navy (Type 191), the Royal Canadian Navy (Type 193) and the RAF (Type 192). The prototype of the Type 192 was first flown on July 5, 1958. Three pre-production machines were then delivered to an RAF Trials Unit in October 1960 for evaluation. The

ABOVE: **The Bristol Belvedere HC Mk1 was designed to meet a Royal Air Force requirement for a medium transport helicopter.**

type entered RAF service as the Bristol Belvedere HC Mk1, and a total of 26 were built, with the final aircraft being delivered in June 1962.

The HC Mk1 was powered by two Napier (Rolls-Royce) Gazelle NGa1 turboshaft engines, which allowed sufficient reserve power to allow the aircraft to fly on a single engine even with a full load. The rotor gearboxes were connected by a synchronizing shaft that not only prevented the blades from clashing strike, but also allowed drive to be taken from either engine. The Belvedere could climb at 49m/160ft per minute on one engine.

The first operational unit, No.66 Squadron, was formed in September 1961 after the Belvedere Trials Unit had accumulated a great deal of expertise on the type during the evaluation phase. Based at RAF Odiham, Hampshire, No.66 was part of RAF Transport Command and was equipped with six Belvederes. The other units were Nos.26 and 72 Squadrons.

LEFT: **A short-wheelbase Land Rover Series II and trailer being lifted during crew training at RAF Odiham, Hampshire.**

LEFT: **The Bristol Type 173 was designed as a 13-seat passenger transport and powered by two Alvis Leonides Major radial piston engines. The Type 173 Mk3 was built to evaluate the four-blade rotor system. Note that on this early machine the tailplane is straight, and is fitted with vertical fins.**

In November 1961, two Belvederes from No.66 Squadron were demonstrated during in The Lord Mayor's Show, London, to deliver troops and equipment on to barges moored on the River Thames. In April 1962, a Belvedere of No.72 Squadron demonstrated the type's lifting capability when it was used to deliver the spire to the top of Coventry Cathedral. In the UK, during the severe winter of early 1963, RAF Belvederes were frequently deployed to carry out emergency and supply flights in parts of the country cut off by heavy snow. The type was used for lifting duties as diverse as retrieving a crashed aircraft from a jungle location to transporting the Honest John battlefield missile for the British Army.

Operational experience with the Belvedere stimulated new thinking by military planners for logistical supply and air mobility. It gave commanders on the ground improved battlefield capabilities in the transport of men (18 fully equipped troops or 12 stretcher cases) and cargo (2,725kg/6,000lb internally or 2,385kg/5,250lb slung below the fuselage).

In the eight years that the Belvedere was in front-line service, it was used in Aden, Borneo, Libya, Malaya and Tanganyika (Tanzania). Many of the missions were to deliver British troops directly into combat areas, including jungle clearings.

In March 1969, the last Belvederes in RAF service were retired when No. 66 Squadron was disbanded at RAF Seletar, Singapore.

ABOVE: **In front-line service, all Bristol Belvedere HC Mk1 helicopters were painted in the standard RAF-pattern camouflage of dark green and medium grey. The type could lift an under slung load of up to 2,385kg/5,250lb.**

Bristol Type 192 Belvedere HC Mk1

First flight: July 5, 1958
Power: 2 x Napier (Rolls-Royce) Gazelle NGa1 turboshaft
Armament: None
Size: Rotor diameter – 14.83m/48ft 8in
Length – 16.56m/54ft 4in
Height – 5.26m/17ft 3in
Weights: Empty – 5,167kg/11,390lb
Take-off – 8,618kg/19,000lb (maximum)
Performance: Speed – 222kph/138mph (maximum)
Service ceiling – 3,050m/10,000ft
Range – 121km/75 miles

Denel AH-2 Rooivalk

The Denel Aviaton AH-2 Rooivalk (red falcon) is a South African-designed and built attack helicopter. Much like the experience that faced US military forces in Vietnam, the South African Defence Force (SADF) was with involved in a conventional war along the country's borders, and defence planners identified a requirement for a dedicated attack helicopter.

In 1984, the Atlas Aircraft Corporation, a predecessor of Denel Aviation, began work on the project, and designed and produced the Atlas XH-1 Alpha test aircraft. The machine was based on the airframe of the Aérospatiale Alouette III and was fitted with the same Turboméca Artouste IIIB turboshaft engine and mechanical components, including

ABOVE: **The Denel AH-2 Rooivalk was purposely designed for operations in the demanding terrain of South Africa's border regions.**

the rotor system. The cockpit was, however, a new design, and followed the tandem layout as used on the Bell AH-1 Cobra and the Hughes AH-64 Apache. To allow the 20mm cannon to be positioned under the nose of

RIGHT: **The main armament on the AH-2 is the French-built Nexter (GIAT) F2, a 20mm single-barrel cannon fed from a magazine containing 700 rounds of ammunition. The South African Air Force (SAAF) procured 12 of the type, and all machines remaining in service are operated by 16 Squadron from their base at AFB Bloemspruit near Bloemfontein in Free State Province.**

the machine, the aircraft was fitted with a tail-wheel undercarriage. Following a first test flight of February 3, 1985, and successful subsequent testing, the development of a production version was confirmed. Part of this development was the decision to utilize the main rotor and the Turboméca Makila 1K2 turboshaft engine from the Atlas Oryx, an upgrade of the Aérospatiale Puma which had been built in South Africa in the face of a UN arms embargo.

The South African Air Force had been operating helicopters for many years in the hostile conditions of the African bush, and demanded that the new attack helicopter could be operated for lengthy periods without sophisticated support. On operations, the AH-2 Rooivalk can be deployed far from base, only requiring a transport helicopter to carry a basic spares supply for support and a ground crew of four to service the machine.

The machine can also carry air-to-air missiles, the South African-produced Mokopa ZT-6 anti-tank missile and 70mm unguided rockets. For defence, the aircraft is designed to have low audio, visual and infra-red signature, and is equipped with an electronic countermeasures suite as well as chaff and flare dispensers.

The Denel AH-2 Rooivalk can carry up to 2,032kg/4,480lb of weapons. The 20mm gas-operated F2 cannon is controlled by sighting equipment fitted on the helmet of the on-board weapons operator. The machine is fitted with infra-red sensors and TV telescopic viewing sights to allow day and night operations. Other sensors and communication equipment makes the Rooivalk a key intelligence link for command and control, to provide the entire operation with shared real time intelligence, potentially lowering the risk of damage from friendly fire.

In the armed reconnaissance role, the helicopter can be deployed to assess enemy positions using long-range sensors to give early warning of any threats. On tactical missions, the Rooivalk will be used to locate the enemy while avoiding detection, provide command with three-dimensional situational awareness, real-time data and identify friendly or enemy forces. Equipment on the helicopter includes a multi-spectral sighting system, allowing military commanders to gain a true 24-hour real-time awareness of the tactical situation. A fully integrated digital management system reduces cockpit workload for the crew, providing more time for battlefield awareness.

ABOVE LEFT: **A salvo of 70mm Folding Fin Aerial Rockets (FFAR) being fired from an AH-2 during a military exercise.** ABOVE: **The Denel AH-2 Rooivalk was designed to be deployed in a remote environment, and requires only a support helicopter to carry spare parts, ammunition and servicing personnel to operate.**

The Denel AH-2 Rooivalk has been purposely developed for the terrain over which the machine is operated, and in this type of combat environment a well-equipped attack helicopter can act as a true force multiplier for the South African military.

A total of 12 AH-2 Rooivalks were ordered, and the type entered service with No.16 Squadron of the South African Air Force in July 1999.

Denel Rooivalk

First flight: February 3, 1985
Power: 2 x Turboméca Makila 1K2 turboshaft
Armament: 20mm F2 cannon, Makopa ZT-6 anti-tank missiles, 70mm FFAR unguided rockets, air-to-air missiles
Size: Rotor diameter – 15.58m/51ft 2in
Length – 16.39m/53ft 9in
Height – 5.19m/17ft
Weights: Empty – 5,730kg/12,632lb
Take-off – 8,750kg/19,290lb (maximum)
Performance: Speed – 309kph/193mph (maximum)
Service ceiling – 6,100m/20,000ft
Range – 740km/437miles

Eurocopter EC665/Airbus HAD Tiger

The concept for the Eurocopter EC665 attack helicopter goes back to 1984, when the Cold War was still dominating military planning in the West. Helicopter gunships were mainly very vulnerable modifications of utility helicopters. The governments of West Germany and France therefore issued a requirement for an advanced multi-role battlefield helicopter with enhanced survivability. The successful design came from MBB (Messerschmitt-Bölkow-Blohm) in West Germany and Aérospatiale in France –

subsequently forming Eurocopter. Five prototypes were built, and the first was flown in April 1991. One of the prototypes was completed as an anti-tank variant for the specific West German requirement, and another was built to reflect the French escort helicopter variant.

Full production of the machine (Tiger in German service; Tigre in French and Spanish service) began in March 2002, and the first production Tigre HAP (Hélicoptère d'Appui Protection – support and escort

ABOVE: **In German Armed Forces service the UHT (from Unterstützungshubschrauber Tiger, German for "support helicopter tiger") can be armed with anti-tank missiles, 70mm /2. in air-to-ground rockets or four AIM-92 Stinger missiles – a 12.7mm /0.50in gunpod can also be fitted.**

helicopter) for the French Army was flown in March 2003. Delivery of the type began in September 2003. Within a few months, deliveries began of the UHT ordered by Germany.

In December 2001, Eurocopter

RIGHT: **The German UHT version was designed from the outset to multi-role to respond to a variety of potential mission demands while having the ability to attack a range of target types.**

LEFT: **All Eurocopter EC665 helicopters in service with the armed forces of Australia, France and Spain are fitted with the French-built 30mm GIAT cannon.**

was awarded a contract to supply the Australian Army with 22 examples of the Tiger ARH (Armed Reconnaissance Helicopter) version, which were fully operational by 2012. The Tiger ARH is an upgraded version of the Tiger HAP with uprated MTR390 engines and a laser designator for the AGM-114 Hellfire II anti-tank missiles. The ARH can also be armed with the 70mm Hydra 70 rocket. The Tigers are replacing the Bell OH-58 Kiowa and the Bell UH-1 Iroquois-based Bushranger gunship in service with the Australian Army.

The Spanish Army's 24 examples of the Tigre HAD (Helicoptero de Apoyo y Destrucción – support and attack helicopter) version are almost identical to the HAP, but with more engine power

available from uprated MTR390 engines and improved airframe protection from ground fire. The French Army subsequently decided to upgrade most of their HAP helicopters to HAD standard.

Some 80 per cent of the airframe is constructed from components manufactured from Carbon Fibre, Reinforced Polymer (CFRP), which allows a weight reduction of up to 30 per cent over a conventional metal structure. This also produces a very smooth surface for improved aerodynamic performance, and is strong enough to withstand 23mm cannon fire.

The airframe is designed to present a low radar signature and minimal infra-red emissions. The machine is equipped with AN/AAR-MILDS

radar, laser targeting, missile warning systems and also a SAPHIR-M chaff and flares dispenser.

The Tiger can be armed with the 68mm SNEB folding-fin rocket, AGM-114 Hellfire missile, 70mm Hydra 70 rocket or Mistral air-to-air missiles. The Stinger anti-aircraft missile can also be carried. The highly accurate and powerful 30mm GIAT30 cannon has set a new standard for helicopter-mounted gun performance – during firing trials a burst of five rounds fired from a range of 1km/ 1.6 miles successfully hit the target.

In July 2009, the French Army began operations in Afghanistan with three Eurocopter EC665 Tigre HAP helicopters, the first active deployment of the type in a war zone. On June 4, 2011, French Army machines operated with AgustaWestland AH-64 Apache Longbow helicopters of the Army Air Corps (AAC) against targets in Libya.

ABOVE: **The MTU/Turboméca/Rolls-Royce MTR390 turboshaft engine and gearbox installation. Note the suppressor fitted to the engine exhaust, which reduces infra-red emissions.**

Eurocopter EC665/ Airbus HAD Tiger

First flight: April 29, 1991
Power: 2 x MTU/Turboméca/Rolls-Royce MTR390 turboshaft
Armament: 30mm GIAT30 cannon, AGM-114 Hellfire missile, Mistral air-to-air missile, 70mm Hydra 70 rocket, 68mm SNEB rocket
Size: Rotor diameter – 13m/42ft 8in
Length – 14m/46ft
Height – 4.32m/14ft 1in
Weights: Empty – 3,060kg/6,746lb
Take-off – 6,000kg/13,228lb (maximum)
Performance: Speed – 315kph/214mph (maximum)
Service ceiling – 3,200m/10,500ft
Range – 800km/497 miles

Eurocopter AS 550 Fennec/Airbus H125M

The Airbus H125M (formerly Eurocopter/Aérospatiale AS 550) Fennec (named after the fennec fox) is a lightweight helicopter used extensively by the French Army and Navy, as well as the navies of Argentina and Malaysia, for reconnaissance, attack and other missions. Both the single engine and twin-engine models have also been ordered by Brazil, Columbia, Denmark, Ecuador,

Indonesia, Kenya, Mexico, Pakistan, Qatar, Tanzania, Thailand, Uzbekistan and Singapore for use as armed scouts and anti-tank helicopters, as well as naval or training aircraft.

There are four single-engined and 11 twin-engined variants, from a basic transport version to a military version armed with a 20mm GIAT M621 cannon and a range of missiles or rockets. It can also be fitted with torpedoes and

ABOVE: **The Royal Danish Air Force (RDAF) operates the Eurocopter AS 550 C2 Fennec for liaison duties. A light-attack helicopter, it can be equipped with a pod-mounted 20mm GAU cannon, and the type can be armed with anti-tank missiles.**

rockets in naval service. The type first entered service in 1990 and was built by Aérospatiale as a development of the AS 350 and AS 355 Écureuil helicopters. In 1990, the military Écureuil series of

RIGHT: **The Eurocopter AS 350B Écureuil is operated by the Army Air Corps as a training helicopter. All operations are flown by No.670 and No.705 Squadrons (AAC) from RAF Shawbury, Shropshire, which is also the base for the Defence Helicopter Flying School (DHFS).**

LEFT: **A Eurocopter AS 550 Fennec in service with the Brazilian Navy on the flight deck of USS** *Pearl Harbor* **(LSD-52) during an exercise off the coast of Argentina.**

helicopters was renamed Fennec. By 2004, a total of 3,640 aircraft had been delivered. The worldwide appeal of the type is due to its versatility and performance. With a maximum ceiling of 7,000m/22,965ft and a mission range of over 645km/348 miles, the Fennec family of helicopters meets the requirements of many civil and military operators.

The latest variant is the AS 550 C3, which has improved protection as it is fitted with self-sealing fuel tanks, energy-absorbing passenger seats and armour protection to the crew seats. If the main gearbox is damaged, it can be run for 45 minutes without lubricant. The rotor blades and hub are designed to be resistant to impact and hits from 7.62mm ammunition. Sophisticated equipment includes a laser and radar warning system, a missile launch detection system and a chaff and flares dispenser to confuse the guidance system of a heat-seeking or radar-guided missile.

The use of composite materials to construct the airframe and finishing the fuselage with infra-red reflective paint reduces radar signature. The main rotor is assembled using the fewest possible number of moving parts to minimize wear and servicing, thus reducing the aircraft's time out of service.

The sophisticated avionics suite enables the crew to fly very low-altitude flight plans safely, utilizing the machine's excellent maneouvrability and power reserves from the Arriel turboshaft engine.

ABOVE: **The naval version of the Eurocopter AS 550 Fennec can be equipped with search radar, the scanner for which is mounted in a radome under the nose of the aircraft.**

Eurocopter AS 550 Fennec/Airbus H125M

First flight: June 26, 1974
Power: 1 x Turboméca Arriel 2B turboshaft
Armament: 20mm GIAT M621 cannon, BGM-71 TOW anti-tank missile, 68mm Brandt rocket, 7.62mm or 12.7mm FNH machine-gun pods
Size: Rotor diameter – 10.69m/35ft 1in
Length – 12.94m/42ft 6in
Height – 3.34m/10ft 11in
Weights: Empty – 1,202kg/2,650lb
Take-off – 2,250kg/4,960lb (maximum)
Performance: Speed – 278kph/178mph (maximum)
Service ceiling – 7,000m/2,2965ft
Range – 645km/348 miles

LEFT: **The UH-72 Lakota is powered by two Turboméca Arriel II turboshaft engines driving a proven hingeless rotor system. This is fitted with advanced technology composite rotor blades which give decreased vibration and noise while enhancing aerodynamic efficiency.**

Eurocopter/Airbus UH-72 Lakota

The Airbus (formerly Eurocopter) UH-72 Lakota is a military version of the technologically advanced and proven multi-mission Eurocopter EC145 helicopter, which was based on the MBB/Kawasaki BK 117 C1. The UH-72 is built by American Eurocopter, a division of EADS North America. Originally marketed as the UH-145, the helicopter was selected by the US Army as the winner for the Light

Utility Helicopter (LUH) programme in June 2006. In October 2006, the manufacturer was awarded a production contract for 345 aircraft. The UH-72 was required to replace Bell UH-1H Iroquois and Bell OH-58A/C Kiowa helicopters in the US Army and Army National Guard (ANG) inventory.

It was quite an achievement for Eurocopter to secure this contract despite very strong competition from

Bell and also McDonnell Douglas who, as the losers, protested the decision. In August, the UH-145 airframe was officially designated UH-72A by the Department of Defense (DoD). After a four-month delay, the first UH-72 was delivered on time. On December 12, 2006, a ceremony attended by General Richard A. Cody, Vice Chief of Staff (Army) and Chief Joe Red Cloud of the Oglala Sioux, Lakota nation, was held to name the aircraft. At the event, the first UH-72A was accepted and named Lokata, continuing a long-standing US Army tradition of using the name of a Native American Indian Tribe for each helicopter type to enter service.

The machines are being built at the American Airbus facility in Columbus, Mississippi. While US production was being established,

LEFT: **A UH-72A of the 121st Medical Company flying over Washington, DC. The unit was the first US military Medical Evacuation (MEDEVAC) unit to receive the helicopter as a replacement for the Bell UH-1H Iroquois.**

LEFT: **On July 18, 2008, the first Eurocopter UH-72 light utility helicopter to enter service with the Army National Guard (ANG) was delivered to the Eastern Aviation Site at Fort Indiantown Gap, Pennsylvania.**

early aircraft were assembled from components manufactured by Eurocopter Deutschland. The 100th Lakota entered service with the US Army in March 2010. During October 2021 the US Army UH-72 fleet passed the one millionth flight hour mark. The UH-72A is equipped with Vehicle and Engine Multi-function Display (VEMD), a system which integrates and synthesizes flight and mechanical information. Hydraulic, electrical and engine control systems are all duplicated, and a crashworthy airframe adds a high level of safety and survivability to the aircraft.

The UH-7A Lakota is designed for a range of missions, from general support to personnel recovery. Army National Guard (ANG) units operate the type on counter-narcotics operations. On delivery to the US Army in January 2007, the first helicopters were sent to the National Training Center at Fort Irwin, California, for MEDEVAC missions. Six months later, in June 2007, the US Army Air Ambulance Detachment (AAD) became the first operational unit. A month later, the Training and Doctrine Command Flight Detachment (TDCFC) at Fort Eustis, Virginia, became the second operational unit.

In January 2009, the United States Military Academy at West Point, New York, received two UH-72As for use as VIP transports. In September 2009, the US Naval Test Pilot School (USNTPS) received the first of five UH-72As as the prime training type for the helicopter training and handling programme.

The UH-72B version that entered US National Guard service in 2021 incorporates the unique Fenestron tail rotor, more powerful engines, enhanced controls and avionics. The UH-72 is also operated by the Royal Thai Army.

LEFT: **A total of 16 Eurocopter UH-72A Lakota helicopters were assigned to the Military District of Washington, DC, based at Davison Army Airfield, Fort Belvoir, Virginia.**

Eurocopter/ Airbus UH-72A Lakota

First flight: June 12, 1999
Power: 2 x Turboméca Arriel IE2 turboshaft
Armament: None
Size: Rotor diameter – 11m/36ft 1in
    Length – 13.03m/42ft 7in
    Height – 3.45m/11ft 9in
Weights: Empty – 1,792kg/3,950lb
    Take-off – 3,585kg/7,903lb (maximum)
Performance: Speed – 269kph/167mph (maximum)
    Service ceiling – 5,791m/18,000ft
    Range – 685km/426 miles

Hiller OH-23 Raven

The Hiller OH-23 Raven was developed from the civilian Hiller Model 360, a three- to four-seat helicopter and was ultimately operated by 26 military air arms around the world. The OH-23 series became the first helicopter of any type to be approved for 1,000 hours of operation between major overhauls.

Stanley Hiller had developed the small but innovative Hiller 360, only the third helicopter qualified by the Civil Aeronautics Administration (CAA), and his company was rare in that it was the first in the US producing helicopters without military sponsorship. Worldwide marketing led to orders from the French, who ordered the production version, the UH-12, for Medical Evacuation duties in the Indo–China war. The UH-12 proved

its military capability with the French under very difficult jungle conditions, and although Hiller had been urging the US Army to consider the UH-12 for their inventory, it took the outbreak of the Korean War to bring large orders. Hiller Aircraft's production line in Palo Alto, California, was soon delivering a helicopter a day for US Army use on the Korean front line. In US military service, the model UH-12 was designated the H-23 Raven, and it served in utility, observation and CASEVAC roles – for the latter it could carry two stretchers. Within a few years, the H-23 was back in combat, scouting with the US Army in Vietnam. The type remained the US Army's primary helicopter trainer until 1965. By the time production ended

ABOVE: **The H-23C was the first of the type to be fitted with a goldfish-bowl-type canopy over the three-seat cockpit.**

in 1965, more than 2,000 examples had been built, with around 300 being exported. Hiller developed and improved the design throughout its service.

In October 1962, pilot Lieutenant Colonel John I. Faulkenberry and mechanic Specialist Fifth Class William Harold Canon broke a US Army distance record for flying a helicopter from one point to another. In nine and a half days they flew 4,345km/2,700 miles. The Hiller would only hold enough fuel for about 80 minutes of flying. With an extra 23 litres/5 gallons of fuel in a can on board, the pair made the trip from airport

LEFT: **The Royal Navy purchased 20 ex-USN HT-2E machines designated as the HT Mk1. A further 21 of the Hiller Model UH-12E were procured, and entered RN service as the HT Mk2.**

to airport, but had to stop only twice at civilian petrol stations along the way for high-test fuel.

The H-23A (UH-12A) had a sloping front window and wooden rotor blades, and was used by both the US Army and US Navy. The H-23B (UH-12B) was designed as a primary helicopter trainer and, although similar to the A model, had the option of skids or a wheeled-type undercarriage and was powered by a Franklin 6V4-200-C33 engine. Versions for the Royal Navy (HT Mk1) and the

US Navy (HTE-2) had wheels. The three-seat H-23D (UH-12D) had a larger engine compared to the earlier UH-12C and had the moulded goldfish bowl-type bubble canopy, reminiscent of the Bell 47, and metal rotor blades. The OH-23G was a dual-control version of the D model, while the OH-23F had a lengthened fuselage with four seats. The G model, powered by a Lycoming piston engine, was the most numerous version with 834 built, followed by the OH-23D, of which 348 were built. The

ABOVE: **The Hiller Model UH-12E-4 was fitted with a larger cabin to accommodate four passengers. The type entered service with the US Army as the H-21F Raven. In 1965, all of the type in service were redesignated OH-23.**

Raven could be armed with two 0.30in M37C machine-guns or two 7.62mm M60C machine-guns.

As well as the US Army and US Navy, operators included Argentina, Biafra, Bolivia, Canada (designated the CH-112 Nomad in Army service), Chile, Colombia, Dominican Republic, France, Germany, Guatemala, Indonesia, Israel, Japan, Mexico, Morocco, the Netherlands, Paraguay, Peru, Sri Lanka, Thailand and Uruguay. The Royal Navy used Hiller HT Mk 1 and 2s for many years, operated by No.705 Naval Air Squadron (NAS), who were tasked with basic flying training of all Fleet Air Arm (FAA) helicopter pilots.

ABOVE: **The cockpit on the Hiller H-23 Raven originally had a sloping front. The type was deployed to Korea for service as a light utility, observation and, when fitted with stretcher panniers, for MEDEVAC duties.**

Hiller OH-23D Raven

First flight: April 3, 1956
Power: 1 x Avco Lycoming VO-540-A1B piston engine
Armament: Usually none
Size: Rotor diameter – 10.82m/35ft 6in
Length – 8.53m/28ft
Height – 2.97m/9ft 9in
Weights: Empty – 824kg/1,816lb
Take-off – 1,225kg/2,700lb (maximum)
Performance: Speed – 153kph/95mph (maximum)
Service ceiling – 4,025m/13,200ft
Range – 330km/205 miles

LEFT: **The distinctive colour scheme of the Indian Air Force Sarang (peacock) helicopter aerobatic display team, which was formed in October 2003.**

HAL Dhruv Mk 1 to 4

The Dhruv is a multi-role helicopter that was developed and manufactured in India by Hindustan Aeronautics Limited, and has been supplied to the Indian Army, Air Force and Navy. In addition, the type has been exported to Bolivia, Ecuador, Israel, the Maldives, Mauritius, Nepal and Suriname. A civilian variant is also available, and has been ordered by numerous customers.

The Advanced Light Helicopter (ALH) programme was announced in November 1984, and was to be the first helicopter designed and built in India. With some technical support from the German company Messerschmitt-Bölkow-Blohm (MBB), the ALH programme progressed, and the first of four prototypes was flown on August 20, 1992. An army version with skid-type undercarriage was then flown, and this was followed by a navalized prototype fitted with a retractable tricycle under-carriage. However, development was delayed due to changing requirements of the main customer, the Indian military. Also, there was a problem with the supply of the engine due to US trade sanctions. Accordingly, the production version was fitted with two Turboméca TM333-2B engines mounted above the cabin.

The cockpit section of the fuselage is manufactured from carbon-fibre reinforced plastic (CFRP), which gives a considerable weight saving over a conventional metal airframe. The high position of the tail boom allows clamshell-type cabin doors to be fitted for easy loading. The four blades of the main rotor are also manufactured from CFRP. Navigation aids include a Global Positioning System (GPS), a Doppler navigation system, distance measuring equipment (DME) and an automatic direction finder.

Deliveries of the Dhruv began in 2002, and 75 had been delivered to the Indian armed forces by 2007. On August 16, 2007, a Dhruv fitted with more powerful HAL/Turboméca Shakti engines was flown for the first time. Following a successful flight test programme, all subsequent production machines were fitted with Shakti engines. By 2017 a total of 228 examples had been produced including 216 for the Indian military.

HAL also developed the Light Combat Helicopter (LCH) based on the Dhruv airframe for the Indian military. The new helicopter is fitted with stub wings with hardpoints for a variety of weapons, including missiles, rockets and gun pods. A turret-mounted machine-gun is fitted to the underside of the cockpit.

LEFT: **US Army troops from the 201st Airborne Aviation Squadron (AAS) leaving an Indian Army Dhruv during a joint military exercise. The Indian Army required the type to be capable of being flown at high altitude, crucial for operations on the Siachen Glacier in Kashmir.**

HAL Dhruv Mk4

First flight: August 20, 1992
Power: 2 x HAL/Turboméca Shakti turboshaft
Armament: Turret gun, rockets, missiles, gun pods
Size: Rotor diameter – 13.2m/43ft 3in
   Length – 15.87m/42ft 1in
   Height – 74.98m/16ft 4in
Weights: Empty – 2,500kg/5,511lb
   Take-off – 5,500kg/12,106lb (maximum)
Performance: Speed – 270kph/168mph (maximum)
   Service ceiling – 4,500m/14,765ft
   Range – 660km/410 miles

LEFT: A US Army TH-55A Osage parked on the flight line at the US Marine Corps Air Station El Toro, California.

Hughes TH-55 Osage

This helicopter is remarkable because it has been in production for more than half a century. Well over 60 years after its first flight it remains in service with military forces around the world as a low-cost training and light utility helicopter.

Hughes, in response to a market demand, developed the Type 269 as a low-cost, lightweight two-seat helicopter. The first prototype was flown on October 2, 1956. The US military were initially interested in the type as a light observation helicopter, and ordered five YHO-2-HU machines. The military rejected the machine for service, but the civilian version went on to be a market leader, being used for operations as diverse as law enforcement and agriculture. The Model 269 was a basic aircraft fitted with a three-blade main rotor, tail rotor and a landing skid-type undercarriage. Flight controls to the rotors were not hydraulically assisted.

By early 1964, some 314 had been built, and later that year, the US Army ordered the Model 269 as a primary training helicopter with the designation TH-55A and named Osage. Within five years, a total of 792 had been delivered, and many remained in service until 1988.

A larger and improved version, the Model 300, was first flown on March 5, 1969, and was further developed as the Model 300C. This was built under licence by Schweizer from 1983 until the company acquired all production rights in 1986. Although Schweizer (later taken over by Sikorsky) made over 250 minor improvements, the basic design of this remarkably long-lived design remained unchanged. Total production of all models, including civil and military versions, was around 3,000. The type has been procured by the Indian Navy and the Greek Army, and also the air forces of Columbia, El Salvador and Peru.

Schweizer further developed the Model 300 by redesigning the fuselage to accommodate a Rolls-Royce 250 turboshaft engine to create the Model 330, which was then further developed as the Model 333 that has been sold to many operators, including the Dominican Air Force.

Northrop Grumman also developed the MQ-8 and MQ-8B Fire Scout as a second generation Unmanned Aerial Vehicle (UAV) for use by the US armed forces from the Model 330 and Model 333 respectively. This remotely controlled helicopter is now in service with the US Navy to provide reconnaissance, situational awareness and precision targeting support. In April 2010, more than 50 years after the first flight of the Model 269, an MQ-8B Fire Scout that was being operated from USS McInerney (FFG-8) while on patrol in the Eastern Pacific was deployed to monitor two vessels suspected of being used for drug smuggling. This resulted in a seizure of cocaine and the arrest of the crews.

LEFT: The Hughes 300 was followed into production in 1969 by the improved Lycoming-engined Hughes 300C (sometimes referred to as the 269C).

Hughes TH-55 Osage

First flight: October 2, 1956
Power: 1 x Lycoming HIO-360-B1A piston engine
Armament: None
Size: Rotor diameter – 8.4m/27ft 6in
Length – 9.2m/30ft
Height – 2.9m/9ft 8in
Weights: Empty – 406kg/896lb
Take-off – 703kg/1,550lb (maximum)
Performance: Speed – 144kph/90mph (maximum)
Range – 375km/233 miles

Hughes OH-6A Cayuse

The basic Hughes Model 369 has become one of the most successful light turbine helicopter designs to have ever been built. In 1960, the US Army announced a contest for the design of a new multi-function Light Observation Helicopter (LOH) for transport, escort, attack, CASEVAC and observation missions. Twelve companies took part in the competition, including Bell and Hiller, but the Hughes design was successful not only by meeting the technical specification, but by also being very competitively priced.

In May 1961, Hughes was contracted to build five prototypes, and the first was flown on February 27, 1962. Originally designated as the YHO-6A by the US Army, under the Department of Defense Joint Designation System (JDS) of 1962, the type became the YOH-6A. In service, the OH-6A was named Cayuse, after the Native American Indian tribe from Oregon. Many nicknames were applied to the odd-looking machine, including the "Flying Egg" and "Loach" – the latter a play on the LOH acronym.

In 1967, during the Vietnam War, the type was rushed into front-line service by the US Army to replace the Hiller OH-23 Raven and Bell OH-13 Sioux helicopters. The OH-6A became and remained the prime scouting helicopter for the duration of the conflict. The type played an extensive role during this period, not only acting as an observation aircraft but also as a target-seeker for Bell AH-1 Cobra gunships escorting troop-carrying Bell UH-1 Iroquois. During the conflict, over one in five of all US military helicopters lost due to ground fire, in operational accidents or destroyed by enemy ground action, was a Cayuse. In March 1973, at the end of the Vietnam War, fewer than 430 of the original 1,420 OH-6A Cayuse helicopters delivered to the US military were still in active service. Veteran pilots and ground crew

RIGHT: From 1971, the OH-6A Cayuse was operated by the Royal Danish Army (RDA), until the operation of all military aircraft became the responsibility of the Royal Danish Air Force (RDAF). Many of the 15 machines originally procured remained in service until 2005.

from the war commended the aircraft for being the most manoeuvrable to fly and the easiest to maintain.

By the mid-1970s, the type was no longer being used for front-line military service, and the remaining aircraft were transferred to the Army National Guard (ANG). During this time, the type began to be used by other organizations, including NASA at the Ames Research Centre and Langley Research Center in Virginia.

In 1966, the OH-6 Cayuse was used to set 22 world records for helicopters, including speed and distance over a closed circuit of 227.69kph/141.48mph over 2,000km/1,243 miles. It also set an all-class helicopter distance record by flying non-stop from Culver City, California, to Ormond Beach, Florida – a distance of 3,561km/2,213 miles in 15 hours, 8 minutes.

This high-profile record-setting, together with an impressive combat reputation, generated considerable market interest. In the early 1980s, Hughes Helicopters was taken over by McDonnell Douglas, and the design was developed as the civil MD 500 light utility helicopter series. This included a range of military helicopters, including the MD 500 Defender. The MH-6B Little Bird, also known as "The Killer Egg", and the heavily armed AH-6C attack variant are both in service with the 160th Special Operations Aviation Regiment (Airborne) (SOAR[A]) of the US Army.

BELOW: **The NH-500E was built under licence in Italy by Breda Nardi. The machine is armed with 70mm Hydra 70 rockets carried in pods.**

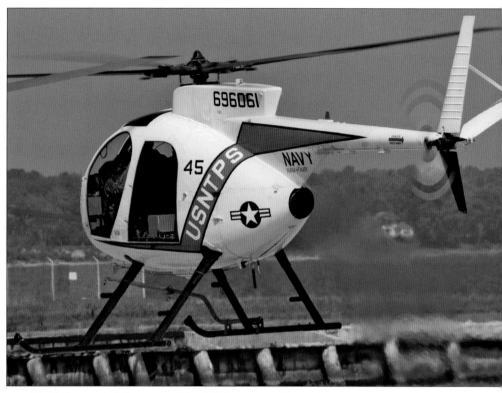

ABOVE: **The US Navy acquired six examples of the TH-6B Cayuse for the US Naval Test Pilot School (USNTPS) at NAS Patuxent River, Maryland. The aircraft were equipped with instrumentation and avionics to train pilots in all aspects of helicopter handling and performance.** BELOW: **Two US Army AH-6J Little Bird versions taking off for a mission at a forward deployed location in southern Iraq during Operation Iraqi Freedom, 2003.**

Hughes OH-6A Cayuse

First flight: February 27, 1962
Power: 1 x Allison T63-A-5A turboshaft
Armament: 7.62mm XM74 machine-gun or 40mm XM75 grenade launcher
Size: Rotor diameter – 8.03m/26ft 4in
Length – 9.24m/30ft 4in
Height – 2.48m/8ft 2in
Weights: Empty – 557kg/1,229lb
Take-off – 1,090kg/2,400lb (maximum)
Performance: Speed – 241kph/150mph (maximum)
Service ceiling – 4,875m/15,994ft
Range – 611km/380 miles

LEFT: **A US Army AH-64 Apache ready to be flown from the flight deck of amphibious assault ship USS *Nassau* (LHA-4) during a joint US Army/ US Navy exercise in the Atlantic.**

Hughes AH-64A Apache

The Hughes YAH-64 was designed to a US Army requirement for an Advanced Attack Helicopter (AAH), and was first flown on September 30, 1975. In 1982, the US Army approved the helicopter, by now designated AH-64A Apache, for production. Deliveries to the

BELOW: **An AH-64 Apache armed with 70mm Hydra 70 rockets in pods on the outboard pylons and AGM-114 Hellfire anti-tank missiles on the inner pylons.**

US Army began in 1986, and to reduce costs and simplify logistics for the US military, the Apache is powered by the General Electric T700 turboshaft, the same engine that is used to power the Sikorsky UH-60 Black Hawk and the Sikorsky SH-60 Seahawk. The Apache is a large, heavily armed helicopter, but is highly manoeuvrable and a major ground-support asset. The type has been used in virtually every US military action

since entry into service, and has also been exported to Egypt, Greece, Israel (the second largest operator after the US), Japan, the Netherlands, Saudi Arabia and the United Arab Emirates. Between 1986 and 1997, a total of 937 were produced.

Although complex, the Apache is designed for ease of maintenance in the field. The airframe and rotor system is designed to withstand hits from 23mm cannon ammunition, and the cockpit is constructed to withstand a crash impact of up to 13m/42ft per second.

The AH-64 Apache is configured to be operated in day or night conditions, and is fitted with a weapons system capable of identifying and attack the enemy position. The stub wings have hardpoints to carry an array of weapons, including the AGM-114 Hellfire missile designed to destroy a tank at a range of up to 20km/32 miles, pod-mounted 70mm Hydra 70 or 70mm AIM-92 ATAS folding-fin high-explosive rockets. A 30mm M230 Chain Gun cannon is mounted in a hydraulically operated turret under the forward fuselage. The gun, which has a firing rate of 625 rounds per minute, is aimed using helmet-mounted sighting equipment. The Apache is equipped with target-designating sensors to enable other helicopters or tanks to lock on and attack. Other electronic equipment fitted includes navigational

LEFT: **A pre-production Hughes YAH-64 Apache. The four-blade main rotor is manufactured to withstand a hit from 23mm ammunition. The co-pilot/gunner is seated in the front, with the command pilot in a raised position behind. The cockpit area, including glazing, is heavily armoured. All fuel tanks on the aircraft are self-sealing.**

aids, communications and various sensors. As defence from an enemy heat-seeking missile, the engine exhaust gases are cooled by being passed through a system of nozzles, thus reducing the infra-red signature.

The AH-64 Apache is designed to be operated from a forward base close to the battlefront and can be re-armed and refuelled in a short time. The type has a combat radius of just 250km/155 miles.

The US Army first deployed the AH-64A Apache in combat during Operation Just Cause, the invasion of Panama, on December 19, 1989. The type amassed 240 combat hours, mainly on night operations, during this action.

In 1991, at the opening of Operation Desert Storm in the first Gulf War, the first shots fired by Allied forces were from eight AH-64A Apaches deployed on missions to destroy parts of the Iraqi radar-defence network, to allow attacking aircraft undetected access to enemy targets. During the ground war phase, a total of 277 of the type were flown in battle and destroyed many Iraqi vehicles, including over 500 tanks. The Israeli Air Force ordered 42 aircraft, and the first was delivered in 1990.

ABOVE: **The AH-64 Apache is fitted a 30mm M230 Chain Gun cannon in a hydraulically operated mounting. The weapon was designed and developed by Hughes, but is now manufactured by Alliant Techsystems.**

AH-64A Apache

First flight: September 30, 1975
Power: 2 x General Electric T700-GE-700 turboshaft
Armament: 30mm M230 Chain Gun, 70mm Hydra 70 or 70mm AIM-92 Stinger, AGM-114 Hellfire, AIM-9 Sidewinder
Size: Rotor diameter – 14.63m/48ft
Length – 14.97m/49ft 2in
Height – 4.66m/15ft 4in
Weights: Empty – 5,165kg/11,363lb
Take-off – 9,525kg/20,995lb (maximum)
Performance: Speed – 293kph/182mph (maximum)
Ceiling – 6,400m/21,000ft
Range – 250km/155 miles

Kaman H-43B Huskie

Charles Kaman's first helicopter, the K-125A first flown in 1947, was fitted with a patented servo-flap-controlled intermeshing rotor system. The two rotors, mounted on separate pylons tilted outwards, were designed to intermesh while rotating in opposite directions. This innovative design meant that the rotors would generate increased lift while eliminating the requirement for an anti-torque tail rotor. The result was a smaller, mechanically simplified and very stable design.

The K-125A design was developed into the K-190, which was flown a year later. The K-225 was the next development, and came to the attention of the US Navy, who took delivery of two machines in 1950. After a thorough evaluation, the USN placed an order for 29 training helicopters designated HTK-1. In 1962, this was changed to T-43E under the Department of Defense Joint Designation System.

RIGHT: **A HOK-1 in service with the US Marine Corps. For operations over South Vietnam, many were painted in jungle-type camouflage.**

While the T-43E was in production, Kaman developed the larger K-600, which was ordered for the US Marine Corps and US Navy as the HOK-1 and HUK-1 (for ship-support) respectively. In 1962, both were redesignated as UH-43C and OH-43D. The distinctively shaped helicopter had a boom-mounted tailplane fitted with three vertical fins for directional control.

ABOVE: **Although the Kaman H-43 Huskie was fitted with an unusual twin rotor system, the type had conventional collective and cyclic flight controls.**

The US Air Force also took delivery of the H-43A (later HH-43A) and named the type Huskie. Deliveries to the USAF began in November 1958. The H-43A was fitted with four vertical tail fins for improved directional control.

In 1951, Kaman had trialed the installation of a small Boeing YT-50 gas turbine engine in one of the development K-225 aircraft, thereby creating the first jet-powered helicopter. With this experience and research, Kaman began to experiment with the installation of a turboshaft engine in a HOK-1 airframe, and flight testing demonstrated significantly improved performance. As a result, the H-43B (later the HH-43B) was developed, and first flew on December 13, 1958.

Powered by an Avco Lycoming T53-L-1B turboshaft mounted on top of the airframe, the B model was larger and had accommodation for up to eight passengers. The significant improvements in performance made this version ideal for the search and rescue role.

A total of 193 were manufactured for the USAF, and this made the H-43B the most numerous variant of all. The USAF used the type primarily for the airfield crash and fire rescue role, and each machine carried a large tank containing 309 litres/63 gallons of chemical foam, a rescue crew wearing firefighting suits, and other special equipment.

The aircraft was fitted with a winch with a lifting capacity of 272kg/600lb. On alert, the crew of an H-43B could be airborne within 60 seconds and were often first in attendance at the scene of a crash. Downwash from the rotors could be used to great effect to deflect flames away from the crashed aircraft.

The H-43 was also exported to a number of foreign air arms under the US Military Assistance Program (MAP), including Burma, Pakistan, Colombia, Morocco and Thailand.

The H-43F was the final production variant. The aircraft was fitted with a more powerful engine and a larger fuselage to accommodate up to 11 passengers, and a total of 40 were supplied to the USAF. A further 17 of the type were built for Iran, and all were specially configured to operate in hot and high conditions.

The H-43F was used in South-east Asia on missions to rescue downed aircrew. The type was especially suited to jungle operations due to the crew being able to fly the aircraft into small clearings. It was also used to resupply US Navy gunboats (part of the so-called

ABOVE: **A Kaman HH-43B equipped with skids mounted on the undercarriage, allowing the machine to land on soft ground or snow.**

"Brown Water Navy") on patrol in the Mekong Delta. On these operations, the aircraft was particularly vulnerable to ground fire from Viet Cong forces, so a machine-gun could be mounted in the door opening for defence.

The H-43 Huskie was flown on more rescue missions during the Vietnam War than any other type of helicopter. In the early 1970s, the H-43 was gradually replaced in US military service by newer types of helicopter.

Kaman H-43B Huskie

First flight: September 27, 1956
Power: 1 x Lycoming 825 T53-L-1B turboshaft
Armament: None
Size: Rotor diameter – 14.43m/47ft
Length – 26.9m/86ft 3in
Height – 7.8m/25ft 7in
Weights: Empty – 2,027kg/4,469lb
Take-off – 3,992kg/8,800lb (maximum)
Performance: Speed – 193kph/120mph (maximum)
Service ceiling – 7,625m/25,000ft
Range – 378km/235 miles

Kaman SH-2 Seasprite

After the considerable success of the earlier H-43 Huskie helicopter, it was a surprise that intermeshing rotor configuration was not used on the company's response to a 1956 US Navy requirement for a long-range search and rescue helicopter.

This helicopter, first flown on July 2, 1959, originally entered USN service as the Kaman HU2K-1. The single-engine helicopter was primarily deployed on USN aircraft carriers in the search and rescue role. In 1962, the type was redesignated UH-2A by the Department of Defense (DoD). By the end of 1965, a total of 190 utility and rescue UH-2A/B versions had been delivered. During the late 1960s, an upgrade programme was initiated, the major part of which was converting the aircraft to a twin-engine

LEFT: **A US Navy UH-2C Seasprite of helicopter Combat Support Squadron HC-1 Det. 19 aboard the aircraft carrier USS Hancock (CVA-19) on a deployment to Vietnam between July 1968 and March 1969.**

configuration. The engines were linked to an uprated gearbox and transmission driving a four-blade rotor, which allowed a substantial increase load-carrying capacity.

The UH-2 Seasprite was ultimately developed as a shipborne combat helicopter with anti-submarine and anti-surface attack capability. In the late 1960s, Light Airborne Multi-Purpose System (LAMPS) was fitted to improve the type's operational capabilities. In operation, a LAMPS-equipped Seasprite was deployed to extend the defensive area around a warship and attack any submarine threat with torpedoes. In the defence role, LAMPS provided early warning of anti-shipping missile attack. LAMPS-equipped Seasprites were designated SH-2D and carried search radar, an Electronic Surveillance Measures (ESM) receiver, an active sonar repeater and a UHF acoustic data-relay transmitter. The type was

ABOVE: **A US Navy Kaman SH-2F Seasprite from Helicopter Light Anti-Submarine Squadron 30 (HSL-30) preparing to land on the destroyer USS Nicholson (DD-982).**

also used for MEDEVAC, SAR, troop transport and supply missions.

The SH-2F was fitted with more powerful engines, an improved rotor, upgraded avionics and was equipped to tow a Magnetic Anomaly Detector (MAD). The tail wheel was moved forward to allow for operations from the decks of smaller ships. After a 16-year gap, the SH-2F was ordered back into production, an extremely rare occurrence in aviation history. From 1982, Kaman manufactured 54 new machines for the US Navy.

In 1987–88, the US Navy deployed the type on Operation Earnest Will (to protect Kuwaiti-owned oil tankers from attack by Iranian forces), the largest naval convoy operation since World War II. The type was used again in 1988 on Operation Praying Mantis (the attack by US naval forces in retaliation for the Iranian mining of a US warship). In 1991, the type was used operationally for the last time on

Operation Desert Storm (the invasion of Iraq). In October 1993, the SH-2F was retired from active USN service. At the time of retirement, the type was reported to require 30 maintenance hours for each hour flown, the highest rate for any aircraft in the US Navy inventory at that time.

Many machines were remanufactured as the SH-2G Super Seasprite, equipped with a much improved electronic warfare capability, and also

ABOVE: **An SH-2G Super Seasprite equipped with the Light Airborne Multi-Purpose System (LAMPS) operated by US Navy Reserve Helicopter Anti-Submarine Squadron (Light) 84 (HSL-84).**

more powerful engines that gave the type the highest power-to-weight ratio of any naval helicopter. The SH-2G entered the US Navy Reserve (USNR) inventory in February 1993, and was retired in May 2001. The SH-2G was also operated by military forces in Egypt, Poland and New Zealand.

ABOVE: **Crew members aboard the battleship USS *Iowa* (BB-61) waiting for a Kaman SH-2F Seasprite to be secured before transporting an injured sailor during NATO exercise North Wedding 86.**

Kaman Seasprite

First flight: July 2, 1959
Power: 2 x General Electric T700-GE-401 turboshaft
Armament: Torpedoes, depth charges, anti-ship or anti–tank missiles, air-to-ground missiles, unguided rockets
Size: Rotor diameter – 13.5m/44ft
Length – 16m/52ft 6in
Height – 4.62m/15ft
Weights: Empty – 3,447kg/7,600lb
Take-off – 6,124kg/13,500lb (maximum)
Performance: Speed – 256kph/159mph (maximum)
Service ceiling – 6,218m/20,400ft
Range – 1,000km/620 miles

Kamov Ka-25

The Ka-25 (NATO codename Hormone) was developed to meet the specification for a Soviet Navy requirement of 1958 for an anti-submarine warfare helicopter that could be operated from the range of vessels in service with the Soviet Navy. In response, Kamov developed the Ka-20 (NATO identifier Harp) from the earlier Ka-15 design. In July 1961, the Ka-20 was first seen in public when it was flown at the Tushino Aviation Day carrying two dummy air-to-surface missiles. The Ka-20 immediately attracted the interest of Western military observers attending the display. Having proven the basic configuration, the type became the prototype for the production Ka-25.

ABOVE: **Two Kamov Ka-25PLs about to land on a Moskva-class cruiser of the Soviet Navy.**

The use of counter-rotating coaxial main rotor alleviates the requirement for an anti-torque tail rotor to be fitted. This allows the fuselage to have a very short tail boom, which saves much-needed deck storage space. The two three-bladed rotors also fold, to save space. The Ka-25 was powered by two Glushenkov GTD-3F turboshaft engines installed side by side above the cabin. In an emergency, the machine could be safely flown on one engine. The three vertical tail fins were fitted to provide directional stability.

A powerful search radar scanner, mounted in a housing under the nose, can detect a surface target as small as the periscope on a submarine. This radar is augmented by Magnetic Anomaly Detector (MAD) sensors,

LEFT: **The Kamov Ka-25T was equipped with a search radar and missiles for the anti-shipping attack role.**

electro-optical sensors and dipping sonar which is lowered into the sea while the helicopter is flown at the hover. Although usually flown unarmed, production aircraft were fitted with an internal weapons bay to carry torpedoes or depth charges (including nuclear type) for anti-submarine attack.

Up to 25 variants of the type are thought to have been built, and among the numerous variations were the Ka-25B/Ka-25PL for anti-submarine warfare and the Ka-25T used for over-the-horizon guidance and targeting of ship-launched missiles. The Ka-25PS was developed as a search and rescue helicopter, and is equipped with a 300kg/660lb capacity winch, sensors to detect a pilot's distress beacon and a powerful searchlight for night operations.

Between 1966 and 1975, some 460 were produced to replace the Mil Mi-4 (NATO identifier Hound) as the primary ASW helicopter in Soviet Navy service. Ka-25s fitted with long-range variable depth sonar to detect enemy submarines were first deployed on board Moskva-class cruisers. The Soviet Navy

ABOVE: **A Kamov Ka-25PL fitted with undercarriage units for flight deck operations on ships of the Soviet Navy. Note the radar scanner housing under the nose.**

received four Kiev-class aircraft carriers which operated Ka-25s in the ASW role.

As well as the Soviet Navy and Russian Federation, the Ka-25 was used by Bulgaria, India, Syria, Ukraine, Vietnam and the former Yugoslavia.

Kamov Ka-25

First flight: 1961
Power: 2 x Glushenkov GTD-3F turboshaft
Armament: Torpedoes, depth charges
Size: Rotor diameter – 15.75m/51ft 8in
　　　Length – 9.75m/32ft
　　　Height – 5.4m/17ft 8in
Weights: Empty – 4,765kg/10,488lb
　　　Take-off – 7,200kg/15,847lb (maximum)
Performance: Speed – 220kph/136mph (maximum)
　　　Ceiling – 3,500m/11,483ft
　　　Range – 400km/248 miles

Kamov Ka-27/Ka-29/Ka-31/Ka-32

Kamov began work on a successor to the Ka-25 in 1967, following requests from the Soviet Navy for a helicopter capable of operating night or day and in all weathers. Although broadly based on the Ka-25, the Ka-27 (NATO identifier Helix) was an all-new helicopter with dimensions similar to the Ka-25, and retaining the distinctive Kamov counter-rotating coaxial main rotor system.

The Ka-27 was flown for the first time in 1973, and remains in Russian Navy service as the standard Anti-Submarine Warfare (ASW) helicopter.

The Ka-27 is fitted with two vertical tail fins mounted on the tailplane at the end of the short tail boom. The type is powered by two Isotov TV3-117V turboshaft engines (well proven in Mil helicopters), which produce twice the power of those used in the Ka-25.

ABOVE: **A Kamov Ka-27 (NATO identifier Helix) from the Russian destroyer _Admiral Vinogradov_ flying near the guided-missile cruiser USS _Vella Gulf_ (CG-72) while on operations in the Gulf of Aden.**

A new type of advanced high-efficiency composite rotor blades and more engine power allows the Ka-27 to lift a payload that is 50 per cent heavier than the earlier design.

The production Ka-27PL ASW version which entered service in 1982 is fitted with a search radar scanner, dipping sonar and sonobouys. An enlarged weapons bay for up to four torpedoes is built into the underside of the fuselage. In action the aircraft is operated in pairs, with one tracking the enemy while the following helicopter launches the attack. Operating in this way, and in all weather conditions, the equipment can be used to detect, track and destroy a target at a submerged

LEFT: **The coaxial rotor assembly and short tail boom are key recognition features of this series of helicopters.**

Although the Ka-27 was an all-new design, it was built to dimensions that were similar to the earlier Ka-25.

troops and cargo. Although specialist transport or combat equipment is usually fitted on the production line, the type is versatile enough to be modified in the field if required. The fuselage can accommodate 16 fully equipped troops or four stretcher cases plus seven seated casualties. Cargo capacity is an impressive 2,032kg/4,480lb. For offensive operations, the armour-protected helicopter can be fitted with four hardpoints to carry rockets, bombs or machine-gun pods. Other loads can be carried in the torpedo bay. The helicopter is also fitted with a 7.62mm machine-gun. In 2001, the Ka-29 was used extensively by Russian forces on operations against Chechen rebels.

The Russian Navy Ka-27M version (upgraded Ka-27PLs) is equipped with radar and tactical command systems that include acoustic sensors, magnetometric sensors, signals intelligence, and a radar mounted under the fuselage providing all-around vision for the search and detection of surface, air, and ground targets.

A 16-passenger civil version, the Ka-32, was built, and some in Aeroflot markings have been seen operating from ships of the Russian Navy. This version is also equipped with a hook under the fuselage for lifting loads. More than 40 of the type are in service in North Korea. In July 2004, that country's air force took delivery of their first Ka-32 to be used for SAR operations.

depth of 500m/1,641ft and running at speeds of up to 75kph/47mph.

The production version of the Ka-27PL also has a lengthened cockpit with additional windows. The lower section of the fuselage is watertight to allow an emergency landing on water. The Ka-27PL has a crew of three, a pilot, a tactical coordinator and an ASW systems operator.

A search and rescue (SAR) version of the Ka-27PS was developed, and on this machine the position for the ASW weapons operator is used by the winchman when operating the

300kg/660lb capacity rescue winch.

Military operators of the Ka-27 include South Korea, Ukraine and Vietnam. A simpler version, the Ka-28 with revised avionics equipment, was exported to China and India. China purchased both the Ka-27 and Ka-28 to be operated from four Russian-built Sovremenny-class destroyers.

A multi-mission naval combat version, the Ka-29, has a wider front fuselage. It was also produced for the Russian military and has been in service since 1985. The type can be used as part of an amphibious assault force to transport

ABOVE: **A Kamov Ka-28 flying over the city of Niz, Serbia, equipped for firefighting – just one of the many roles that can be carried out by this versatile type of helicopter.**

Kamov Ka-27PL

First flight: 1973
Power: 2 x Klimov TV3-117V turboshaft
Armament: Torpedoes, depth charges
Size: Rotor diameter – 15.90m/52ft 2in
Length – 12.25m/40ft 2in
Height – 5.4m/17ft 8in
Weights: Empty – 6,100kg/13,338lb
Take-off – 12,600kg/27,778lb (maximum)
Performance: Speed – 250kph/155mph (maximum)
Ceiling – 5,004m/16,405ft
Range – 800km/496 miles

Kamov Ka-50/Ka-52

The Ka-50 (NATO identifier Hokum), was developed in the 1980s from the Kamov V-80Sh-1 prototype and was first seen in public at the Zhukovsky Air Show, near Moscow, in August 1992. The following month, the second production machine was displayed in the UK at the Farnborough Air Show. In November 1993, four production machines were delivered for trials with the Russian Army. In the late 1980s, large orders for the Ka-50 had appeared

to be imminent, but the collapse of the Soviet Union in 1991 threw defence procurement into chaos. Only 12 of the type were delivered to the Russian Army in August 1995, not the expected hundreds. Production of the KA-50 was restarted in 2006, but only to complete five machines that were not delivered during the Soviet era.

Soviet military experience in Afghanistan showed that although the Mil Mi-24 was an excellent attack

ABOVE: **The two-seat Kamov Ka-52 Alligator (NATO identifier Hokum-B) was designed to be the lead aircraft guiding a battle formation of Kamov Ka-50 Black Shark helicopters to the target.**

helicopter, it was found to be too large and lacked manoeuvrability. Also during hazardous low-level operations, the type was found to be vulnerable to ground fire. A specification was issued by the military detailing a requirement for a compact, well-armed and manoeuvrable helicopter with an airframe that could absorb a lot of battle damage. The Ka-50, named Black Shark by the manufacturer, has an aircraft-type fuselage with a vertical tailfin, and is extremely manoeuvrable. The type is cleared to be aerobatic.

The lack of a tail rotor also greatly improves combat survivability. During the war in Afghanistan, many helicopter crews found that any damage to the tail boom or tail rotor could be catastrophic. The main gearbox is also safely mounted between the engines and is well protected.

LEFT: **The Kamov Ka-50 Black Shark (NATO identifier Hokum) can carry an impressive array of weapons, including 30mm cannon pods, unguided ground-attack rockets and anti-tank missiles.**

LEFT: **The Kamov Ka-50 Black Shark was the first production helicopter fitted with an ejection seat. Explosive charges detach the rotor blades before the rocket-powered seat is fired.**

The cockpit is protected by 55mm/ 2.1in bullet-proof glass and armour plating strong enough to sustain hits from 20mm ammunition.

The Ka-50 was the first production helicopter to be fitted with an ejection seat. The rotor blades are blown off by explosive charges before the NPP Zvezda K-37-800 rocket-powered seat is fired.

The helicopter is relatively light and consequently has an excellent power-to-weight ratio, allowing an impressive

amount of weaponry to be carried on the two stub wings. Each wing has two hardpoints and a mounting on on each wingtip to carry rockets, missiles or gun pods. A heat suppressor mounted over each engine exhaust duct is designed to reduce the aircraft's infra-red signature, reducing the possibility of a strike by a heat-seeking missile. The Ka-50 can be flown on one engine in the event of battle damage.

In January 2001, the Ka-50 was first used in combat in an attack

on Chechen positions, operated within a force of Ka-29 and Mi-24 attack helicopters.

The Ka-52 (NATO identifier Hokum-B), a two-seat development, was first flown in June 1997, and retains some 85 per cent of the original Ka-50 airframe. The type is intended to be deployed on the battlefront as the lead aircraft to a force of Ka-50s. The type is known as the Alligator, and is thought to be in limited service with the Russian special forces.

The Ka-52 saw extensive service during the 2022 Russian invasion of Ukraine with a number being shot down by Ukraine forces.

ABOVE: **The Kamov Ka-50 Black Shark and the Ka-52 Alligator Alligator were only operated by the Egyptian Air Force and the Russian Air Force, which at its peak had a combined fleet of over 60 machines.**

Kamov Ka-50

First flight: July 27, 1982
Power: 2 x Klimov TV3-117VMA turboshaft
Armament: 30mm cannon AA-8 Aphid, AA-11 AAM, Archer, AT-9 Ataka or AT-16 Vikhr anti-tank, AS-10 Karen anti-radiation, AS-12 Kegler air-to-surface
Size: Rotor diameter – 14.5m/47ft 7in
Length – 16m/52ft 6in
Height – 4.93m/16ft 2in
Weights: Empty – 9,800kg/21,605lb
Take-off – 10,800kg/23,810lb (maximum)
Performance: Speed – 310kph/193mph (maximum)
Ceiling – 5,500m/18,030ft
Range – 460km/286 miles

MBB/Eurocopter Bo105

The Bo105 is light, two-engine, multi-purpose utility helicopter originally designed and developed by Bölkow in Germany. The type was manufactured by Messerschmitt-Bölkow-Blohm (MBB) until 1991, when the company became a part of Eurocopter.

Production of the Bo105 continued until 2001, by which time over 1,500 military and civil versions had been produced. The type is fitted with an advanced rigid-rotor system (designed in association with Aérospatiale) and two turboshaft engines, allowing the Bo105 to be highly manoeuvrable and fully aerobatic. The cockpit is designed to allow the crew excellent visibility through large unobstructed windows. The Bo105 is equipped for all-weather operation.

Design of the type began in 1962 and the prototype, powered by two Allison turboshaft engines, was first flown on February 16, 1967, with MBB test pilot Wilfried von Engelhardt at the controls. Civil certification was granted in 1970, and the machine entered production for German civil and law enforcement services, as well as for overseas customers.

RIGHT: **A Bo105E-4 in service with the Albanian Air Force, one of the many nations who ordered the type.**

The Bo105C version was developed during 1972, and the Ministry of Defence in West Germany ultimately chose the type for the light observation military helicopter programme and ordered 100 machines in 1977.

The German Army also procured 212 of the Bo105 PAH-1, an anti-tank version armed with six HOT missiles, a second-generation, long-range anti-tank missile system.

ABOVE: **A Bo105 PAH-1 equipped with HOT missiles of the German Army Aviators School from Heeresflugplatz Celle (Celle Air Base).**

An infra-red sight for the missile system, mounted on top of the cockpit directly above the pilot, allows the crew to observe potential targets at night and in all weathers, while the helicopter is held at the hover behind covering terrain.

ABOVE: **A salvo of 2.75in rockets being fired from a Bo105 of the Mexican Navy at the ex-USS *Connolly* (DE-306) target ship during the multi-national naval exercise Unitas Gold.**
RIGHT: **A Bo105 from Multi-Purpose Helicopter Squadron 40 (MH-40) being held at the hover prior to landing on USS *Essex* (LHD-2).**

The German Army Aviation Corps (Heeresfliegertruppe) was the largest operator of the type, with a total of over 300 in service. The type was also used in the battlefield observation and transport role. Bulky cargo was carried by a hook mounted under the fuselage. The load could be jettisoned instantly by operating an emergency release in the cockpit.

Other operators have included the Albanian Air Force, Chilean Air Force and Navy, Colombian Navy, Indonesian Air Force and Navy, Iraqi Air Force, Mexican Navy, Royal Netherlands Air Force, Philippine Air Force and Navy, Republic of Korea Army, Spanish Army, Swedish Air Force and Army and the Uruguayan Navy. Many overseas customers have deployed the Bo105 in the maritime patrol role. For the CASEVAC/ MEDEVAC role, the helicopter can be fitted to carry two stretchers mounted behind the crew. Clamshell doors at the rear of the fuselage give access to the cargo compartment.

The civil version of the Bo105 has been used for many duties, including emergency rescue, law enforcement, ambulance, SAR (fitted with infra-red sensors and a powerful searchlight) and mountain rescue.

MBB Bo105

First flight: February 16, 1967
Power: 2 x Allison 250-C20B turboshaft
Armament: HOT anti-tank missiles
Size: Rotor diameter – 9.84m/32ft 4in
Length – 11.86m/38ft 11in
Height – 3m/9ft 10in
Weights: Empty – 1,280kg/2,820lb
Take-off – 2,400kg/5,290lb (maximum)
Performance: Speed – 242kph/150mph (maximum)
Service ceiling – 5,185m/17,000ft
Range – 585km/363 miles

LEFT: **Development of the Mil Mi-1 (NATO identifier Hare) commenced at the end of World War II. In many ways it was an advanced machine, being built with an all-metal monocoque-type fuselage. The type was enormously important for the future of Soviet helicopter development.**

Mil Mi-1

Designed by Mikhail Mil, the Mi-1 was the first Soviet helicopter to go into series production, and the first helicopter to enter service with the Soviet military. During World War II, Mil led the Soviet experimental helicopter section, having had pre-war experience working with Nikolai Ilyich Kamov, a pioneer in Soviet helicopter development. The prototype, designated GM-1 (Gelikopter Mil), was built and flown in 1948 with test pilot M. K. Baikalov at the controls. The machine was fitted with a single main rotor, a fully enclosed cockpit (for a pilot and up to three passengers) and an all-metal monocoque-type fuselage. Baikalov was later killed in one of the prototypes when it crashed due to the failure of a weld in the tail-rotor bearing assembly. The aircraft was powered by a single Ivchenko AI-26V radial petrol engine.

The rotor blades were constructed from steel and plywood with fabric covering. An anti-torque rotor with wooden blades was fitted at the rear of the tail boom. A long skid was fitted under the end of the tail boom to protect the tail rotor from damage during take-off and landing. The underside of the nose was glazed to give the pilot the best possible view on landing. Production versions were equipped with a radio altimeter, the aerial for which was mounted under the tail boom. Fuel in all versions was carried in a 240-litre/53-gallon aluminium tank. To allow an increase in range, a 160-litre/35-gallon auxiliary fuel tank could be carried externally on the starboard side of the fuselage.

The type was already in Soviet military service when eight were displayed in public for the first time at the 1951 Tushino Aviation Day. Production of the Mi-1 (NATO identifier Hare) took place over a 16-year period

ABOVE: **This Mil Mi-1M, once operated by the Hungarian Air Force, is fitted with enclosed stretcher-carrying panniers. The machine is displayed at the Museum of Hungarian Aviation, Szolnok.**

ABOVE AND RIGHT: **The Mil Mi-1 was widely used in many Warsaw Pact countries, including Poland. A total of some 1,500 were manufactured in Poland as the SM-1.**

in the Soviet Union, where some 1,000 were built. Production of the type, designated SM-1, by WSK PZL at Swidnik in Poland began in 1955, and over 1,500 airframes were completed. Aviation commentators at the time observed the similarities between the Mi-1 and the US-built Sikorsky S-51, as well as the British-built Bristol Type 171 Sycamore. The type was widely exported to be used by the military air arms of other Warsaw Pact countries and other Soviet-friendly nations. The Mil Mi-1 was used in a variety of roles, including reconnaissance, transport, SAR, MEDEVAC (fitted with external temperature-controlled stretcher panniers mounted on the sides of the fuselage), training and observation. Float-equipped versions were also produced.

This was a period of development and innovation in helicopter technology so as production of the type continued, it was improved and refined, leading to a major improvement in reliability. In keeping with most Soviet equipment, the helicopter was designed to operate in cold, harsh conditions, being fitted with de-icing systems for both the rotor and cockpit windscreen.

Overseas military operators included the Afghan Air Force, Albanian Air Force, Algerian Air Force, People's Republic of China, Cuban Air Force, Czechoslovak Air Force, East German Air Force, Egyptian Air Force, Finnish Air Force, Hungarian Air Force, Iraqi Air Force, Mongolian People's Air Force, North Korean Air Force, Romanian Air Force and Syrian Air Force.

ABOVE: **The Mi-1 had a fixed nosewheel landing gear equipped with brakes. The machine is fitted with an auxiliary fuel tank on the side of the fuselage to provide an increase in range.**

Mil Mi-1

First flight: September 20, 1948
Power: 1 x Ivchenko AI-26V piston engine
Armament: None
Size: Rotor diameter – 14.35m/47ft 1in
Length – 12.09m/39ft 8in
Height – 3.30m/10ft 10in
Weights: Empty – 1,700kg/3,740lb
Take-off – 2,330kg/5,126lb (maximum)
Performance: Speed – 205kph/127mph (maximum)
Ceiling – 3,500m/11,480ft
Range – 590km/367 miles

LEFT: **The Mil Mi-2 (NATO identifier Hoplite) was based on the airframe of the earlier Mi-1. T he machine was fitted with two turboshaft engines driving a single gearbox installation positioned above the cabin.**

Mil Mi-2

Just a few years after the first true helicopter designs were in service, it was clear that the turboshaft engine gave designers the ability to build bigger, more efficient helicopters. The Mi-2 (NATO identifier Hoplite) was based on the Mi-1, but was fitted with an all-new two-turboshaft engine and gearbox installation (designed by Isotov) positioned on top of the helicopter, driving a three-blade main rotor and a two-blade tail rotor. This arrangement allowed much more cabin space. The new powerplant installation also made the helicopter less affected by changes to the Centre of Gravity (CoG)

from cabin cargo or passengers. The aircraft was fitted with a nose-wheel-type tricycle undercarriage.

With more power and lighter engines, the Mi-2 offered a significantly improved weight-carrying capability compared to the earlier machine, and the type was soon being developed for a range of both military and civilian roles. The Mi-2 became the Bell UH-1 of the Soviet Union.

The V2 prototypes had been flown in Russia but all production of the Mi-2 was undertaken by PZL-Swidnik, near Lublin in Poland. The first Polish-built machine flew on November 4, 1965.

Over the following 26-year manufacturing period, a total of 5,080 machines were produced, mainly for military use.

The type was widely exported outside the Soviet Union. Military operators included Afghanistan, Albania, Algeria, Armenia, Azerbaijan, Belarus, Bulgaria, China, Cuba, East Germany, Hungary, Czechoslovakia and Poland. Many were transferred to other states, including Djibouti, Estonia, Ethiopia, Cambodia, Georgia, Ghana, Indonesia, India, Iraq, Latvia and Liberia. The type was also delivered to Lesotho, Libya, Lithuania, Mongolia, Mexico, Myanmar, Nicaragua, North Korea, Peru, Syria and Turkey.

LEFT: **The main rotor blades on the Mi-2 are constructed from a metal spar and ribs covered with aluminium. The main and tail rotors are fitted with an electrically heated de-icing system, essential for the harsh weather conditions of the Soviet Union.**

LEFT: **In Polish service, the Mi-2URP-G is armed with 9M14 Malutka anti-tank and Strela-2 anti-aircraft missiles.** MIDDLE LEFT: **The Mi-2 URP-G can carry pod-mounted 7.62mm machine-guns.**

PZL developed 25 versions for both military and civilian use from firefighting to training, ambulance (with four stretchers mounted side-by-side), SAR, photographic survey and reconnaissance.

The Mi-2URN Zimija (viper) was a gunship version armed with two pods, each containing 16 unguided rockets, a fixed 23mm NS-23 cannon on the starboard side of the fuselage, plus a cabin-mounted machine-gun to be fired by a crew member. The later Mi-2US was armed with two pod-mounted 7.62mm PKT machine-guns, as well as a fixed 23mm NS-23 cannon and a cabin-mounted machine-gun. The Mi-2URP Salamandra (salamander) was an anti-tank version armed with four AT-3 Sagger (9M14M Malyutka) wire-guided guided missiles with four "reload" missiles carried in the cabin. The Mi-2 URP-G Gniewosz carried four Strela 2 air-to-air missiles (AAM) for missions as an escort helicopter. In this dangerous role, the Mi-2URP-G was equipped with a radar warning receiver system to alert the pilot to any threat from enemy radar.

Many Mi-2s remain in front-line military service around the world. In the USA, a Cold War museum is reported to have operated four of the type on air-experience flights for their visitors. The US Army also operated the Mi-2 as part of a training programme for pilots to learn the flight characteristics of Soviet-era helicopter types.

Mil Mi-2

First flight: November 4, 1965
Power: 2 x Isotov GTD-350P turboshaft
Armament: None
Size: Rotor diameter – 14.56m/47ft 9in
Length – 11.94m/39ft 2in
Height – 3.75m/12ft 4in
Weights: Empty – 2,402kg/5,485lb
Take-off – 3,700kg/8,140lb (maximum)
Performance: Speed – 210kph/130mph (maximum)
Service ceiling – 4,000m/13,125ft
Range – 170km/105 miles

ABOVE: **The Mil-2 can carry 700kg/1,545lb in the cabin, or 800kg/1,765lb in a cargo net suspended from a hook mounted on the underside of the fuselage.**

Mil Mi-4

In 1951, Stalin had demanded a "sudden, great advance in Soviet helicopters", having noted the successful use of helicopters during the Korean War. The Mil design team may well have examined a Sikorsky S-55 as a source of inspiration but produced a machine that, although similar in appearance, was larger and had a better lift capacity. The Mil Mi-4 (NATO codename Hound) was developed in an impressively short time and was first flown by May 1952. The type was first displayed to the public at the 1953 Tushino Aviation Day in Moscow. By 1954, the Mi-4 was in military service, thus providing the Soviet leader with the advance in helicopter technology he had demanded.

The layout of the Mi-4 was, like the S-55, designed with ease of maintenance in mind. The engine, a proven Shvetsov Ash-82V radial piston engine (developed from the US-built Wright Cyclone), was installed at an angle in the nose behind large doors for easy access. The four-blade rotor was driven from the gearbox through a drive shaft that passed between the crew seats to the rotor hub. Unlike the Sikorsky S-55, the Mil Mi-4 had clamshell rear doors that not only made loading of freight much simpler, but were removable to enable infantry (up to 14 fully equipped troops could be carried) to exit rapidly during an airborne assault. In place of troops,

up to 1,600kg/3,530lb of cargo could be carried in the cabin, and often included small vehicles or light artillery.

At first, serious problems with the rotor kept the Mi-4 out of service. The wood-skinned and Bakelite (an early plastic) blades had a very short life of 100 hours before having to be replaced. In 1954, design and material improvements had allowed this time period to be increased to 300 hours, and by 1957 to 600 hours. By 1960, when all-metal rotor blades were fitted, this was increased to 1,500 hours.

The basic version of the Mi-4 was the 12–14 passenger military transport. Among the numerous variants produced was the Mi-4PLO, an anti-submarine warfare version fitted with a radome under the nose, a ventral observer station, dipping sonar, depth charges, sonobuoys and Magnetic Anomaly Detection (MAD) equipment. The Mi-4A was a military assault version with a ventral gun position on the underside of the fuselage fitted with a 12.7mm machine-gun with 200 rounds of ammunition. The Mi-4KP was an airborne command post, and the Mi-4M was an attack version armed with a chin gun turret in the nose and external rocket pods.

The Mi-4 was widely used by the Soviet armed forces (army, air force and navy), as well as by Warsaw Pact or Soviet-friendly nations. Albania, which phased out the type in 2005, is believed to have been the last military user of the Mi-4. Other operators were the Afghan Air Force, Algerian Air Force, Angola People's Air Defence Force, Bangladesh Air Force, Bulgarian Air Force and Navy, Burkina Faso, Cambodian Air Force, Cameroon

LEFT: The Mi-4M was one of few helicopters ever to be equipped with a gun turret as well as rocket pods.

Air Force, People's Republic of China and the Fuerza Aérea Revolucionaria in Cuba. Other military operators included the Egyptian Air Force, Finnish Air Force, Indian Air Force, Indonesian Air Force, Iraqi Air Force, Mongolian People's Air Force and the North Korean Air Force. The type was also used by Sierra Leone, Somali Air Corps, South Yemen, Tajikistan, Syrian Air Force, Sudanese Air Force, Vietnam People's Air Force and the Yemen Air Force.

ABOVE: **The Mil Mi-4 was the first Soviet-built helicopter designed to be fitted with hydraulically boosted flight controls.**

When Soviet production ended in 1964, some 3,200 military and civil versions had been produced. From 1959 to 1965 in China, Harbin built a further 545 of the type under licence as the Z-5, powered by an HS7 radial piston engine. The prototype of the Z-5 was first flown on December 14, 1958.

BELOW: **Between 1959 and 1965, the Mi-4 was built by Harbin in the People's Republic of China as the Z-5. The machine was powered by a Chinese-built HS7 radial piston engine.**

Mil Mi-4

First flight: May, 1952
Power: 1 x Shvetsov ASh-82V piston engine
Armament: 12.7mm machine-gun
Size: Rotor diameter – 21.00m/68ft 11in
   Length – 25.02m/82ft 1in
   Height – 5.18m/17ft
Weights: Empty – 6,626kg/14,608lb
   Take-off – 7,534kg/16,610lb (maximum)
Performance: Speed – 200kph/124mph
   (maximum)
   Service ceiling – 5,486m/18,000ft
   Range – 500km/313 miles

Mil Mi-6

The Mi-6 (NATO identifier Hook) was first flown in June 1957. For some time it was both the largest helicopter in the world and, with a speed of 300kph/186mph, the fastest. It was also the first turboshaft-powered helicopter to be designed and built in the Soviet Union. The enormous five-blade main rotor has a diameter of 35m/114ft 10in and the overall length of the machine with the rotor turning is 41.74m/137ft, larger than the wingspan of a Lockheed C-130 Hercules. Between 1957 and 1980, some 800 were built for military and civil operators.

Originally developed to meet a joint Soviet Air Force/Aeroflot requirement for a heavy-lift helicopter, the Mi-6 is a complex aircraft and has a flight crew of two pilots, a flight engineer, a navigator and a radio operator. The Soviet Union had remote, undeveloped areas without airfields that had to be accessed quickly for both military and commercial reasons. The Mi-6 had a specially developed rotor de-icing system for operations in sub-zero conditions. The tail rotor (larger than the main rotor of some helicopters) was fitted with electric heating in early versions, but this was replaced with

ABOVE: **The Mil Mi-6 transport helicopter (NATO identifier Hook) was seen in public for the first time during September 1957.**

chemical de-icing in later versions. The main rotor blades had a steel main spar and were covered with aluminium. The tail rotor blades also had a steel spar but were covered with Bakelite plastic. The Mi-6 is powered by two Soloviev D-25V turboshaft engines driving the main rotor through a single gearbox which weighs 3,200kg/7,040lb.

The Mi-6 has a very large cabin for a helicopter and can carry up 70 fully equipped troops on seats fitted along the cabin sides and on a line of seats down the centre of the cabin. The type can be fitted for the MEDEVAC role to carry 41 stretchers and two medical attendants. The maximum internal payload is 12,000kg/26,450lb (more than a Sikorsky CH-54 Tarhe), and a cargo of 8,000kg/17,637lb can be carried slung under the helicopter. In October 1957, the type was used to set a new weight-to-height record by lifting 10,174kg/22,400lb to altitude. In 1961, on another record flight, this was increased to 20,117kg/44,800lb to a height of 2,745m/9,000ft.

LEFT: **The Mil Mi-10 flying crane was developed from the Mi-6, and entered service in 1963. It was built in both short-undercarriage (Mi-10K) and long-undercarriage (Mi-10R) versions.**

Large clamshell rear doors facilitate the loading of bulky cargo, including the PT-76 tracked carrier mounted with a FROG-7 battlefield missile, trucks or heavy artillery. The Mi-6 was designed to carry all types of armoured personnel carriers, armoured cars and light mechanized infantry vehicles in service with Soviet military forces.

Special versions included the Mi-6PS search and rescue helicopter developed in 1966 for the recovery of Vostok, Voshkod and Soyuz space vehicles. The Mi-6VKP was equipped as a command post and fitted with specialized electronic warfare equipment – a T-shaped antenna is mounted on the tail boom.

In addition to service with the Soviet military, the Mi-6 was operated by a number of Warsaw Pact and Soviet-friendly nations, including Afghanistan, Algeria, Azerbaijan, Belarus, Bulgaria, People's Republic of China, Egypt, Ethiopia, Indonesia, Iraq, Kazakhstan, Lao People's Liberation Army Air Force, Peru, Poland, Syria, Ukraine, Uzbekistan, Vietnam and Zimbabwe.

Between 1979 and 1989, ten of the type were lost in accidents or to enemy fire during Soviet operations in Afghanistan.

ABOVE: **Troops exiting a Peruvian Air Force Mi-6 as another lands during an air-assault exercise.**

Mil Mi-6

First flight: June 5, 1957
Power: 2 x Soloviev D-25V turboshaft
Armament: 12.7mm machine-gun
Size: Rotor diameter – 35m/115ft
Length – 41.74m/137ft
Height – 9.86m/32ft
Weights: Empty – 27,240kg/59,928lb
Take-off – 42,500kg/93,700lb (maximum)
Performance: Speed – 300kph/186mph (maximum)
Service ceiling – 4,500m/14,750ft
Range – 620km/384 miles

RIGHT: **The size of this Mi-6 can be appreciated as it dwarfs nearby cars. Note the large shoulder wings, which generate up to 20 per cent of the aerodynamic lift.**

LEFT: **The main rotor blades on the Mil Mi-8 (NATO identifier Hip) are manufactured from an aluminium alloy and fitted with an electro-thermal de-icing system. The blades also have an internal gas pressurization system to aid the detection of cracks caused by metal fatigue.**

Mil Mi-8

Powerful, easy to maintain and economical to operate, the Mi-8 (NATO identifier Hip) has been produced in greater numbers than almost any other helicopter, and has served in more than 50 air arms around the world. More than 11,000 have been built, including the Mi-17 variant (by comparison, Sikorsky built some 1,500 Sea Kings), and it has been operated in a variety of roles, from troop carrier, gunship,

search and rescue to command post. When the type was first displayed in 1961, it was larger and appeared as powerful as any Western-built helicopter. The popular notion that the Soviet Union was somehow only capable of copying Western designs was laid to rest.

Intended to succeed the Mi-4, the V-8 prototype was a single-engine design that evolved into the Mi-8. However, both

Aeroflot (the Soviet state airline) and the Soviet military required two engines for extra power and operational safety. Mil then designed and produced a twin-engine version of the V-8 with two turboshafts mounted (as on the Mi-6) above the cabin. The first test flight,

BELOW: **Two Mil Mi-8 helicopters delivering Egyptian infantry during an air-assault exercise in desert conditions.**

RIGHT: **Ease of maintenance and comparatively low operating costs made the Mi-8 an attractive buy for many export customers. Production of the Mi-8 was carried out by Mil plants at Kazan and Ulan-Ude.**

on September 17, 1962, was successful, and the design was refined and perfected until the Mi-8 was ready for production in 1965. The type entered Soviet Air Force service in 1967. Export orders followed soon after the Mi-8 was demonstrated at the 1965 Paris Air Show.

The Mi-8 has been built in a large number of military variants, the most numerous being the tactical assault helicopter which accounted for some 9,000 of the total production run. Other versions included utility, electronic warfare and border surveillance when equipped with special sensors. The gunship variant was armed with a nose mounted gun, unguided rockets and anti-tank missiles carried on external pylons. Other military versions have been produced for mine laying and clearance, CASEVAC, tactical reconnaissance, photographic duties and spacecraft recovery.

The Mi-8 has been deployed for combat in many very different

BELOW: **An Mi-17 of the Macedonian Air Force. The Mi-17 is the export version of the Mi-8MT.**

environments at locations around the world. The troop transport version was widely used to launch many infantry assaults by Soviet forces during the 1979–89 war in Afghanistan. Some 40 of the type were shot down by Taliban forces. The Mi-8 was extensively used by Russian forces in Chechnya.

The Mil-8 was deployed during the Arab–Israeli war of 1973–74, where the Egyptian Air Force made extensive use of the type to land tactical assault troops. The Mi-8 was used by Iraqi forces in the protracted Iran–Iraq war of 1980–88, and again during the Gulf War of 1991. The type saw action on both sides following the 2022 Russian invasion of Ukraine.

Between April and May 1986, a large number of Mi-8s were used to drop radiation-absorbing material on the reactor area at the devastated Chernobyl nuclear power plant. The majority of these helicopters were abandoned near the site after becoming contaminated with radioactive dust.

The Mi-17 is an improved version with uprated engines and can be identified by the tail rotor being positioned on the port side of the tail boom. An additional starboard door is fitted and the clamshell doors at the rear of the cargo hold replaced. The Mi-17 can carry up to 36 fully equipped troops able to exit the helicopter in three groups through the two side doors and a ramp at the rear.

Many civilian and military versions remain in service around the world. The enormous scale of production and the type's longevity of service must define the Mi-8 as one of the world's greatest helicopters.

Mil Mi-8

First flight: September 17, 1962
Power: 2 x Klimov (Isotov) TV-2-117A turboshaft
Armament: Rockets or anti-tank missiles
Size: 21.29m/69ft 11in each
    Length – 25.24m/82ft 9in
    Height – 5.65m/18ft 6in
Weights: Empty – 7,160kg/15,752lb
    Take-off – 12,000kg/26,400lb (maximum)
Performance: Speed – 250kph/155mph (maximum)
    Service ceiling – 4,500m/15,000ft
    Range – 500km/311 miles

Mil Mi-14

The Mi-14 (NATO identifier Haze) was developed from the successful Mi-8 as a dedicated naval helicopter for service within the Soviet Union, and was produced in anti-submarine, mine-countermeasures and search and rescue versions. The type was first flown in September 1969, and after a protracted development programme entered service in the mid-1970s as a replacement for the ageing Mi-4 helicopters. The Mi-14 was in

the main land-based, being too large to be stowed on the Kiev-class aircraft carriers then in service with the Soviet Navy.

One of the main differences between the Mi-14 and the Mi-8 was that the fuselage was designed with a boat-type hull for amphibious operations. Sponsons were fitted on the rear fuselage for stability on water. An additional small float was fitted on the underside of the tail boom

ABOVE: **More powerful engines were required to compensate for the extra weight of the amphibious hull and undercarriage retraction equipment.**

to keep the tail rotor clear of the water. The box-shaped item mounted on the underside of the tail boom is a Doppler navigation radar scanner.

The Mi-14PL is an anti-submarine warfare version and is equipped with a chin-mounted radar scanner, dipping

LEFT: **Normally, the Mi-14 has a crew of three, but the Mi-14PL has a crew of four – two pilots, a flight engineer and a systems operator.**

sonar and a towed APM-60 Magnetic Anomaly Detection (MAD) system to detect enemy submarine activity far below the ocean surface. When not in use, the MAD "sled" is stowed outside the rear of the main cabin.

A weapons bay in the hull carried OKA-2 sonobuoys to aid in the detection of submarines together with a retractable search radar. The Mi-14 was also armed with torpedoes and depth charges. A nuclear depth bomb, developed at the height of the Cold War, was part of the weapons inventory. The Mi-14PL can also be armed with air-to-surface missiles for use against surface vessels. In Polish service this type was designated Mi-14PW, and only the SAR version was available for

export. An improved ASW version was developed, the Mi-14PLM, with more powerful engines and improved detection equipment.

The Mi-14PS was the dedicated SAR version developed from the Mi-14PL but with an enlarged cabin door and a rescue hoist. A powerful searchlight was also fitted to enable rescues at night and in adverse weather conditions. The Mi-14PS carried ten 20-place life rafts. Ten survivors could be accommodated on board the helicopter and the empty life rafts towed behind the machine.

For mining operations the Mi-14BT was developed to tow a minesweeping sled to clear shipping channels of acoustic, magnetic and contact mines in preparation for an amphibious

landing. A seat for the tow operator was positioned in the rear fuselage. The winch was fitted to the rear of the fuselage mounted inside an aerodynamic fairing. This version of the Mi-14 could also be used to lay mines carried in the weapons bay.

By 1991, some 230 had been produced, and in addition to those supplied to the Soviet Air Force and Soviet Navy, many were exported to Warsaw Pact forces, including the Bulgarian Navy, East German Air Force, East German Navy, Polish Navy and the Yugoslav Air Force. The Mi-14 was also operated by the Cuban Navy, Ethiopian Air Force, Georgian Air Force, Libyan Air Force, North Korean Air Force, Syrian Naval Aviation, Ukrainian Naval Aviation and Yemen. Many of the type remain in service with these air arms or their successors.

ABOVE **The type has been produced in anti-submarine, search and rescue, firefighting, minesweeping and transport versions.**

Mil Mi-14PL

First flight: September, 1969
Power: 2 x Klimov (Isotov) TV3-117MT turboshaft
Armament: Torpedoes, bombs
Size: Rotor diameter – 21.29m/69ft 11in
Length – 25.3m/83ft
Height – 6.93m/22ft 9in
Weights: Empty – 8,900kg/19,625lb
Take-off – 14,000kg/30,865lb (maximum)
Performance: Speed – 230kph/143mph (maximum)
Service ceiling – 3,500m/11,500ft
Range – 1,135km/704 miles

Mil Mi-24

The Mil Mi-24 (NATO identifier Hind) is a large helicopter designed for attack duties, such as anti-tank operations and close air support, but with accommodation to transport up to eight fully armed troops. Over 2,000 have been delivered over the past 40 years. In 2007, the Russian Air Force announced its intention to replace all Mi-24s in service with Mi-28 and Ka-50 attack helicopters. The Mi-24has been operated by around 50 nations and

has given a number of nicknames by aircrew, such as "The Flying Tank", "Crocodile" (due to its style of camouflage) and "Glass" (after the distinctive double-bubble canopy over the tandem cockpit).

The Mi-24 entered service in 1969 with the closest comparative transport model at the time being the Bell UH-1A Iroquois, used for moving US troops to and from battlegrounds throughout the Vietnam War. During this period,

ABOVE: **There are at least 10 variants of the basic Mi-24, including the Mi-25 and Mi-35.**

the US military was investigating ways of improving individual helicopter types to advance efficiency in built-for-purpose roles (e.g. attack, gunship or transport). The Soviets were examining

BELOW: **Mil Mi-35 helicopters of the Afghan National Air Corps taking off in formation, to practise for the Afghan National Day in Kabul.**

RIGHT: **A Mil Mi-24 in service with the Macedonian Air Force about to take off for a tactical training mission with Bulgarian forces.**

ways of combining roles within one type of helicopter. The Mi-24 was based on the same configuration as the Mi-8, two turboshaft engines positioned on top of the fuselage driving a five-blade main rotor and a three-blade tail rotor. The airframe is covered with anti-impact armour able to withstand hits from 0.50in ammunition. The rotor blades are constructed from titanium and can absorb hits from similar calibre ammunition. The cockpit canopies are moulded in armoured glass and are designed to resist 37mm cannon fire.

After significant combat experience during Soviet operations in Afghanistan between 1979 and 1989, the combined role of troop transport and gunship was finally discontinued due to the weight penalty. With less weight, the Mi-24 became more manoeuvrable and is commonly compared to the Sikorsky S-67 Black Hawk in service with US forces. The Mi-24 was designed to be fast – to reduce risk to on-board troops and to provide the adequate fire support to ground troops. To achieve this, the design team included a retractable tricycle landing undercarriage to reduce drag. The fuselage was streamlined and the stub wings also provided some lift at high speed. To create a more stable firing platform, the main rotor was tilted a few degrees to the right of the fuselage and the landing gear positioned to the left. The tail rotor was also asymmetrical to produce enough side force to compensate for the tilted main rotor.

The combat history of the Mi-24 is unparalleled by any other helicopter, Russian or otherwise. Since the 1970s, the type has been operated in numerous conflicts. During the 2022 Russian invasion of Ukraine, the type has seen action on both sides and a number have been destroyed in action.

LEFT: **The Cyprus Air Command operates 11 examples of the Mi-35P, the export version of the Mi-24P.**

ABOVE: **Early versions of the Mil Mi-24 were armed with a Yakushev-Borzov 12.7mm YaK-B Gatling-type rotary machine-gun in a remote-controlled turret. The gun was linked to a sighting system mounted under the nose of the aircraft.**

Mil Mi-24

First flight: September 19, 1969
Power: 2 x Isotov TV3-117 turboshaft
Armament: 12.7mm machine-gun, 23mm cannon, rocket-launcher pod, cannon pod, grenade launcher, bomb, anti-tank missiles
Size: Rotor diameter – 17.3m/57ft
Length – 21.35m/70ft 1in
Height – 6.5m/21ft 3in
Weights: Empty – 8,500kg/18,740lb
Take-off – 12,000kg/26,500lb (maximum)
Performance: Speed – 335kph/208mph (maximum)
Service ceiling – 4,500m/14,750ft
Range – 750km/465 miles

LEFT: **Venezuela was among the large number of nations to procure the Mil Mi-26 (NATO identifier Halo) for military operations.**

Mil Mi-26

The Mil Mi-26 (NATO identifier Halo) is a true heavy-lift helicopter. In fact, it is the world's largest production helicopter. It has twice the take-off weight of the Boeing CH-47 Chinook and an internal capacity similar in size to that of a Lockheed C-130 Hercules. This gigantic machine was first flown on December 17, 1977, and entered service with the Soviet military as a replacement for the Mil Mi-6 during 1983. The type remains operational, and over 300 have been built in both civil and military versions. The Mi-26 has been to exported to customers in more

than 30 countries around the world.

In the early 1970s, a technical specification was issued for a helicopter with an empty weight (without fuel), which was not to be more than 50 per cent of the maximum take-off weight. The result was the Mil Mi-26, designed by Marat Tishchenko, a protégé of Mikhail Mil, the founder of the design bureau. The helicopter is powered by two Lotarev D-136 turboshaft engines mounted on top of the fuselage, which drive the unconventional eight-blade main rotor through a gearbox. The five-blade tail rotor is mounted on

a fin at the end of the tail boom.

In 1982, the heavy-lift capability of the Mi-26 was demonstrated when a total mass of 56,768.8kg/124,948lb was raised to an altitude of 2,000m/6,562ft. The type is available in any of 16 different variants, including the Mi-26P, a civil air transport with accommodation for 63 passengers in airliner-type seating. The same variant was used as a military transport with

BELOW: **The Mil Mi-26 is fitted with a distinctive eight-blade main rotor system. The type has a five-blade tail rotor.**

a capacity for 65 fully equipped troops.

The Mi-26MS is fitted out for the MEDEVAC role and can carry up to 65 stretchers and four/five attendants. An Anti-Submarine Warfare (ASW) version (Mi-26NEF-M) equipped with search radar and Magnetic Anomaly Detector (MAD) equipment is also in service. Other versions are the Mi-26TP for firefighting operations, the Mi-26PK/TM flying crane and the Mi-26TZ air-to-air refuelling tanker. Access to the interior of the machine is through three clamshell doors at the rear of the fuselage; two of them hinge outward while the third has an integral ramp for loading.

In 2002, after Operation Anaconda in Afghanistan, Lt Col Chuck Jarnot was instructed to organize the recovery of two US Army Chinook helicopters which had been shot down during the action and abandoned on a mountainside. With no heavy-lift capability available within the US military, Jarnot contacted a civilian operator of the Mi-26 based in Belgium. Six weeks later, the aircraft arrived in Afghanistan, flown by an East European crew. The operation was carried out using the under-fuselage cargo hook (lifting capacity 30,000kg/66,138lb) to recover the aircraft. The only Mi-26 in North America is a civilian version being operated for the oil industry in Canada.

The type has been used not only for recovery missions but, significantly, for the transport of heavy equipment to remote regions affected by disaster. In May 2008, an earthquake hit the Sichaun province in China, and Mil Mi-26 helicopters were used to airlift in earth-moving tractors to remove landslides which had blocked rivers causing severe flooding over vast areas, threatening the lives of the local population. Military operators of the type have included the Belarus Air Force, Royal Cambodian Air Force, Air Force of the Democratic Republic of the Congo, Indian Air Force, Kazakh Air Defence Forces, Mexican Air Force, Peruvian Army, Russian Air Force, Russian Army, Ukrainian Air Force, Ukraine Army and the Venezuelan Air Force.

LEFT: **One of two Mil Mi-26TC helicopters based in Greece and equipped for firefighting operations. A large volume of water or fire-retardant chemical is being carried under the machine in a purpose-designed hopper to be discharged over the fire.**

ABOVE: **Current operators of the Mil Mi-26 include the air forces of India, the Russian Federation and Ukraine. Aeroflot, the national airline of Russia, has also operated the type.**

Mil Mi-26

First flight: December 14, 1977
Power: 2 x Lotarev D-136 turboshaft
Armament: None
Size: Rotor diameter – 32m/105ft
Length – 40.025m/131ft 4in
Height – 8.15m/26ft 9in
Weights: Empty – 28,200kg/2,170lb
Take-off – 56,000kg/123,450lb (maximum)
Performance: Speed – 295kph/183mph (maximum)
Service ceiling – 4,600m/15,100ft
Range – 1,920km/1,190 miles

LEFT: **The Mil Mi-28 (NATO identifier Havoc) has a crew of two personnel seated in separate heavily armoured cockpits. The structure, including the windows, is manufactured to withstand direct hits from up to 12.7mm ammunition.**

Mil Mi-28

The Mil Mi-28 (NATO identifier Havoc) is a day or night all-weather attack helicopter. Whereas the Mil Mi-24 had a secondary troop transport capability, the Mi-28 is only designed for attack. Development of the type began in 1972, when both sides in the Cold War were trying to learn from operational experience in the Vietnam War in terms of the effectiveness of the helicopter in the attack role or as a gunship. The outline design was informed by the need to improve performance and speed on Soviet helicopters tasked with ground attack. The Mi-28 is often considered to be the Russian equivalent of the AH-64 Apache. The first of three Mi-28A prototypes was flown on November 10, 1982.

The Mi-28 has a conventional helicopter gunship cockpit layout with the crew sitting in tandem, the gunner in front of the pilot. A 30mm Shipunov 2A42 cannon in a barbette mounting is positioned under the nose of the aircraft. The wings on the machine each have two hardpoints to carry a variety of weapons, including

the Sheksna anti-tank missile, Ataka-V or S-8/13 unguided rocket, 23mm Gsh-23L gun pod, Igla-V or Vympel R-73 air-to-air missile and the KMGU-2 mine dispenser.

The Mi-28N (N – Night) version was launched and first flew on November 14, 1996. Described in the company's sales literature as a "round-the-clock operation combat helicopter", the

type is equipped to locate and attack enemy armour and also low-speed air targets (including other helicopters). On-board avionics enable the crew to accurately navigate by day or night and in all weather conditions. Computer-aided terrain-following flight systems permit low-altitude operation. To locate targets, the crew use an infra-red imaging and target search

ABOVE: **The configuration of the Mil Mi-28 is essentially the same as other attack helicopters. The use of a tail-wheel-type undercarriage allows a gun and mounting to be positioned under the cockpit.**

ABOVE: **The Mil Mi-28 can carry the B-8 pod, which contains 80mm folding-fin unguided missiles and eight AT-9 anti-tank missiles on each stub wing.**

LEFT: **A Shipunov 30mm 2A42 cannon is positioned in a mounting under the forward fuselage.**

radar – the sight is mounted on a mast above the rotor head to allow the helicopter to be held at the hover below a tree line or buildings, not exposed to enemy fire. Radar and laser illumination warning systems alert the crew to any enemy radar threat or heat-seeking missile attack.

The helicopter is powered by two Klimov TV-3-117VMA turboshaft engines mounted in pods above each wing root for protection against ground fire. Manufactured from composite materials, the downward deflecting nozzles shroud the engine exhausts to minimize the heat signature. The cockpit is compatible with Night Vision Goggles (NVG), and the sensor package includes a laser rangefinder and optical sights for weapon aiming.

The cockpit is protected by titanium and ceramic armour, and the window glass can withstand hits from 12.7mm ammunition. At the trailing edge of the port wing, a hatch provides access to a compartment with space for three personnel. The Mi-28 is a helicopter designed to be air-portable and is often transported in Antonov An-22 and Ilyushin Il-76 aircraft of the Russian Air Force.

The first two prototypes were delivered to the military in 2004 for testing. In 2006, the first production Mil Mi-28N was delivered to the Russian military. By early 2012, there were 52 operational, and the type is now the standard attack helicopter in Russian service.

The Mi-28N was deployed by Russia during the 2022 invasion of Ukraine and a number were destroyed by Ukrainian defenders. Iraq and Algeria have both acquired examples of the type.

Mil Mi-28

First flight: November 28, 1992
Power: 2 x Klimov TV3-117VMA turboshaft
Armament: 30mm cannon, Ataka-V anti-tank missiles, S-8 rocket, S13 rocket, 23mm Gsh-23L gun pods, Sheksna and 9A-2200 anti-tank missile
Size: Rotor diameter – 17.2m/55ft 1in
Length – 17.01m/55ft 5in
Height – 3.82m/12ft 7in
Weights: Empty – 8,094kg/17,844lb
Take-off – 12,000kg/26,455lb (maximum)
Performance: Speed – 304kph/189mph (maximum)
Service ceiling – 5,700m/10,702ft
Range – 450km/279 miles

NH Industries NH90

The NH90 is a versatile twin engine helicopter developed by NH Industries partnership (Airbus Helicopters, Leonardo Helicopters, and Fokker Aerostructures) and was designed to meet a NATO requirement for a medium multi-role military helicopter that provides the benefits of type standardization for both land and maritime operations. The helicopter is available in two versions, the NATO Frigate Helicopter (NFH) and the Tactical Transport Helicopter (TTH).

The prototype NH90 was first flown on December 18, 1995, and the production TTH helicopter was first flown in May 2004. After a two-year production delay, deliveries of the NH90 began in December 2006, when three TTH transport helicopters were handed over to the German Army. In August 2007, the NFH version was flown for the first time.

The airframe of the NH90 is constructed from composite materials to reduce the number of parts, and

ABOVE: **The NH90 is built in two versions – the NFH for naval operations and the TTH tactical transport.**

structural weight with increased strength, improved fatigue life and resistance to corrosion and battle damage. The blades of the main rotor are also manufactured from composite materials for strength, damage tolerance and improved fatigue life.

The helicopter is equipped with fly-by-wire flight controls with no mechanical back-up, which reduces the overall weight,

LEFT: **An NH90 Tactical Transport Helicopter (TTH) in service with the German Army. The machine is held in the hover, which causes the tips of the main rotor blades to generate vortices in the moist air over the forest.**

LEFT: **The NATO Frigate Helicopter (NFH) version of the NH90 in service with Aéronavale, the air arm of the French Navy. The NFH is built primarily as an Anti-Submarine Warfare (ASW) helicopter, but can be used for many other roles.**

maximizes performance and lessens crew workload. Maintenance and inspection requirements are also greatly reduced compared with those for a conventional control system. In December 2003, the NH90 became the first medium-sized transport helicopter to fly with full fly-by-wire controls. The aircraft has a full glass cockpit, with all flight, aircraft systems and maintenance data being displayed to the crew (in colour) on five multi-function LCD screens. All are compatible with Night Vision Goggles (NVG) and helmet-mounted display systems.

The NH90 is designed to operate in confined spaces such as the deck of a ship (NFH), but has cabin large enough to accommodate 20 fully equipped troops (TTH). The primary role of this version is the transportation of troops, but it can easily be adapted to carry more than 2,500kg/5,511lb of cargo. The type is also equipped for the SAR mission and can be quickly adapted for MEDEVAC/CASEVAC duties to carry up to 12 stretchers. In Finnish and Swedish service, the TTH is designated TTT (Tactical Troop Transport).

The primary missions of the NFH version are in the Anti-Submarine Warfare (ASW) and Anti-Surface unit Warfare (ASuW) roles, and it can be armed with a variety of weapons, including anti-submarine torpedoes, air-to-surface missiles and air-to-air missiles.

On ASW operations, a typical four-hour mission is made up of a 35-minute flight to the area of operation, 20 minutes dropping sonobuoys, two hours on surveillance, 30 minutes releasing torpedoes and 35 minutes for the return flight to the frigate. In a typical four-hour screening operation, the helicopter would take 15 minutes to reach the area of operation, three hours and 30 minutes in the area executing 11 consecutive cycles of ten-minute sonar dipping, then 15 minutes to return to the home ship.

In the anti-surface warfare role, the helicopter is equipped with an Over The Horizon (OTH) capability to detect, track, identify and attack an enemy vessel. Secondary roles include Anti-Air Warfare (AAW), Vertical Replenishment (VertRep), SAR, troop transport and mine laying. The helicopter has a crew of three – a pilot, a Tactical Coordinator (Tacco) responsible for mission management and a Sensor Systems Operator (Senso) – and can be operated day and night and in all weather conditions.

Many of the aircraft being operated in Europe are fitted with a counter-measures and self-protection suite which includes a missile approach warning system, integrated radar warning and laser warning receivers. Chaff and flare dispensers are also standard

equipment. Other sensors fitted include Forward Looking Infra-Red (FLIR), Magnetic Anomaly Detector (MAD) and sonar equipment.

The NFH version is powered by two Rolls-Royce Turboméca RTM322-01/9 turboshaft engines. Those ordered for service with Italian and Spanish forces are powered by General Electric T700/T6E1 turboshaft engines.

Although the NH90 was developed for and is in service with NATO countries, it has been ordered by a number of other countries around the world. More than 440 NH90s have been delivered to 18 customers in 14 countries and the type had, by mid 2021, accumulated more than 265,000 flight hours.

NH Industries NH90 NFH

First flight: December 18, 1995
Power: 2 x Rolls-Royce Turboméca RTM322 turboshaft
Armament: Martel Mk2/S anti-ship missile, torpedoes
Size: Rotor diameter – 16.3m/53ft 6in
Length – 19.56m/64ft 2in
Height – 5.31m/16ft 5in
Weights: Empty – 6,400kg/14,109lb
Take-off – 10,600kg/23,369lb (maximum)
Performance: Speed – 300kph/186mph (maximum)
Ceiling – 6,000m/19,686ft
Range – 900km/559 miles

Piasecki YH-16 Transporter

In the post-war years, as the Strategic Air Command (SAC) arm of the USAF was being increased in size and worldwide operations, so grew a requirement for an aircraft to rescue any aircrew shot down or forced to abandon their aircraft far from base. In 1946, the USAF detailed a requirement for a large long-range helicopter for this role, and issued a contract to the Piasecki Helicopter Corporation to build two development machines in 1949. Known to the company as the PV-15, now designated XH-16A (serial number 50-1269), it was first flown on October 23, 1953, with test pilots Harold Peterson and Phil Camerano at the controls.

At the time, the XH-16A was the largest helicopter in the world, and each of the two overlapping rotors had a diameter of 25m/82ft. The fuselage was as capacious as that of a Douglas DC-4 transport aircraft. The YH-16A could carry up to 40 fully equipped troops or three light trucks loaded into the aircraft up a ramp through a rear door.

The helicopter (officially named Transporter) was initially powered by two Pratt & Whitney R-2180-11 radial piston engines and was the world's first twin-engine helicopter. First flown in 1955, the YH-16A (the Y prefix denotes an experimental aircraft) was powered by two Allison YT38-A-10 turboshaft engines and was the first helicopter in the world to be powered in this way. The three blades of each rotor were assembled from a milled aluminium outer skin, an aluminium honeycomb core and a leading edge balance weight which acted as a form of mechanical fastener. The slow rotating speed (125rpm) of the rotors made the blades almost visible when turning. Each engine drove an individual rotor. The proposed YH-16B was to have been powered by two Allison YT56-A5-2 turboshaft engines and to transport up to 69 passengers. One development designed by Piasecki for the YH-16B was a large load-carrying pod fitted under the fuselage to carry equipment. This required the undercarriage to be lengthened.

Although impressive, the helicopter was underpowered and lacked the

ABOVE: **The US Air Force tested the Piasecki YH-16, but the programme was abandoned after the crash of the second prototype. Various pods were designed for special functions, including a field operating room, an electronics centre and a mobile repair centre.**

required performance. The USAF decided against procuring the YH-16A, but the US Army continued testing the machine until the second XH-16A suffered a catastrophic mechanical failure, broke up and crashed in December 1956.

Piasecki XH-16A Transporter

First flight: October 23, 1953
Power: 2 x Pratt & Whitney R 2180-11 radial piston engines
Armament: None
Size: Rotor diameter – 25m/82ft
Length – 23.79m/78ft
Height – 7.62m/25ft
Weights: Empty – 14,534kg/32,041lb
Take-off – 20,893kg/46,060lb (maximum)
Performance: Speed – 198kph/123mph (maximum)
Ceiling – 5,490m/18,000ft
Range – 370km/230 miles

LEFT: **For ease of maintenance, the fuselage was designed to allow the engine and mounting, fan cowling and oil system to be removed as a single unit through a roof hatch. The HUP-2 entered service with the US Navy and US Marine Corps in 1949.**

Piasecki HUP Retriever/UH-25 Army Mule

In 1945, US Navy Board of Aeronautics issued a specification for a helicopter suitable for operations from aircraft carriers, battleships or cruisers and other large vessels in the US Fleet. The Piasecki Helicopter Corporation and Sikorsky Aircraft Corporation were issued with contracts to design and build prototypes. After evaluation, the Sikorsky XHJS-1 was cancelled and Piasecki were contracted to build two prototypes designated XHJP-1 (Model PV-14).

The XHJP-1 was first flown in March 1948. After extensive trials, the HUP-1 Retriever (Model PV-18) entered production for the US Navy. In 1949, the type began to enter USN service, and in February 1951 the first operational aircraft were in service with Helicopter Utility Squadron 2 (HU-2) "Fleet Angels" as part of Carrier Group Six. The aircraft was powered by a Continental R975-46 radial piston engine driving overlapping tandem rotors. The HUP-1 had a

two-man crew and could accommodate up to five passengers or three stretchers. By 1952, Piasecki had delivered 32 of the type to the USN.

The second production version was the HUP-2, which had the more powerful Continental R975-46A engine and was the first production helicopter to be fitted with a Sperry-manufactured auto-pilot. The HUP-2S was equipped with dipping sonar equipment for anti-submarine warfare operations. The HUP-2S was found to be underpowered for the demanding ASW role, resulting in the sonar equipment being removed and the aircraft being used for SAR and transport missions.

A total of 193 were built, of which 15 were supplied to France for service with the navy.

A version of the HUP-2 was developed for the US Army and designated H-25A Army Mule (UH-25C in 1962). This model was fitted with large doors

and power-boosted controls, as well as a strengthened cabin floor to carry a heavier payload. A total of 70 were delivered from 1953, but were judged to be unsuitable for front-line deployment. Consequently, from 1955, a total of 50 machines were transferred to the USN and designated HUP-3. The Navy was already operating a number of Retrievers which had been upgraded to HUP-3 standard. By 1958, those that remained on the US Army inventory were used for training purposes and withdrawn from service. The Royal Canadian Navy (RCN) also took delivery of three HUP-3s.

During the Korean War, the type was used extensively for transport and rescue missions by US forces. A total of 339 had been built when the production line was closed in July 1954. The type was finally withdrawn from service in 1964.

LEFT: **The Piasecki HUP-3 Retriever was fitted with a large rectangular hatch, offset to the right, to allow a rescue winch with a capacity of up to 181kg/399lb to be operated.**

Piasecki HUP-3 Retriever

First flight: March, 1948
Power: 1 x Continental R-975-46A radial piston engine
Armament: None
Size: Rotor diameter – 10.67m/35ft
 Length – 17.35m/56ft 11in
 Height – 3.84m/12ft 7in
Weights: Empty – 1,786kg/3,938lb
 Take-off – 2,767kg/6,100lb (maximum)
Performance: Speed – 169kph/105mph (maximum)
 Ceiling – 3,048m/10,000ft
 Range – 547km/340 miles

Piasecki H-21 Workhorse/Shawnee

The H-21 was developed from the all-metal HRP-2 which, in turn, was a development of the HRP-1 Rescuer, the original "Flying Banana" flown by the US Navy, US Marine Corps and US Coast Guard. It was the fourth tandem rotor machine designed by the Piasecki Helicopter Corporation to enter production for the United States military.

The helicopter was designed in response to a United States Air Force (USAF) specification for a helicopter to operate in the long-range rescue role in Arctic conditions. The XH-21 was first flown on April 11, 1952. The

USAF, having already ordered 18 pre-production YH-21As in 1949 for evaluation, placed a production order for 32, designated H-21A Workhorse. They were to serve in the search and rescue role with the Military Air Transport Service Air Rescue (MATSAR). The first production H-21A flew in October 1953, and a further six aircraft were built for the Canadian military under the Military Assistance Program (MAP) to be deployed in support of the DEW (Distant Early Warning) line radar installations across the Canadian Arctic.

ABOVE: **A pre-production YH-21A flight test machine being flown for the first time in front of a crowd of Piasecki employees.**

The second version to be developed was the H-21B Workhorse for the USAF Troop Carrier Command (TCC). This aircraft was fitted with an uprated Curtis-Wright R-1820-103 Cyclone radial piston engine, the rotor blades were extended by 15cm/6in, and it was equipped with a Sperry autopilot. The machine had a significantly higher maximum take-off weight and could accommodate 20 fully equipped troops or 12 stretchers in the CASEVAC role. The H-21B was operated by the USN (10) and by the Japanese Self-Defense Force (JSDF), which also had 10 in service.

The US Army version of the H-21B was designated H-21C Shawnee (CH-21C after July 1962). A number of these machines were exported to the French Army (98) and Navy (10), Canada (6) and to the then West Germany (32). The C model was fitted with a large hook under the fuselage to enable a load of up to 1,814kg/4,000lb to be lifted.

LEFT: **Although the Piasecki H-21B was developed for long-range rescue operations, the type could be used to lift loads such as a light military vehicle.**

LEFT: **The Piasecki H-21C Workhorse was fitted with two external auxiliary tanks when being deployed for a long-range rescue mission. Six of the type were supplied to the Royal Canadian Air Force (RCAF) to be used as support aircraft for the Distant Early Warning (DEW) line of radar installations sited across northern Canada.**

In the mid-1950s, French forces were embroiled in the Algerian War, and both the French Air Force and Army were keen to explore the use of the helicopter in the ground-attack role. As a result, some of their H-21Cs were trialled on the battlefront with fixed, forward-firing machine-guns and rockets. A few were trialled with bomb racks fitted, but the machine's manoeuvrability and performance were found to be unsuitable for ground-attack. The H-21C continued to be used as a troop transport by French forces. Most were fitted with a door-mounted machine-gun or 20mm cannon for self-defence during high-risk ground operations. The French military

BELOW: **The H-21 was an early successful example of a multi-role helicopter, and could land on wheels, skis or floats.**

also found that the Shawnee was less vulnerable to ground fire due to the location of the fuel tanks. Although not suited for ground-attack, by the end of the Algerian War the French had developed very effective large-scale counter-insurgency tactics, in which the H-21C Shawnee troop transports were deployed alongside ground-attack Sikorsky H-34 Choctaws.

The US Army also explored the potential of the H-21C as a gunship or ground-attack helicopter, either armed with machine-guns mounted under the nose or with a gun mounting in each door opening. In US Army service, the H-21C was, however, most extensively used as a troop or supply transport. In August 1954, a US Army H-21C named "Amblin' Annie" became the first helicopter to be flown non-stop across

the USA, being refuelled in flight via a very basic hose system trailed from a de Havilland (Canada) U-1A Otter.

After Vertol acquired Piasecki in 1959, Sweden ordered two of the Model 44 (civilian H-21B) helicopters for their air force and nine of the same machines for the navy.

In December 1961, the H-21C Shawnee was deployed to South-east Asia for service with the 8th and 57th Transportation Companies of the US Army. Relatively low speed and unprotected control cables and fuel lines made the H-21C vulnerable to ground fire. In Vietnam, despite some early losses, the type provided the US Army with a reliable supply and transport helicopter until 1964, when it was replaced with the Bell UH-1 Iroquois. All Piasecki CH-21 helicopters in US military service had been retired by the end of 1964.

Piasecki CH-21C Shawnee

First flight: April 11, 1952
Power: 1 x Curtis-Wright R-1820-103 Cyclone radial piston engine
Armament: None
Size: Rotor diameter – 13.41m/44ft
  Length – 26.31m/86ft 4in
  Height – 4.70m/15ft 5in
Weights: Empty – 3,629kg/8,000lb
  Take-off – 6,668kg/14,700lb (maximum)
Performance: Speed – 211kph/131mph (maximum)
  Service ceiling – 2,360m/7,750ft
  Range – 644km/400 miles

PZL W-3 Sokól

First flight: November 16, 1979
Power: 2 x WSKPZL Rzeszów PZL-10W turboshaft
Armament: 23mm GSz-23 cannon on W-3W
Size: Rotor diameter – 15.7m/51ft 6in
Length – 14.21m/46ft 8in
Height – 5.14m/16ft 10in
Weights: Empty – 3,850kg/8,488lb
Take-off – 6,400kg/14,119lb (maximum)
Performance: Speed – 260kph/161mph (maximum)
Service ceiling – 5,100m/19,680ft
Range – 745km/463 miles

PZL W-3 Sokól

Manufactured by PZL-Swidnik (now AgustaWestland Swidnik), the W-3 is the first Polish-designed helicopter to enter series production. The project began in 1973 and the first prototype was flown on November 16, 1979. Development took some time to get underway, but production began in 1985 and the 100th aircraft was completed in June 1996.

The helicopter is built in both civil and military versions, and four of the type have been operated by Polish forces in Iraq. Military versions include the W-3T unarmed transport (operated by the Polish, Czech Republic and Myanmar Air Forces). A VIP passenger (W-3S) and a flying command centre (W-3P SOT) version are operated by the Polish military. An armed version

LEFT: **The W-3WA is a version used by the Polish Land Forces. It is armed with two 23mm cannon and four pylons to carry weapons, including anti-tank missiles and unguided rockets. "Sokól" is Polish for "falcon".**

(W-3W) fitted with two 23mm GSz-23L cannon and four weapons pylons is in service. The MEDEVAC version (W-3R) is operated by the Polish and Czech Republic Air Force. The Polish Air Force (W-3RL) and Polish Navy (W-3RM) operate the type in the search and rescue (SAR) role.

Robinson R22/R44

The Robinson R22 is a compact two-seat light utility helicopter designed in 1973 by Frank Robinson, and has been in production since 1979. The R22 is relatively cheap to purchase and maintain, making the type popular with the civilian market, and has been purchased by some military customers.

Military operators include the Dominican Republic Army and the Philippine Navy. In 2003, the US Navy procured four examples of the Maverick, an Unmanned Aerial Vehicle (UAV) developed by Boeing from the R22 for Special Operations Forces. The first four-seat R44 Astro was flown on March 31,

1990. This was followed in January 2000 by the R44 Raven, fitted with hydraulically assisted flight controls. The R44 Raven II has a more powerful engine and enhanced performance. The type has been delivered to military operators, including the Bolivian Air Force, Dominican Republic Army, Estonian Air Force, Hungarian Air Force and Lebanese Air Force.

LEFT: **The Robinson R44 Raven entered service in January 2000, and is operated by a small number of air forces as a training and communications helicopter.**

Robinson R22

First flight: August 28, 1975
Power: 1 x Lycoming O-320-A2B piston engine
Armament: None
Size: Rotor diameter – 7.7m/25ft 2in
Length – 8.7m/28ft 8in
Height – 2.7m/8ft 11in
Weights: Empty – 361kg/796lb
Take-off – 621kg/1,370lb (maximum)
Performance: Speed – 189kph/117mph (maximum)
Service ceiling – 4,267m/14,000ft
Range – 386km/240 miles

LEFT: **G-ALUF was the second Skeeter built and featured improvements, including a more powerful engine, increased rotor diameter and a redesigned tail boom.** BELOW: **The Federal German Army operated Skeeter Mk50s.**

Saunders-Roe Skeeter

The Saunders-Roe Skeeter was a two-seat training and scout helicopter that became the first rotary-wing aircraft to be operated by the Army Air Corps (AAC).

The design was originally conceived in 1947 by the Cierva Autogiro Company. The Cierva W.14 Skeeter 1, powered by a Jameson FF-1 engine, was first flown on October 8, 1948. However, it was not until late 1956 that the type finally entered service. This protracted development period meant that the type was outdated and virtually obsolete before it had entered service. The delays were initially due to the lack of power from the Jameson engine. The Skeeter 2, powered by a de Havilland Gipsy Major 10, was first flown in 1949. This machine was destroyed on the ground due to resonance problems which caused a catastrophic failure of the rotor assembly and airframe. To alleviate this problem, the Skeeter 3 was powered by a Blackburn Cirrus Bombardier fuel-injected engine.

Saunders-Roe Limited took over Cierva in 1951, and built the improved Skeeter 7 powered by a de Havilland Gipsy Major 215. After evaluation, the British Army placed an order for 64 of the Skeeter AOP.12 (Air Observation Platform), which entered service with the AAC in October 1956. The Royal Air Force ordered the dual-control version, the Skeeter T13, to train helicopter instructors for the AAC. The type was retired from the Army Air Corps in the late 1960s.

The Skeeter Mk50 was produced for the Federal German Army (6), while the Mk51 was supplied to the Federal German Navy (4). Saunders-Roe was acquired by Westland Aircraft Limited in 1960 and a proposed turbine-powered Skeeter was cancelled. However, the project did lead to the P531 helicopter, which in turn was developed as the Westland Scout and Wasp.

LEFT: **The Skeeter became the first operational helicopter for the Army Air Corps (AAC), but limited performance and lack of external load capacity led to it being used mainly as a training machine.**

Saunders-Roe Skeeter AOP 12

First flight: October 8, 1948
Power: 1 x de Havilland Gipsy Major 215 piston engine
Armament: None
Size: Rotor diameter – 9.76m/32ft
   Length – 11.88m/39ft
   Height – 2.99m/9ft 10in
Weights: Empty – 794kg/1,750lb
   Take-off – 1,066kg/2,350lb (maximum)
Performance: Speed – 194kph/121mph (maximum)
   Service ceiling – 3,902m/12,800ft
   Range – 389km/242 miles

LEFT: **This R-4B serial 43-46506 is preserved at the National Museum of the United States Air Force at Dayton, Ohio.**

Sikorsky R-4

The Vought-Sikorsky VS-300 experimental helicopter was a pioneering design, being the first to be fitted with cyclic controls for the rotor and an anti-torque tail rotor. The prototype was first flown in tethered flight on September 14, 1939, with Igor Sikorsky at the controls. On May 13, 1940, the VS-300 was free-flown by Sikorsky for the first time. Continued success with flight trials resulted in a commitment by the United States Army Air Forces (USAAF), in 1941, to proceed with the development of the XR-4 (X – Experimental, R – Rotorcraft).

The fuselage was constructed from steel tubing that was covered almost entirely with fabric. The rotor blades were of conventional spar and rib construction, also covered with fabric. The enclosed cockpit had side-by-side

seating accommodation for a crew of two and had dual controls. The XR-4 was first flown on January 14, 1942, powered by a Warner R-500-1 Super Scarab radial piston engine.

In May 1942, serial number 41-18874, was flown 1,225km/761 miles in stages from Bridgeport, Connecticut to Wright Field, Ohio in just over 16 hours. The XR-4 went on to break all previous helicopter endurance, altitude and speed records. The US Army was sufficiently impressed to order 29 pre-production machines for evaluation in January 1943. Designated YR-4, all were fitted with the more powerful Warner R-550-3 engine and lengthened rotor blades. Evaluation of these machines led to further improvements, including an increased fuel capacity. The tailwheel was moved further to the

rear of the tail boom to improve stability on the ground. These machines were designated YR-4B.

In 1943, one of the pre-production machines was used to execute the first-ever landing of a helicopter on a ship at sea, when being operated from the deck of USS *Bunker Hill* (CV-17).

In April 1944, a YR-4B flown by US Army pilot Lt Carter Harman was deployed to carry out the very first helicopter combat rescue. In the humid, high-altitude conditions of Burma, Lt Harman rescued the pilot and three passengers from a USAAF liaison

BELOW: **The more streamlined R-6 was known as the HOS-1 or Hoverfly II. Note the wheel mounted underneath the tail boom root, to keep the tail rotor well clear of the ground.**

RIGHT: **In British service, the R-4 was known as the Hoverfly. The fuselage was a space frame constructed from steel tubing and covered with fabric. The end of the tail boom was left uncovered to allow access to the tail rotor assembly.**

aircraft that had landed in the jungle. It took four flights as only one passenger could be carried at a time, but all were airlifted to safety. Lt Harman was only the seventh US Army pilot to be helicopter-qualified.Over the following weeks, he flew another 15 jungle rescue missions.

Six ships of the US Navy (USN), each carrying two YR-4B helicopters, were sent to the South Pacific to serve as floating Aviation Repair Units (ARU) for damaged US aircraft. When not

BELOW: **The Sikorsky R-6A was operated by the US Navy as the HOS-1. The type was also used by British military services as the Hoverfly II.**

required for parts delivery flights, the helicopters were available for MEDEVAC duties. In 1948, all of the R-4Bs remaining in US service were redesignated H-4B.

The first production (R-4B) batch of 100 machines was fitted with the more powerful Warner R-550-3 engine. Of these, 35 were delivered to the USAAF for liaison and observation duties. The US Navy took delivery of 20 designated HNS-1 for reconnaissance, transport and air sea rescue duties. The Royal Navy had been very interested in development of the type and had received some YR-4B pre-production machines for evaluation. By the end of the World War II, there were

a number of development and production machines in Great Britain, including 45 production machines supplied under the Lend-Lease Programme. In Royal Air Force service, where it was known as the Hoverfly I, the type was flown by the Helicopter Training School at RAF Andover, Hampshire, No. 529 Squadron at RAF Henley-on-Thames, Oxfordshire, and was operated by The King's Flight from RAF Benson in Oxfordshire. The Fleet Air Arm (FAA) of the Royal Navy was the main operator of the type. The Hoverfly I remained in service into the mid-1950s, with the Joint Experimental Helicopter Unit (JHEU) established on April 1, 1955.

First flown on October 15, 1943, the R-6 was an improved version with a streamlined part metal fuselage and a more powerful Franklin 0-405-9 piston engine. In USN service the R-6 was designated HOS-1, and in British service as the Hoverfly II.

Sikorsky R-4B

First flight: January 14, 1942 (XR-4)
Power: 1 x Warner R-550-3 Super Scarab radial piston engine
Armament: None
Size: Rotor diameter – 11.6m/38ft 1in
　　Length – 14.65m/48ft 1in
　　Height – 3.78m/12ft 5in
Weights: Empty – 952kg/2,098lb
　　Take-off – 1,171kg/2,581lb (maximum)
Performance: Speed – 120kph/75mph (maximum)
　　Service ceiling – 2,438m/8,000ft
　　Range – 209km/130 miles

Sikorsky S-51

Building on the confidence gained from the R-4 helicopter and responding to a United States Army Air Forces requirement for a far more capable machine, Sikorsky Aircraft Corporation developed the VS-337, a two-seater helicopter powered by a radial engine. Designated XR-5, the type was powered by a Pratt & Whitney R-985 Wasp Junior radial piston engine, and was flown for the first time on August 18, 1943. After a successful test programme, the helicopter entered service with the USAAF as the H-5. The US Navy procured the HO2S, and the US Coast Guard the HO3S. The type was to become widely known as the Sikorsky model number S-51.

In US Army service, the H-5 was used for spotting and communications work, but it is perhaps best known as a rescue aircraft during the Korean War. The S-51 afforded the military a new means of extracting personnel from behind enemy lines or from the sea. Early H-5s were fitted with a litter (stretcher) carrier on each side for casualty evacuation duties and, later, a rescue hoist. This allowed battlefield casualties to be recovered rapidly and transported for medical treatment.

RIGHT: **Survivability in the event of an emergency water landing was a key consideration in the development of the type.**

On November 29, 1945, the first successful air sea rescue by helicopter was carried out by test pilot Dimitry Viner flying an H-5 when he lifted two seamen to safety from a sinking ship, a short distance from the Sikorsky plant in Stanford, Connecticut. The last H-5 and HO3S-1 helicopters were retired from active US military service in 1957. US production lasted until 1951, by which time Sikorsky had built a total of 285.

ABOVE: **The success of the Dragonfly gave Westland the confidence to adapt and develop other Sikorsky designs. The British company rapidly developed into a major helicopter manufacturer.**

In 1946, Westland Aircraft Limited negotiated a licence agreement with Sikorsky that led to production of the type in the UK. The first Westland-built S-51 was flown for the first time in 1948. The S-51 Dragonfly was an almost

ABOVE: **A US Navy Sikorsky HO3-S1 parked in front of a Royal Air Force Handley-Page Hastings transport aircraft.**

complete redesign by Westland and was powered by a British-built Alvis Leonides radial piston engine.

In 1953, production ceased after 139 machines had been completed. The Dragonfly was the first UK-built helicopter to enter service with the British military. The Royal Navy was the first UK military operator with the HR.1, an Air Sea Rescue (ASR) version. The first RN squadron to fly the Dragonfly was No.705 Naval Air Squadron (NAS) formed at Royal Naval Air Station Gosport (HMS *Siskin*), near Portsmouth. The rescue version of the type was equipped with a powered hoist with a lifting capacity of 170kg/375lb.

The HC.2 operated by the Royal Air Force was similar to the RN version but fitted with carriers for the casualty evacuation role. The prime ASR version in Royal Navy service was the HR.3, and a total of 58 were built. This machine and the HC.4 in RAF service were fitted with all-metal rotor blades and hydraulic servo-assisted controls.

During the Malaya Emergency, RAF machines were deployed on operations from 1950, and in three and a half years the type was used to evacuate 675 casualties, transport over 4,000 passengers and move 38,100kg/84,000lb of supplies in some 6,000 sorties.

The Widgeon was developed from the Dragonfly by Westland as a private venture, but although it was an excellent machine, only a small number (15) were built.

The Sikorsky S-51 and the Westland Dragonfly were exported to Argentina, Australia, Belgium, Brazil, Canada, Ceylon, Egypt, France, Iraq, Italy, Japan, the Philippines, Thailand and Yugoslavia.

An early pre-production YH-5A, serial number 43-46620, is preserved at the National Museum of the US Air Force at Wright Patterson Air Force Base in Ohio.

ABOVE: **A Westland S-51 Dragonfly during flight trials with stretcher-carrying panniers mounted on each side of the aircraft. The type was used operationally by the RAF.**

Sikorsky S-51

First flight: August 18, 1943 (XR-5)
Power: Pratt & Whitney radial piston engine
Armament: None
Size: Rotor diameter – 14.63m/48ft
    Length – 17.4m/57ft 1in
    Height – 3.96m/13ft
Weights: Empty – 1,718kg/3,780lb
    Take-off –2,193kg/4,825lb (maximum)
Performance: Speed – 171kph/106mph (maximum)
    Service ceiling – 4,390m/14,400ft
    Range – 580km/360 miles

Sikorsky H-19 Chickasaw

In May 1949, the Sikorsky Aircraft Corporation was given what appeared to be the impossible task of designing an all-new helicopter for the US Air Force in just seven months. The new machine, Sikorsky model S-55, had to carry ten passengers as well as a crew of two. The task was achieved, and on November 10, 1949, the first of five YH-19 prototypes was flown for the first time. The YH-19 was the first large helicopter manufactured by the company, and was to remain in military service into the 1990s.

After successful trials, the USAF ordered a batch of 55, designated H-19A and fitted with the same Pratt & Whitney R-1340-57 Wasp radial piston engine used to power the prototype machines. On this and all later models, the engine was accessed through distinctive clamshell doors, which made routine servicing a relatively easy task – an engine change would take just two hours. The location of the engine in the nose allowed the cockpit to be positioned at the centre of gravity, thereby allowing a range of loads to be carried within the helicopter without stability being affected. The

engine was linked to the main rotor gearbox by a long drive-shaft.

Ease of maintenance and versatility were fundamental to the design of the machine. For example, each undercarriage leg was fitted with an independent shock absorber which improved stability during landing and take-off.

The S-55 was of pod-and-boom design, and was constructed with the extensive use of magnesium and aluminium to reduce the structural weight and therefore enhance performance. Early examples can be identified by the lack of a distinctive triangular-shaped fillet where the tail boom meets the fuselage, and by the

ABOVE LEFT AND RIGHT: **The YH-19 prototype lacked the triangular fillet that connected the fuselage to the tail boom, which featured in production machines. The prototype's horizontal stabilizer on the starboard side of the tail was replaced by two anhedral fins in production machines.**

addition of the inverted fins on the underside of the tail boom – these were fitted to improve lateral stability.

Production continued for the USAF, with 270 examples of the H-19B powered by the Wright R-1300-3 Cyclone radial piston engine driving a larger-diameter main rotor. An order for 72 of the H-19C followed from the US Army and, following tradition, the type was named Chickasaw. In 1962,

RIGHT: **Each of the four legs on the wide stable undercarriage was fitted with a shock absorber for maximum stability during take-off, landing and taxiing. Floats could be fitted or permanent amphibious landing gear could be installed.**

ABOVE: **The Sikorsky H-19B was powered by a Wright R-1300-3 Cyclone radial piston engine driving a larger-diameter main rotor.**

ABOVE: **The engine on the S-55 was mounted at an angle in the nose behind clamshell doors for easy servicing. The drive-shaft to the gearbox ran through the cabin.**

under the Department of Defense (DoD) directive, the type was redesignated UH-19C and UH-19D. The type was the first transport helicopter to enter service with the US Army.

The US Navy also procured versions of the S-55, having signed a contract in April 1950. Between 1950 and 1958, the USN took delivery of 119, including ten HO4S-1 (H-19A) and 61 of the HO4S-2 (30 of these were built for the US Coast Guard as the HO4S-3G). The US Marine Corps received 90 of the HRS-2 and 84 of the HRS-3, which were used as troop transports and built to the same specification as the HO4S. Although the SAR variant was deployed by the USN towards the end of the Korean War and saw limited service, the USMC gained operational experience with the type on assault missions. The UH-19 Chickasaw

remained in service during the early years of the Vietnam War.

In Korea, the type proved to be so versatile that it allowed the US military the opportunity to develop various operational techniques, including landing troops in enemy territory, transport and recovery of damaged vehicles, moving equipment and for aircrew rescue. On September 13, 1951, helicopters were used for the first time to transport troops into combat when US Marines were deployed to a hill under attack by Chinese forces. In the CASEVAC role, up to six stretchers could be accommodated.

In March 1952, the type was certified for civilian operations and offered in two versions, the S-55A powered by a Pratt & Whitney R-1340 Cyclone radial piston engine and the S-55B powered by a

Wright R-1300-3 Wasp radial piston engine. Later that year, the type was flown by Sabena, the national airline of Belgium, on the first commercial rotary wing services when the type was operated between Belgium, the Netherlands, France and Germany.

A total of 1,067 of all military versions built were operated by the air services of some 30 nations. In the UK, Westland Aircraft built 547 under licence. Licence production was also carried out in France by SNCA, and many of these machines were used by French forces during the war in Algeria.

ABOVE: **The US Marine Corps used the type to develop air assault operations in the Korean War. The type went on to serve for a short period in Vietnam.**

Sikorsky H-19B Chickasaw	

First flight: November 10, 1949
Power: 1 x Wright R-1300-3 Wasp radial piston engine
Armament: None
Size: Rotor diameter – 16.16m/53ft
Length – 12.85m/42ft 2in
Height – 4.07m/13ft 3in
Weights: Empty – 2,381kg/5,250lb
Take-off – 3,583kg/7,900lb (maximum)
Performance: Speed – 180kph/112mph (maximum)
Service ceiling – 3,940m/13,000ft
Range – 580km/360 miles

Sikorsky CH-37 Mojave

The Sikorsky CH-37 Mojave (company designation S-56) was the first heavy-lift helicopter built for the US Marine Corps, and was for a decade the largest helicopter flying outside of the Soviet Union. Until late 1961, the CH-37 was the largest helicopter in the US military inventory.

The type was produced to meet a USMC requirement for an assault helicopter with the capacity to transport 26 fully equipped troops, and was the first twin-engine type designed by Sikorsky.

The machine was powered by two Pratt & Whitney R-2800 Double Wasp radial piston engines of the type used by many World War II combat aircraft. The engines were not positioned inside the fuselage but were fitted in nacelles, which also housed the retractable main undercarriage, mounted on stub wings. If gunfire hit the five-blade rotor main rotor, it was designed to continue providing lift with one blade missing. For transportation, the main rotor blades were folded back along the top of the

ABOVE: **For many years, the Sikorsky CH-37A Mojave was the largest helicopter in service with the US military forces.**

fuselage. A large four-blade anti-torque rotor was mounted at the tail. This was a unique approach to designing a heavy-lift helicopter. The XHR2S-1 prototype was first flown on December 18, 1953.

The engine arrangement gave an unobstructed cargo area in the fuselage, and up to three jeep-type light vehicles loaded through large clamshell doors in the nose could be transported. Alternatively, up to 907kg/2,000lb of cargo could be carried. Two 1,136-litre/300-gallon auxiliary fuel tanks containing extra fuel for the engines were mounted flush with the fuselage in line with the undercarriage.

The US Army had also evaluated the prototype in 1954, and were sufficiently impressed to order 94 machines designated H-37A Mojave. Deliveries to the 4th Medium Helicopter Transportation Company (MHTC) began in 1958, and all deliveries were completed by mid-1960. All US Army

LEFT: **The CH-37B Mojave was fitted with an auto-stabilizer system manufactured by Lear.**

machines were later upgraded to B standard by the installation of crash-proof fuel tanks and auto-stabilization equipment manufactured by Lear, which allowed the H-37A to be loaded and unloaded while held in the hover.

In 1962, all military aircraft in US service were given standardized designations, and under this system the type became the CH-37C.

Two machines in US Navy service were converted to HR2S-1W configuration by fitting an AN/APS-20E radar scanner in a radome mounted under the nose for evaluation for Airborne Early Warning (AEW) operations. Airframe vibration was a severe problem, and the trials were cancelled.

In 1963, the US Army briefly deployed four CH-37Bs to Vietnam for the recovery, often from behind enemy lines, of downed US aircraft. The CH-37 had a comparatively short service life, being phased out in the late 1960s. All of the type were replaced in US Army service with the Sikorsky CH-54 Tarhe, a lighter

ABOVE: **The engines of the CH-37 Mojave were mounted in nacelles which also housed the retractable undercarriage.**

machine powered by two turboshaft engines, which had a lifting capacity five times greater than the CH-37.

In developing the CH-37 Mojave, the Sikorsky team gained valuable experience which they were able to use in the design and production of later large single-rotor helicopters for the US military. Total production of the CH-37, including prototypes, amounted to 150 airframes, 94 delivered to the US Army and 55 to the USMC.

ABOVE: **The CH-37 Mojave was used to transport light vehicles and troops, as well as to carry larger items, including light aircraft as an under slung load. The type was the last large helicopter to be piston-engine-powered.**

Sikorsky CH-37B Mojave

First flight: December 18, 1953
Power: 2 x Pratt & Whitney R-2800-54 Double Wasp radial piston engines
Armament: None
Size: Rotor diameter – 21.95m/72ft
Length – 19.59m/64ft 3in
Height – 6.71m/22ft
Weights: Empty – 9,449kg/20,831lb
Take-off –14,090kg/31,063lb (maximum)
Performance: Speed – 209kph/130mph (maximum)
Service ceiling – 2,650m/8,700ft
Range – 233km/145 miles

Sikorsky H-34 Choctaw

The Sikorsky H-34 (company model S-58) was originally designed for anti-submarine warfare, later serving in transport and firefighting, rescue of astronauts, disaster recovery and even flying presidents. The machine was flown for the first time on March 8, 1954, and in September of that year the first of them entered service with the US Navy, initially designated HSS-1 Seabat (anti-submarine) and HUS-1 Seahorse (transport). The USN designations for the type included those in service with the US Marine Corps and US Coast Guard. In 1962, a Department of Defense (DoD) common designation system for US military aircraft was introduced, and the H-34 became the SH-34 Seabat, the UH-34 Seahorse and the CH-34 Choctaw.

The Sikorsky H-34 was built as a larger, more powerful single-engine successor to the H-19 Chickasaw and was one of the last piston-engined helicopters to enter service with the military.

ABOVE: **The Sikorsky S-58 was sold to military and civilian operators around the world. The US Marine Corps (USMC) operated the type as the HUS-1 and UH-34D.**

The USN machines were used for the recovery of capsules and astronauts during the NASA Mercury space programme. An SH-34G Seabat rescued Alan B. Shepard, Jr. from the sea after his historic suborbital flight in 1961. Later in the same year, the hatch on the Mercury 4 capsule opened too early and the capsule filled with water. Although the Seabat was renowned for an excellent weight-lifting capability, the capsule, Liberty Bell 7, proved too heavy and it was released and sank beneath the waves.

The airframe of the CH-34 used magnesium in the structure, and as this is a particularly flammable metal, the type was therefore vulnerable to ground fire. This is perhaps one of reasons that the US Army never deployed any of the type to Vietnam, choosing to operate the Piasecki CH-21 Shawnee before the introduction into service of the Bell UH-1 Iroquois. Ironically, however, a number of the type had been sold

LEFT: **A damaged Cessna L-19 Bird Dog liaison and observation aircraft being attached to a Sikorsky CH-34 Choctaw. The lifting capability was impressive.**

LEFT: **A Sikorsky UH-34D Seahorse viewed over South Vietnam from the door gunner's position of an accompanying UH-34D. Both helicopters are from Marine Medium Transport Squadron 162 (HMM-162). The aircraft is armed with a 7.62mm M60 machine gun.**
ABOVE: **A US Army CH-34C Choctaw in flight.**

to the Army of the Republic of Vietnam (ARV), although it is reported they were not widely used due to a lack of spare parts and maintenance problems. However, despite being phased out of US Army service, the USMC continued to use the CH-34 even after the Tet Offensive in 1968. The H-34 was highly regarded by USMC aircrews, who liked the aircraft's simplicity and reliability – so much so that the phrase "give me a HUS" or "cut me a HUS" came to mean "help me out" in common Marine parlance, referring to the HUS Seahorse. All H-34s were retired from US military service by the early 1970s.

In June 1967, the CH-34 was deployed to great effect during the Israeli Six-Days War. In 1959, Israel received 24 S-58s (the civil variant of the H-34), which had been originally intended for West Germany but diverted to the Levant. By 1967, the Israeli Air Force had No.124 (Rolling Sword) Squadron established with a complement of 28 aircraft. As the war continued over the week of June 5–10, these helicopters went from merely evacuating stranded pilots after a crash to dropping Israeli paratroops behind enemy lines to capture Sharm-El-Sheik in Egypt, as well as the Golan Heights in Syria.

Although the piston Choctaws were only in military use for about 20 years, they were manufactured under licence in both France and in the United Kingdom as the Westland Wessex.

Sikorsky H-34A Choctaw

First flight: March 8, 1954
Power: 1 x Wright R-1820-84 radial piston engine
Armament: Machine-gun, rockets
Size: Rotor diameter – 17.0m/56ft
Length of fuselage – 17.27m/56ft 7in
Height – 4.85m/15ft 11in
Weights: Empty – 3,583kg/7,900lb
Take-off – 6,350kg/14,000lb (maximum)
Performance: Speed – 198kph/123mph (maximum)
Service ceiling – 2,900m/9,515ft
Range – 397km/250 miles

ABOVE: **A number of CH-34 airframes were remanufactured and converted to turbine power for military and civilian operators as the T-58. The fuselage was lengthened and fitted with a Pratt & Whitney Canada PT6T-3 Twin-Pac turboshaft engine installation.**

LEFT: **An impressive formation of US Navy SH-3H Sea King Anti-Submarine Warfare (ASW) helicopters from Helicopter Anti-Submarine Squadron (HS-12). The ASW role was the Sea King's original purpose, but it has proved to be a most versatile design.**

Sikorsky SH-3 Sea King

In 1957, the Sikorsky Aircraft Corporation was awarded a contract to design and develop an all-weather amphibious helicopter for the US Navy. The Sikorsky XHSS-2 (company model S-61) was flown for the first time on March 11, 1959. In 1962, the company received an order to build seven YHSS-2 development aircraft. A production order for 245 machines was placed, and the HSS-2 became operational with the USN in June 1961. In 1962, under a directive from the Department of Defense (DoD), the type was designated SH-3.

The SH-3 was powered by two General Electric T58-GE-10 turboshaft engines driving a five-blade main rotor and a conventional tail rotor.

For transport and stowage, the main rotor folded back along the fuselage. The tail boom also folded. The lower fuselage (hull) was boat-shaped to allow amphibious operation. A sponson on each side housed the retractable main undercarriage and inflatable flotation bags. A 272kg/600lb capacity rescue winch is mounted above the main door. In the transport role the SH-3 can accommodate 28 fully equipped troops, and in the SAR role up to 22 passengers or nine stretchers and

LEFT: **A very high-profile search and rescue mission – an SH-3A from HC-1 preparing to recover the Apollo 17 space capsule and crew after the last flight to the moon, December 19, 1972.** RIGHT: **A US Navy SH-3G Sea King being refuelled from the deck of a warship while at the hover.**

two attendants can be carried. A load of 3,630kg/8,003lb can be lifted by an automatic touchdown release cargo hook mounted under the fuselage.

The Sea King was primarily developed to locate and attack submarines of the Soviet Navy. The aircraft was unique in that it could carry both Anti-Submarine Warfare (ASW) detection equipment and the weapons to attack – a mission that normally required two aircraft. The SH-3 was equipped with AQS-13B/E dipping sonar, ARR-75 sonobuoy receiver, ASQ-81 Magnetic Anomaly Detector (MAD) and an AKT-22 data link. The ASW dipping sonar is lowered through a hatch in the hull. An "attitude-hold" autopilot and sonar coupler link to a radar

altimeter, and Doppler radar are fitted to allow the aircraft to be hovered at the exact altitude over a target. In the anti-submarine role, the SH-3 is armed with Mk 44/46 torpedoes and even the B-57 nuclear depth charge. The Sea Eagle or Exocet missile is carried for attack against enemy shipping.

The SH-3A is flown by US Marine Corps unit HMX-1 to operate transport flights under the call sign "Marine One", for the President of the United States. A replacement for the SH-3A is currently being sought under the VXX programme.

The type has been operated by many military forces, including those of Argentina, Brazil, Denmark, India, Iran, Iraq, Malaysia, Peru, Saudia Arabia and

ABOVE: **A Brazilian Navy SH-3 Sea King and an SH-3H from Helicopter Anti-Submarine Squadron 9 (HS-9). Dipping sonar is being lowered from both machines during a joint anti-submarine warfare exercise.**

Spain. At the time of writing, a number of the type remain in service with military operators around the world.

The Canadian military procured 41 machines to be assembled by United Aircraft of Canada and designated CH-124. The Sea King was built under licence in Italy by Agusta as the AS-61 and by Mitsubishi, again under licence, in Japan as the S-61. Westland Helicopters obtained a licence to produce the type in the UK and went on to develop a UK Sea King.

Between 1959 and 1980, Sikorsky built some 800 of the type in a number of variants for the military and civilian markets.

ABOVE: **The type was built under licence in Italy by Agusta as the AS-61 for the Italian Navy. For stowage on board a ship, the main rotor blades can be folded back, and part of the tail boom also folds to reduce space.**

Sikorsky SH-3H Sea King

First flight: March 11, 1959
Power: 2 x General Electric T58-GE-10 turboshaft
Armament: Depth charges, anti-shipping missiles, torpedoes
Size: Rotor diameter – 18.9m/62ft
Length overall – 22.15m/72ft 8in
Height – 5.13m/16ft 9in
Weights: Empty – 4,428kg/9,762lb
Take-off – 9,526kg/21,000lb (maximum)
Performance: Speed – 267kph/166mph (maximum)
Service ceiling – 4,481m/14,700ft
Range – 1000km/621 miles

Sikorsky HH-3E Jolly Green Giant

TheS-61R helicopter was derived from the CH-3 (S-61) Sea King which had been in service with the US Navy since 1961. In 1958, the Sikorsky Aircraft Corporation began design and development of the type as a private venture. The fuselage was redesigned to be much larger, with a rear cargo door and a loading ramp. The lower fuselage was boat-shaped, as on the SH-3, and manufactured to be watertight. On June 17, 1963, the prototype S-61R was flown for the first time. Before the development flying programme was completed, the US Air Force placed an order for 22 aircraft, designated CH-3C, to be operated by rescue and recovery squadrons. A total of 133 were built.

The USAF ordered 42 of the CH-3E, an improved version for long-range rescue missions, and also 41 of the earlier CH-3C were remanufactured to CH-3E specification. Eventually all of these machines would be converted to HH-3E standard. The USAF then purchased 50 of the HH-3E version for specialized Combat Search and Rescue (CSAR) operations in South-east Asia. The MH-3E was a specifically equipped version for missions operated by US Special Forces.

In August 1965, the US Coast Guard (USCG) ordered 40 of the HH-3F version equipped with AN/APN-195 search radar for all-weather Air Sea Rescue (ASR) operations. USCG crews operating the HH-3F named the type "Pelican".

TOP: A Sikorsky HH-3E Jolly Green Giant is the specialized version built for Combat Search and Rescue (CSAR) operations. ABOVE: An early production Sikorsky CH-53E Jolly Green Giant on a flight near the Pentagon, the headquarters of the US Department of Defense (DoD) in Arlington County, Virginia.

ABOVE: **The Sikorsky HH-3F was given the name "Pelican" for its service in the US Coast Guard.**
RIGHT: **On May 6, 1994, the type was withdrawn from service, marking the end of USCG amphibious operations. Serial number 1430 was the first HH-3F to enter service with the USCG.**

The HH-3E was fitted with titanium protective armour and a defensive armament of three 7.62mm M60 machine-guns. The type was fitted with two external fuel tanks which could be jettisoned, self-sealing fuel tanks under the cabin floor and a high-speed rescue hoist. The HH-3E could accommodate 25 fully equipped troops or 15 stretchers and two attendants. The HH-3E was given the name "Jolly Green Giant" by crews operating the type in Vietnam.

The HH-3E was the first helicopter to be produced with a retractable fuel probe for air-to-air refuelling, and when fitted with external fuel tanks had a range limited only by the endurance of the crew. In 1967, to demonstrate the long-range capability of the type, two were flown non-stop from New York to the Paris Air Show, a distance of 6,872km/4,270 miles. This operation, during which each machine was air-to-air refuelled nine times, set a long-distance record for helicopters.

In 1967, the first aircraft of the type arrived in Vietnam, and were operated by the USAF from Udorn Air Base in

Thailand and Da Nang Air Base in South Vietnam. The long-range HH-3E enabled the USAF helicopters to conduct CSAR operations in Laos, Cambodia, South Vietnam and even North Vietnam. In 1970, US Army Special Forces were flown in an HH-3E Jolly Green Giant as part of a force which attempted the rescue of captured US personnel from a Prisoner of War (PoW) camp at Son Tay, located 37km/23 miles to the west of Hanoi, the capital of North Vietnam.

Twenty-five years later, during Operation Desert Storm (first Gulf War) in 1991, the HH-3E Jolly Green Giant was deployed to operate CSAR missions, during which 251 Coalition forces aircrew were rescued.

A licence was agreed between Sikorsky and Agusta to build the HH-3F in Italy as the AS-61R. In 1974,

production began, and 22 machines were built to replace Grumman HU-16 Albatross amphibious aircraft used in the SAR role by the Italian Air Force.

By 1995, all of the type in US service had been retired and replaced with the Sikorsky HH-60G Pave Hawk.

Sikorsky HH-3E

First flight: June 17, 1963
Power: 2 x General Electric T58-GE-10 turboshaft
Armament: 7.62mm M60 machine-gun
Size: Rotor diameter – 18.79m/62ft
    Length overall – 22.15m/72ft 8in
    Height – 5.46m/18ft 1in
Weights: Empty – 4,429kg/9,763lb
    Take-off – 10,002 kg/22,050lb (maximum)
Performance: Speed – 262kph/164mph (maximum)
    Service ceiling – 3,636m/12,000ft
    Range – 965km/600 miles

Sikorsky CH-54 Tarhe

The S-60 prototype powered by two Pratt & Whitney R2800-54 radial piston engines (as used on the H-37 Mojave) was flown for first time on March 25, 1959. The machine crashed on April 3, 1961, but Sikorsky had already commenced development of the larger and more powerful S-64 which could lift an impressive 5,443kg/12,000lb payload. The first of six pre-production YCH-54As ordered by the US Army was flown on May 6, 1962. The machines were powered by two Pratt & Whitney T73-P-1 turboshaft engines driving a six-blade main rotor. Following a successful test-flying programme, the US Army placed an order for 54 of the production CH-54As. The West German armed forces evaluated the type but did not proceed with an order. The US Army then went on to order 37 of the heavier CH-54Bs fitted with the more powerful Pratt & Whitney T73-P-700 turboshaft engine, which had sufficient power to allow single-engine operations. Following a US Army tradition, the type was named "Tarhe" after a chief of the Wyandot, a Native American Indian tribe.

The CH-54 was an early example of modular design, as the power unit and even the cockpit section could be easily removed and fitted to another airframe in the field. A window across the rear wall of the cockpit allowed the co-pilot to operate the cargo winch and observe loading operations. Cargo could be handled in this manner with the helicopter held in the hover. The Universal Military Pod (UMP), a multi-purpose cargo container specifically designed to fit under the fuselage of a CH-54, could accommodate 87 fully equipped troops for helicopter assault operations. The UMP could also be configured as a combat command post or as a field hospital. Later, the UMP was fitted with a cargo hook to carry an under-slung load. On November 4, 1971, a CH-54B was flown to a world record altitude for helicopters of 11,010m/36,122ft.

The CH-54B was deployed around the world by the US Army, and in Vietnam the type was used operationally by the 478th and the 291st Aviation Companies to recover 380 downed US military aircraft.

ABOVE: **The Tarhe retained the rear-view window for the co-pilot first fitted in the S-60. On November 4, 1971, a CH-54B set the record for the highest level helicopter flight at 11,010m/36,122ft.**

The specialized BLU-82B Daisy Cutter, a 6,000kg/15,000lb bomb design to flatten an area of forest or scrub, was test dropped from a CH-54A Tarhe over Vietnam. The weapon was later dropped only from the Lockheed C-130 Hercules.

Budget cuts led to the cancellation of the Heavy Lift Helicopter (HLH) programme. Operations with the CH-54B Tarhe continued, but were supplemented by the Boeing CH-47 Chinook which eventually replaced the type in the heavy lift role.

The type had also been manufactured by the Sikorsky Aircraft Corporation for the civilian market as the S-64 Skycrane. Many ex-military machines were purchased by civilian operators. Erickson Air-Crane Inc. of Portland, Oregon, negotiated to buy the production rights and certification from the Sikorsky Aircraft Corporation, and continues to manufacture the type

as the Erickson S-64 Aircrane. The company also operates the largest fleet of S-64 helicopters in the world which are used to lift large loads. Machines in the Erickson fleet can be equipped with water-bombing equipment for firefighting operations.

The five-blade rotor, tail rotor and drive system from the CH-54B were used basically unchanged on the very successful Sikorsky S-65 (CH-53) series of helicopters. In 1958, the same equipment had been licensed by Westland Helicopters for use on the Westminster helicopter, of which only two prototypes were built. First flown on June 15, 1958, the type was eventually scrapped and the parts returned to Sikorsky.

ABOVE: The Sikorsky CH-54 was an ingenious design – to save airframe weight and for ease of servicing, the engines, gearbox and drive to the tail rotor were left uncovered. BELOW: The Universal Military Pod (UMP) multi-purpose container was specifically designed for the CH-54. The UMP was used to transport troops or cargo, or could be equipped as a command post or a portable field hospital.

Sikorsky CH-54B Tarhe

First flight: May 9, 1962
Power: 2 x Pratt & Whitney T73-P-700 turboshaft
Armament: None
Size: Rotor diameter – 21.95m/72ft
 Length – 26.97m/88ft 6in
 Height – 7.75m/25ft 5in
Weights: Empty – 8,981kg/19,800lb
 Take-off – 21,319kg/47,000lb (maximum)
Performance: Speed – 241kph/150mph (maximum)
 Service ceiling – 5,587m/18,330ft
 Range – 370km/230 miles

LEFT: **A US Marine Corps CH-53 Sea Stallion approaching the flight deck of the Nimitz-class aircraft carrier USS *Harry S. Truman* (CVN-75) for landing. Note the fixed refuelling probe in position on the nose of the aircraft.**

Sikorsky CH-53 Sea Stallion

In 1960, the US Navy began the process of identifying a replacement for the Sikorsky CH-37 Mojave in the heavy-lift role. In January 1961, a Tri-Service Assault Transport Program (TSATP) was proposed, and the type selected for development was the Vought-Hiller-Ryan XC-43, a four-engine tilt-wing experimental aircraft. The Bureau of Naval Weapons (BuWeps), acting on behalf of the USMC, initiated the Heavy Helicopter Experimental Program (HHXP). In August 1962, a decision was made to contract Sikorsky to develop the S-65A as the

YHC-53A. The type was first flown on October 14, 1966, at the Sikorsky airfield in Stratford, Connecticut. Deliveries of the production CH-53A to the USMC began in 1966.

Sikorsky decided to use the proven six-blade main rotor system, gearbox, transmission and tail rotor from the S-64 Skycrane/CH-54 Tarhe. The fuselage was of similar dimensions to that of the HH-3 and, although watertight, it was designed only for an emergency landing on water. A door was fitted in the starboard side and armour was fitted to crew areas

and to protect vital equipment. The mechanical flight controls were backed up by three hydraulic systems. On US Navy and USMC machines, the main rotor and tail boom were designed to fold for stowage on board a ship.

The first USMC squadron (HMH-463) to receive the type was deployed to South-east Asia, and from mid-January 1967 operated a four aircraft detachment from a base near Da Nang, South Vietnam. On January 25, a CH-53A was deployed to recover a damaged Sikorsky UH-34 Choctaw from a ship and airlift the machine to a land base for repair. By the end of May, the four helicopters had been used to carry out over 100 successful recovery operations of 72 Sikorsky UH-34 Choctaws, 13 Piasecki CH-46 Sea Knights, 16 Bell UH-1E Iroquois and a number of fixed-wing aircraft.

LEFT: **A Sikorsky CH-53G in service with the German Army. All the machines are being upgraded to allow the type to remain in front-line service for more years than originally planned.**

LEFT: **Large and relatively slow-moving helicopters can be vulnerable to attack from heat-seeking missiles. Here, decoy flares are being fired from a CH-53D Sea Stallion during testing of the AN/ALC-39 Countermeasures Dispensing System (CDS).**

The fact that just four helicopters were able to retrieve such a large number of valuable military assets in such a short period was proof of the wisdom of developing this very capable heavy-lift helicopter. On May 22, 1967, the rest of the squadron arrived and with a total of 26 helicopters on strength, the unit was called on to undertake a wider range of heavy-lift duties, including transporting up to 38 combat troops or moving heavy artillery weapons slung under the fuselage on a cargo hook.

Despite an impressive combat record, only some 150 of the CH-53A were built. The D model was fitted with the more powerful General Electric T64-GE-413 turboshaft engine, which allowed up to 55 fully equipped troops or a heavier cargo load to be transported. Delivery of the improved CH-53D began in March

1969. Compared to other types, the CH-53D had a relatively short production run, which ended in early 1972 after some 120 had been completed. Virtually all of these helicopters were deployed to the war in South-east Asia.

The USN operated the RH-53D, equipped with an air-to-air refuelling probe, for mine-countermeasures operations. Only the US Air Force operated the CH-53C for Special Forces missions and later as a cargo transport. The CH-53D was built for the (West) German army, and the first 20 were assembled from Sikorsky-supplied parts by VFW-Fokker. The German company Speyer then assembled a further 90 machines. In total, 112 were acquired (including two supplied by Sikorsky) and were designated CH-53G. Versions of the CH-53D were also exported to

Austria and sold on to Iran (RH-53D), Israel (S-65C-3) and Mexico (S-65C-3), which were purchased from Israel.

The Sikorsky CH-53D Sea Stallion was used extensively for seaborne and land-based operations, and was to remain the prime heavy-lift helicopter for the USMC until the Sikorsky CH-53E Super Stallion, an improved three-engine variant, entered service in 1981. The CH-53D continued to be used in front-line service to transport combat equipment and personnel, and was used extensively during Operation Desert Storm (first Gulf War) in 1991.

In 2012 the US Marine Corps retired the CH-53 after forty years of service, and in 2021 the Israeli Ministry of Defense announced the selection of the CH-53K to replace the nation's S-65C-3 Ya'sur fleet.

ABOVE: **A CH-53A Sea Stallion on a recently installed landing mat at a USMC fire support base positioned on the top of a mountain in South Vietnam.**

Sikorsky CH-53A Sea Stallion

First flight: October 14, 1964
Power: 2 x General Electric T64-6 turboshaft
Armament: 7.62mm M60 or 12.7mm machine-guns
Size: Rotor diameter – 22.02m/72ft 3in
Length (with rotors turning) – 26.9m/86ft 3in
Height – 7.6m/24ft 11in
Weights: Empty – 10,181kg/22,444lb
Take-off – 16,965kg/37,400lb (maximum)
Performance: Speed – 315kph/196mph (maximum)
Service ceiling – 6,401m/21,000ft
Range – 869km/540 miles

Sikorsky UH-60 Black Hawk

The Sikorsky UH-60 Black Hawk tactical assault helicopter is one of the most significant military helicopters ever to be produced. The type has been operational for over 40 years and continues in service with the US military and other forces around the world. In 1991, during Operation Desert Storm (first Gulf War), it was reported that over 1,000,000 troops were transported by Sikorsky UH-60 Black Hawk helicopters.

In 1972, the US Army initiated the Utility Tactical Transport Aircraft System (UTTAS) competition for find a replacement for the Bell UH-1 Iroquois. The design selected was the Sikorsky S-70. The prototype YUH-60A was first flown on October 17, 1974, and after

extensive flight and development testing the type entered US Army service the 101st Airborne Division as the UH-60A in June 1979. Following a US Army tradition, the type was named "Black Hawk" after the Native American Indian tribe.

The UH-60A was flown by a crew of two pilots and two crewmen, and accommodated 11 fully equipped troops. Operating in battlefront conditions is dangerous, and during a mission a helicopter could easily sustain serious damage, sometimes enough to cause the aircraft to crash. With this is mind, Sikorsky built a number of survivability features into the machine. The rotor head and rotor blades were designed to take and survive direct machine-gun

ABOVE: **A UH-60L Black Hawk helicopter flying a low-level mission over Iraq. The L model is a UH-60A with upgraded engines, stronger gearbox and an updated flight control system.**

fire. Speed is vital when dropping troops (large cabin doors aid rapid egress), and the undercarriage was designed to take a vertical impact of up to 45kph/28mph. The engine exhausts are covered by infra-red suppressors to disguise the heat signature of exhaust gases and reduce the threat from a heat-seeking missile. The engines are mounted apart, again to reduce the risk of battle damage. The fuselage has a low-profile shape to reduce target area. The UH-60A Black Hawk can also carry a substantial cargo load internally or slung on cargo hooks mounted on the underside of the fuselage.

In 1987, the US Army ordered the improved UH-60L and included all the modifications and upgrades previously made to the UH-60A in service. The UH-60L was fitted with the more powerful General Electric T700-GE-701C engine, allowing the cargo lifting capacity to be increased by 454kg/1,000lb up to an impressive 4,100kg/9,000lb. This was a vital improvement as troops were equipped with more and heavier equipment. Sikorsky began production of the UH-60L Black Hawk in 1989.

Work on the further improved UH-60M began in 2001, with the intention of keeping the type as a front-line

ABOVE: **Two UH-60 Black Hawk helicopters taking off after delivering supplies and troops to the 155th Brigade Combat Team positioned at Forward Operating Base Hotel, near Najaf, Iraq.**

helicopter into the 2020s. The UH-60M was fitted with the upgraded General Electric T700-GE-701D engine. Other improvements included a strengthened cabin floor, impact absorbing crew seats, jettisonable cockpit doors and a wire strike protection system. An avionics upgrade included the fitting of a Global Positioning System (GPS) and an Automatic Direction Finder (ADF). For transportation or stowage on board a ship, the main and tail rotor blades, tail boom and stabilator are designed to be foldable. In July 2006, the first UH-60M Black Hawk was delivered to the US Army for evaluation, and this was followed by an order for 1,227 machines.

The Black Hawk can be fitted with stub wings on the upper fuselage to mount a range of additional weapons, including unguided rocket pods, anti-tank missiles or machine-gun pods. External fuel tanks can be carried, which substantially increase the operational range of the type.

The US Army first used the UH-60 in battle during Operation Urgent Fury, the invasion of Grenada, October 25, 1983,

RIGHT: **The UH-60Q operated by the US Army is a sophisticated air ambulance fitted to carry six casualties on stretchers. The type has an oxygen-generating system and other specialized emergency treatment equipment.**

and then for Operation Just Cause, the invasion of Panama, December 20, 1989. In 1991, during Operation Desert Storm, the US Army deployed some 300 of the type in the largest-ever air-assault operation. The UH-60 was used on the battlefield again during Operation Iraqi Freedom, the invasion of Iraq, in September, 2003. The type was also used in Afghanistan during the Operation Enduring Freedom. The UH-60 has also been used in action by US forces in Somalia, the Balkans and Haiti. Export customers include the Columbian National Police, Air Force

and Army, who use the helicopter in the war against drug operators and guerrilla forces. A gunship version has been developed for these operations. The Israeli military have used ex-US Army UH-60 Black Hawk helicopters for air operations against targets in Lebanon. The Mexican Air Force acquired the type for Special Forces operations against drug runners; the Federal Police and Mexican Navy also operate the type. The S-70i Black Hawk, an international military version, is assembled by PZL Mielec, a subsidiary of Sikorsky, in Poland.

LEFT AND ABOVE: **The tail rotor is angled at 20 degrees off the vertical. It creates thrust to allow for changes to the machine's centre of gravity as fuel is used and the aircraft becomes lighter. The automatic all-flying stabilator senses changes in airspeed and operates during the hover to keep the helicopter stable.**

Sikorsky UH-60A Black Hawk

First flight: October 17, 1974
Power: 2 x General Electric T700-GE-700 turboshaft
Armament: 7.62mm machine-gun
Size: Rotor diameter – 16.36m/53ft 8in
Length – 19.76m/64ft 10in
Height – 5.13m/16ft 10in
Weights: Empty – 4,819kg/10,624lb
Take-off – 9,185kg/20,250lb (maximum)
Performance: Speed – 296kph/184mph (maximum)
Ceiling – 5,700m/19,000ft
Range – 600km/370 miles

Sikorsky HH-60G Pave Hawk

Since 1987, the HH-60G Pave Hawk has been the prime rescue helicopter in United States Air Force service. The type is operated by many elements of the USAF, including Air Combat Command (ACC), Pacific Air Force (PAF), Air Education and Training Command (AETC), US Air Force Europe (USAFE), Air National Guard (ANG) and the Air Force Reserve

Command (AFRC). During Operation Desert Storm, Pave Hawks provided combat search and rescue coverage for coalition forces in western Iraq, along the coast of Kuwait, the Persian Gulf and Saudi Arabia. The type was also deployed to execute emergency evacuation for US Navy SEAL combat teams inserted into Kuwait before the invasion was launched.

ABOVE: **The HH-60G Pave Hawk has an impressive performance, and is one of the few rescue helicopters equipped with an attack capability.**

The HH-60G Pave Hawk is primarily operated in the Combat Search and Rescue (CSAR) role to recover downed aircrew or any forces that have become isolated in enemy territory, day or night and in all weather conditions.

LEFT: **A rescue swimmer jumping from an HH-60J during a demonstration flight.** ABOVE: **The Sikorsky HH-60J Jayhawk is based on the SH-60 Seahawk helicopter, and replaced the HH-3F Pelican in US Coast Guard service.**

The HH-60G is a highly modified version of the UH-60 Black Hawk, and features an upgraded navigation suite that includes integrated Inertial Navigation System (INS), Global Positioning System (GPS) and Doppler navigation. The type is fitted with satellite, secure voice and Have Quick communications equipment. All HH-60G machines have an automatic flight control system, a Night Vision Goggles (NVG) facility and Forward Looking Infra-red (FLIR) sensors that allow the crew to fly the helicopter at low level on night operations. Additionally, the type is equipped with all-colour weather radar and an anti-icing system for the engine and main rotor blades, allowing the machine to be operated in all weather conditions.

Mission equipment includes a retractable inflight refuelling probe, internal auxiliary fuel tanks, two 7.62mm or 0.50in machine-guns, and a 3,600kg/8,000lb capacity cargo hook mounted under the fuselage. All are fitted with folding rotor blades for transportation (or stowage on board a ship), allowing a number to be carried in a Boeing C-17 Globemaster II or Lockheed C-5 Galaxy transport aircraft.

For improved survivability in combat conditions, all types have a radar warning receiver, infra-red jammer and a flare/chaff countermeasures dispensing system. Rescue equipment includes a hoist with a lifting capacity of 272kg/600lb and a personnel locating system which provides range and bearing information, and is compatible with the PRC-112 survival radio.

During the Kosovo war, Pave Hawks provided continuous CSAR coverage for NATO air forces, and were successfully used to recover two USAF pilots shot down and isolated behind enemy lines.

In March 2000, three HH-60G Pave Hawk helicopters were deployed to Mozambique in support of an international flood relief operation, and in 17 days a total of 240 missions were flown to deliver more than 162,752kg/358,400lb of humanitarian supplies. After Hurricane Katrina in September 2005, more than 20 of the type from USAF Reserve (USAFR) and Air National Guard (ANG) units were deployed in support of recovery operations in New Orleans and surrounding areas. Pave Hawk

ABOVE: **Two Sikorsky HH-60G Pave Hawk helicopters during Angel Thunder, a Combat Search and Rescue (CSAR) exercise held at Davis-Monthan Air Force Base (AFB) in the Arizona desert.**

crews flew operations around the clock for nearly a month, saving more than 2,900 civilians from the post-hurricane devastation.

The HH-60G was among the many different types of helicopter flown by the US military during Operation Iraqi Freedom in 2003. The type also saw service on the battlegrounds of Afghanistan and is being replaced by the UH-60M-derived HH-60W.

Sikorsky HH-60G Pave Hawk

First flight: October 17, 1974
Power: 2 x General Electric T700-GE-700 turboshaft
Armament: 7.62mm or 0.50in machine-gun
Size: Rotor diameter – 14.1m/53ft 7in
  Length – 17.1m/64ft 8in
  Height – 4.4m/16ft 8in
Weights: Empty – 7,260kg/16,000lb
  Take-off – 9,900kg/ 22,000lb (maximum)
Performance: Speed – 296kph/184mph (maximum)
  Service ceiling – 4,627m/14,000ft
  Range – 933km/580 miles

Sikorsky SH-60 Seahawk

The Seahawk is the standard anti-submarine helicopter operated from ships of the US Navy. In the late 1970s, the US Navy issued a requirement for an updated Light Airborne Multi-Purpose System (LAMPS) helicopter to operate from smaller naval escorts, and both Boeing and Sikorsky submitted design proposals. Following a fly-off,

the Sikorsky machine, a development of the UH-60A Black Hawk, was named the winner. While the SH-60 used the same basic airframe and components of the UH-60A, the type was far more expensive and complex due to the fitting of extensive avionics equipment and weapons systems. The USN took delivery of the SH-60B Seahawk in 1983.

ABOVE: An AGM-119 Penguin anti-shipping missile being launched from a Sikorsky SH-60 Seahawk. The Norwegian-built missile is designed to skim the surface at high speed, and has a range of 55km/34 miles.

The SH-60 is designed to be operated day and night at sea and in all weather conditions. The primary mission for the type is to search for enemy submarines or surface vessels that may pose a threat. The SH-60B Seahawk is equipped for anti-submarine warfare with a complex system of sensors, including a towed Magnetic Anomaly Detector (MAD) and air-launched sonobuoys (from a Sikorsky-designed launcher). The SH-60B is also used for Anti-Shipping Surveillance and Targeting (ASST) to extend the defensive radar range, and is operated from aircraft carriers, cruisers, destroyers and frigates of the USN. The SH-60 has a range of 600km/373 miles and can remain on station for several hours. The internal fuel tanks hold 2,250 litres/ 496 gallons, but the machine can be fitted with an inflight refuelling system. However, this can only be used when the helicopter is held in the hover.

LEFT: The Forward Looking Infra-Red (FLIR) turret is positioned on a mounting fitted to the nose of the SH-60 Seahawk. An ARN-146 positioning indicator forms part of the equipment.

LEFT: **A US Marine Corps Seahawk hovering above the ground to evacuate a simulated casualty during an exercise.**

unit fitted with a laser designator.

The SH-60B is operated by a pilot, a co-pilot/Airborne Tactical Officer (ATO) and an enlisted Aviation Systems Warfare Operator (ASWO). The type's roles includes SAR, Vertical Replenishment (VertRep) at sea and MEDEVAC missions. The SH-60B Seahawk completed its last US Navy active-duty deployment for the US Navy in April 2015 afer 32 years and over 3.6 million hours of service.

The SH-60F is produced only for carrier-based ASW and SAR operations. The type differs from the SH-60B by being fitted with AQS-13F dipping sonar in place of MAD equipment, and is not armed with anti-shipping missiles. The SH-60F carries 14 sonobuoys rather than the 25 carried by an SH-60B. It is capable of carrying the Mk 46 ALT and an M-60D, M-240 or GAU-16 machine-gun mounted in the cabin door opening for defence.

The Sikorsky SH-60 Seahawk has been exported and operated by the navies of Australia, Brazil, Greece, Taiwan, Thailand, Turkey, Singapore and Spain. In Japan, Mitsubishi Heavy Industries built the SH-60K under licence, fitted with more powerful engines and upgraded avionics, for the Japanese Maritime Self-Defense Force (JMSDF).

Sensors and related equipment include an APS-124 search radar, UHF direction finding system, infra-red jammers and a radar altimeter. For defence, the SH-60 is equipped with a chaff/flare dispenser and missile warning sensors. Optional equipment includes a nose-mounted Forward Looking Infra-Red (FLIR) turret, and an ARN-146 position indicator to alert the sonar operator when the helicopter is directly over a submerged submarine. The primary attack weapon is the Mk 46 or Mk 50 Advanced Lightweight Torpedo (ALT) and the AGM-114 Hellfire missile. For defence, an M-60D or GAU-16 machine-gun can be mounted in the cabin door space.

To deal with surface threats, the SH-60 carries the AGM-119B Penguin anti-shipping missile. Target acquisition is carried out using a thermal imaging

Sikorsky SH-60B Seahawk

First flight: December 12, 1979
Power: 2 x General Electric T700-401 turboshaft
Armament: AGM-84 Harpoon, AGM-114 Hellfire, AGM-119 Penguin, Sea Skua, Mk 46 or Mk 50 torpedo, Mk 36 mine, Mk 35 depth charge
Size: Rotor diameter – 16.36m/33ft 8in
Length – 19.76m/64ft 10in
Height – 5.18m/17ft 10in
Weights: Empty – 6,190kg/13,650lb
Take-off – 9,925kg/ 21,884lb (maximum)
Performance: Speed – 235kph/145mph (maximum)
Service ceiling – 5,790m/19,000ft
Range – 600km/373 miles

ABOVE: **An SH-60H Seahawk being used to transport ordnance from the Military Sealift Command ship USNS *Walter S. Diehl* (T-AO-193) to USS *Nimitz* (CVN-68) during a Vertical Replenishment.**

Sikorsky MH-60G Pave Hawk

The United States Air Force describes the primary wartime mission for the MH-60G Pave Hawk as "the infiltration, extraction and resupply of Special Operations forces", which of course includes deployment of the type to rescue aircrew shot down over enemy territory.

In 1981, the USAF selected the Sikorsky UH-60 Black Hawk as a replacement for the Sikorsky HH-53E Jolly Green Giant and began an immediate programme to upgrade the type by fitting the PAVE electronics system, air-to-air refuelling probe and improved fuel capacity.

In December 1987, the more sophisticated UH-60A Credible Hawk entered service with the USAF 55th Aerospace Rescue and Recovery Squadron (ARRS) at Eglin Air Force Base (AFB), Florida. Later, all were upgraded to the same standard as new-build MH-60G machines.

ABOVE: **The airframe of the Sikorsky MH-60G Pave Hawk is designed to absorb battle damage. The main rotor blades are manufactured from titanium and composite materials, and can take direct hits from up to 23mm ammunition.**
LEFT: **A Sikorsky MH-60G Pave Hawk on a rescue training mission over the Nevada desert. For operations after dark, the flight crew are equipped with the Night Vision Goggles (NVG) facility and a Forward Looking Infra-Red (FLIR) system.**

The type could be transported in a large aircraft such as the Lockheed C-5A Galaxy (up to five MH-60Gs can be carried), Boeing C-17 Globemaster II or on a logistics transport ship. The blades of the main rotor were designed to fold back to reduce stowage space. A ground crew were able to prepare the helicopter for loading in less than an hour. Off-loading and re-assembly was achieved in less than two hours. The fuel system on the MH-60G allowed the type to be refuelled using a pressure or gravity feed system at Forward Area Arming and Refuelling Points (FAARP).

Avionics fitted in the MH-60G include terrain-following radar, voice altitude warning system and Forward Looking Infra-Red (FLIR) radar. With these, the crew can fly the machine in all weathers, day or night and at low level below enemy radar. The type is also equipped with Global Positioning System (GPS), an Inertial Navigation System (INS) and Doppler radar. The MH-60G is fitted with an automatic flight control system to stabilize the aircraft in flight. To operate over hostile airspace, the helicopter is fitted with an APR-39A(V)1 radar warning receiver, an ALQ-144A infra-red jammer

and an M130 chaff dispenser as defence against enemy radar and heat-seeking missiles. To locate downed aircrew, a range and bearing receiver compatible to the PRO-112 survival radio is fitted. A Hover Infra-red Suppressor System (HISS) is fitted to reduce the heat signature of the engine exhausts.

In 1991, during Operation Desert Storm, the USAF operated the type on Combat Search and Rescue (CSAR) missions, flying deep into enemy territory to locate and rescue any downed pilot. These missions were typically supported and defended by aircraft of the Coalition invasion force. The MH-60G was deployed by the USAF for CSAR duties in support of NATO forces engaged in Operation Allied Force, the large-scale bombing campaign to destroy the Yugoslav military infrastructure. During these operations, two USAF pilots were rescued from enemy territory.

The MH-60G can accommodate 12 fully equipped US Special Forces troops if internal auxiliary fuel tanks are not carried. When internal fuel tanks are fitted, this capacity is reduced to 10 troops. The rescue hoist fitted on the MH-60G has a 76m/250ft cable

ABOVE: **A Sikorsky MH-60G Pave Hawk landing during a Combat Search and Rescue (CSAR) mission. The type is equipped for day or night operations and in all weather conditions. The machine is fitted with a fixed air-to-air refuelling probe.**

and a lifting capacity of 272kg/600lb. If a landing to extract troops is impossible, Special Patrol Insertion-Extraction (SPIE) netting is hung from the helicopter to allow the troops to clip-on and be lifted to safety. An External Stores Support System (ESSS) is fitted under the fuselage to lift up to 3,629kg/8,000lb of supplies and equipment.

Sikorsky MH-60G Pave Hawk

First flight: October 17, 1974
Power: 2 x General Electric T700-GE-701C/D turboshaft
Armament: 0.50in GAU-18/A machine-gun
Size: Rotor diameter – 16.36m/53ft 8in
  Length – 17.1m/64ft 8in
  Height – 4.4m/16ft 8in
Weights: Empty – 6,400kg/14,109lb
  Take-off – 9,979kg/22,000lb (maximum)
Performance: Speed – 299kph/186mph (maximum)
  Ceiling – 4,267m/14,000ft
  Range – 716km/445 miles

Sikorsky CH-53E Super Stallion

In 1962, the US Marine Corps initiated the Heavy Helicopter Experimental (HHX) competition, which was won by the Sikorsky Aircraft Corporation with a three-engine development of the proven CH-53 Sea Stallion. The prototype XCH-53E was flown on March 1, 1974, and the first pre-production YHC-53E was flown on December 12, 1975. An initial order for 33 was placed by the USMC, followed by an order for 16 from the US Navy. The CH-53E Super Stallion entered service with the USMC on June 16, 1981.

The aircraft is powered by three General Electric T64-GE-416 turboshaft engines driving a seven-blade main rotor fabricated (as are the tail rotor blades) from a titanium and glass-fibre composite material. A total of 172 machines were built (the last in November 2003) and the majority deployed with USMC units in the Pacific and Atlantic Fleets. Those in USN service operate in the transport role.

The CH-53E is the largest and heaviest helicopter in service with US military forces. The type is operated for the transportation of troops and equipment during the initial assault phase of an amphibious operation, then to deliver reinforcements and supplies in subsequent operations. The CH-53E can be operated from ships by day or night, and in the most adverse weather conditions.

ABOVE: **A USMC Sikorsky CH-53E Super Stallion from HMH-461 Det. A flying over the Red Desert in Kandahar Province, Afghanistan.**

The helicopter is capable of lifting up to 16,257kg/35,840lb at sea level, and transporting the load over an operational radius of 93km/58 miles. A typical cargo would be a 7,258kg/16,000lb M198 howitzer, the gun's crew and ammunition, or an eight-wheeled Light Armoured Vehicle (LAV-25) weighing 11,794kg/26,000lb.

Flight instrumentation includes a four-axis autopilot, an auto-stabilized digital flight control system, an attitude and heading reference system, a Global Positioning System (GPS) and an AN/APN-217 Doppler radar.

RIGHT: **A CH-53E Super Stallion from Marine Heavy Helicopter Squadron 361 (MHM-361) high above the Pacific Ocean, on the way to perform a daytime tactics training exercise.**

RIGHT: **US Marines boarding a CH-53E Super Stallion helicopter on the amphibious assault ship USS *Bataan* (LHD-5) in the Persian Gulf. The helicopter is operated by Medium Marine Helicopter Squadron 264 (HMH-264).**

The cockpit is equipped with Pilot Night Vision System (PVNS) and Integrated Helmet and Display Sighting System (IHADSS) to allow the type to be flown on low-altitude operations at night or in adverse weather conditions.

The cabin can be configured in a number of ways and although it is fitted with 37 folding canvas seats along the sides as standard, the addition of a centre row increases the total capacity to 55. Up to seven standard cargo pallets can be accommodated, loaded through a door in the rear of the fuselage. A hydraulically operated rear ramp for the loading of freight is fitted. An external load lift system, developed by Skyhook Technologies Inc., mounted on the underside of the fuselage, allows loads of to up to 16,330kg/36,000lb to be carried.

The machine is equipped with a radar warning system and M130 chaff/flare dispensers as defence against heat-seeking missiles. The cowlings covering the engines and transmission are fabricated from a Kevlar laminate as protection against gunfire. The self-sealing fuel tanks are housed in the forward section on each side of the lower fuselage sponson. Further fuel can be carried in drop tanks which are mounted on each sponson. For long-range positioning flights, seven additional fuel tanks can be carried in the cabin. The CH-53E is also equipped with an air-to-air refuelling probe and is fitted with a hose-hoisting system to allow the aircraft to be refuelled from a surface ship without landing.

Armament comes in the form of a ramp-mounted weapon system developed and evaluated by the US Marine Corps. A 0.50in GAU-21/A reduced-recoil machine-gun, which can be installed and removed in less than two minutes, is "soft-mounted" on the cargo-loading ramp.

In January 1990, during Operation Eastern Exit, two Super Stallions carrying US Marines were flown from USS *Guam* (LPH-9) to rescue US and foreign nationals from the US Embassy in Mogadishu, the war-torn capital of Somalia. The mission was flown at night over a distance of 858km/533 miles, the helicopters being air-to-air refuelled twice en route. On June 8, 1995, two CH-53Es were deployed from USS *Keersage* (LHD-3) to rescue Capt. Scott O'Grady (USAF), an F-16 Fighting Falcon pilot who was shot down behind enemy lines in the province of Bosnia, Yugoslavia.

ABOVE: **Two CH-53E Super Stallion helicopters carrying cargo in nets being refuelled from a Lockheed C-130 Hercules during a long-range supply operation.**

Sikorsky CH-53E Super Stallion

First flight: March 1, 1974

Power: 3 x General Electric T64-GE-416 turboshaft

Armament: 0.50in GAU-21/A machine-gun

Size: Rotor diameter – 24.08m/79ft
Length – 20.19m/99ft 1in
Height – 8.97m/29ft 5in

Weights: Empty – 15,071kg/33,226lb
Take-off – 33,340kg/73,500lb (maximum)

Performance: Speed – 315kph/196mph (maximum)
Service ceiling – 5,634m/18,500ft
Range – 925km/574 miles

Sikorsky MH-53J Pave Low

The US Air Force used the MH-53 to penetrate enemy territory for special operations and aircrew recovery for more than 40 years. Capable of operating day or night or in bad weather, these large two-engine helicopters were used to conduct long-range, low-level missions to insert, extract and resupply US Special Operations Forces around the world.

The MH-53 helicopters were originally HH-53 helicopters used by the US Air Force in the Vietnam War which, over decades of service, received many upgrades and improvements. After the 1960s, all were essentially remanufactured, with the airframe being completely reskinned and the engines and rotor systems replaced. Along with the new lease of life came a new designation – MH-53 (M – Multi-mission and H – Helicopter).

The most significant enhancement to the helicopter was the Pave Low electronics programme which modified the type for operating at night and during bad weather. Equipped with Forward Looking Infra-Red (FLIR) sensors, Global Positioning System, Inertial Navigation System (INS) and terrain-following radar, the MH-53 could be flown on clandestine, low-level missions in all weathers, day or night, anywhere in the world. Folding rotor blades made the MH-53 aircraft carrier-compatible. If a clearing was not available when operating in jungle conditions, a device known as a Forest Penetrator, a type of heavy folding seat, could be lowered through the tree canopy to facilitate the rescue.

In the late 1980s, the USAF launched the Pave Low III programme, in which nine MH-53Hs and 32 HH-53s were modified for night and adverse weather operations. During the programme, the following items were improved or fitted: AN/AAQ-29A FLIR radar, GPS, INS, terrain-following radar and other integrated avionics to enable the crew

ABOVE: **A Sikorsky MH-53J Pave Low III on a training flight. The machine is from the US Air Force 20th Special Operations Squadron based at Hurlburt Field, Florida. The Pave Low III programme to modify HH-53 and MH-53 helicopters for night and all-weather operations began in the late 1980s.**

to navigate precisely to and from a target area. The USAF designated these modified aircraft as the MH-53J, the largest and heaviest helicopters in the USAF inventory and the most technologically advanced in the world.

The MH-53 carried a crew of six, consisting of two pilots, two flight engineers and two gunners manning a combination of 7.62mm Minigun or 0.50in M218 machine-guns. In the transport role, 38 fully equipped troops or 14 stretchers could be carried. An external cargo hook with a lifting capacity of 9,072kg/20,000lb was mounted under the fuselage.

In 1990, during Operation Desert Storm, MH-53s of the USAF provided the lead for US Army AH-64 Apaches during airstrikes on Iraqi defences to destroy the early warning radar system at the start of the bombing campaign. Infiltration, exfiltration and resupply missions for US Special Forces went on throughout the war. The type was also deployed in Iraq, Saudi Arabia, Kuwait and the Persian Gulf,

to provide search and rescue coverage for the air forces of the Coalition. In 2003, the MH-53 was once again deployed to Iraq to support US Special Forces missions during Operation Lasting Freedom.

The MH-53M Pave Low IV system gave the aircrew instant access to the total battlefield situation on a colour digital map screen compatible with Night Vision Goggles. Using signals from satellite links,

ABOVE: **A Sikorsky MH-53J Pave Low III being prepared for the last operational flight of the type at an airfield in Iraq. All MH-53 helicopters were retired from US Air Force service on September 30, 2008.**

the system displayed virtually real-time information to identify potential hazards along the flight route or enemy radar.

In 2008, the US Air Force Special Operations Command (AFSOC) decided to retire the MH-53 from service, as it was no longer economically viable to keep the aircraft maintained in combat-ready condition. The type was replaced in service by the Bell Boeing CV-22B Osprey.

ABOVE: **A Sikorsky MH-53M Pave Low IV being refuelled from a Lockheed MH-130P Combat King aircraft during a training exercise. All MH-53 helicopters have been replaced in US Air Force service by the V-22 Osprey. Note the large rigid refuelling probe.**

Sikorsky MH-53J Pave Low

First flight: October 15, 1964
Power: 2 x General Electric T64-GE-7A turboshaft
Armament: 7.62mm Minigun or 0.50in M218 machine-gun
Size: Rotor diameter – 22.02m/72ft
Length overall – 28m/88ft
Height – 5.22m/17ft 2in
Weights: Empty – 10,691kg/23,570lb
Take-off – 19,051kg/42,000lb (maximum)
Performance: Speed – 315kph/196mph (maximum)
Service ceiling – 4,900m/16,000ft
Range – 868km/540 miles

Sikorsky MH-53E Sea Dragon

The MH-53E Sea Dragon is a version of the CH-53E developed for the US Navy for the Airborne Mine Countermeasures (AMCM) role, with a secondary mission of shipboard delivery. The AMCM mission includes minesweeping, floating mine destruction, channel marking and towing of small surface craft. Operating from aircraft carriers and other warships, the MH-53E Sea Dragon can carry up to 55 fully equipped troops or a 16,257kg/35,840lb payload over a distance of 93km/58 miles, or a 10,161kg/22,400lb payload over 926km/580 miles. Additional capabilities include SAR, air-to-air refuelling and refuelling at the hover. The machine is fitted with an external cargo hook for Vertical Replenishment (VertRep) operations.

The prototype MH-53E was first flown on December 23, 1981. The first of some 50 deliveries to the USN began in 1986, and the type entered front-line service in April 1987. The MH-53E is heavier and has a greater fuel capacity than the CH-53E (12,112 litres/3,200 gallons), which is carried in larger sponsons each of which is fitted with two fuel tanks.

RIGHT: **A post-tsunami humanitarian mission in Indonesia. Civilians and crew are unloading food, clothing and relief supplies from the rear cargo ramp of an MH-53E Sea Dragon of Helicopter Mine Countermeasures Squadron 15 (HM-15).**

Although the Sea Dragon retains some 80 per cent commonality with the CH-53, it differs from the earlier version by being fitted with rear escape hatches, an improved tail rotor system and airframe structural reinforcement.

The MH-53E Sea Dragon can be used to deploy a formidable range of AMCM equipment. The aircraft is flown above the surface of a waterway, towing electronic or magnetic equipment to locate and clear mines. The main type of sweep used is the hydrofoil sled. This equipment (too large to be carried in the helicopter), which is towed at a relatively high speed across the water, is capable of detonating both acoustic and magnetic mines.

ABOVE: **A rainbow is formed in the ocean mist as a Helicopter Mine Countermeasures Squadron 15 (HM-15) Sikorsky MH-53E Sea Dragon conducts mine-countermeasures operations.**

The MH-53E can also operate the AN/SPU-1/W, a single magnetized orange pipe minesweeping system towed as a single unit or three units in tandem to detonate mines by magnetic influence. In contrast, the purely mechanical Mk-103 system is used for sweeping moored mines. This system is a wire-type sweep trailed from the helicopter and fitted with cutters to slice through mooring cables so that the submerged mines float to the surface to be neutralized.

The Airborne Laser Mine Detection System (ALMDS) is an airborne electro-optical system that is capable of rapid detection and classification of floating and moored mines located in relatively shallow water. With input from GPS, accurate navigation data is provided to determine target location. Using these systems can enable significant areas of sea to be rendered safe for friendly shipping. Perhaps these capabilities are best illustrated by the statistic from Operation Desert Storm in 1991, that one USN squadron

ABOVE: **Preparing to launch MK-103 minesweeping equipment from the rear ramp of an MH-53E Sea Dragon helicopter over the Persian Gulf.** RIGHT: **An MH-53E Sea Dragon towing a Mk 105 hydrofoil minesweeping sled while conducting simulated mine clearance operations.**

operating the MH-53E cleared over 1,000 Iraqi mines. For AMCM missions, the MH-53E is operated by a crew of seven: pilot, co-pilot, safety observer, two AMCM equipment handlers and two ramp operators.

In the cockpit, the pilots are assisted by a dual-digital automatic flight control system controlled by two computers that continually cross-check one another and disable any potential false inputs. If one computer fails, the other automatically doubles output, eliminating any degradation in automatic flight control performance.

The MH-53E was also procured by Japan directly from Sikorsky, and this version is designated S-80M-1 by the manufacturer.

ABOVE: **A Sikorsky MH-53E of Helicopter Mine Countermeasures Squadron 15 preparing to launch from the amphibious assault ship USS *Nassau* (LHA-4). The Sea Dragon is fitted with AN/ALE-39 Countermeasures Dispensing System (CDS), which can be mounted internally or externally and is designed to dispense chaff, infra-red decoy flares or expendable jammers.**

Sikorsky MH-53E Sea Dragon

First flight: December 23, 1981
Power: 3 x General Electric T64-GE-419 turboshaft
Armament: 0.50in M218 machine-gun
Size: Rotor diameter – 24.08m/79ft
  Length – 30.19m/99ft 1in
  Height – 8.6m/28ft 4in
Weights: Empty – 16,667kg/36,745lb
  Take-off – 31,616kg/69,700lb (maximum)
Performance: Speed – 278kph/173mph (maximum)
  Service ceiling – 3,048m/10,000ft
  Range – 1,931km/1,200 miles

Sikorsky Superhawk/CH-148 Cyclone

The Sikorsky H-92 was developed for military operation in parallel with the successful civil S-92 helicopter. The type has an airframe that incorporates some of the best design elements from the successful and proven Black Hawk, Seahawk and CH-53 series of military helicopters. The H-92 was first flown on December 23, 1998.

The H-92 can transport 22 fully equipped troops, or perform lift operations using the cargo hook with a lifting capacity of 4,536kg/10,000lb. The exceptionally large cabin offers a range of interior options to maximize flexibility, and it can accommodate vehicles or palletized stores up to a total weight of 4,421kg/9,748lb. The inbuilt cargo handling system has a 1,814kg/4,000lb capacity cargo winch and a floor-roller system to ease the loading and unloading of bulky items. A rear ramp allows easy and rapid loading and unloading of cargo and troops. Six stretcher cases plus medical attendants can be accommodated.

The airframe of the helicopter has been purposely designed for strength and enhanced extreme mission endurance. The H-92 has also been designed to be transportable in Lockheed C-5A Galaxy or Boeing C-17 Globemaster II transport aircraft, and takes less than two hours to prepare, load and deploy. Advanced military avionics include a Night Vision Goggles (NVG) compatible cockpit and Head-Up Display (HUD); and aircraft

ABOVE: **Safety features on the Sikorsky H-92 Superhawk include a high-visibility cockpit, crashworthy passenger seats and high-energy-absorbing landing gear.**

survivability systems include designed-in crashworthiness and ballistic tolerance to direct hits from small arms.

RIGHT: **The H-92 is a military development of the civilian S-92. A number of government operators around the world have acquired versions for transport or military duties.**

RIGHT: **The H-92 is a large helicopter capable of accommodating 22 troops or freight internally, while having the capability to lift 4,536kg/10,000lb as an underslung load.**

The Canadian government selected the H-92 to satisfy a unique and challenging naval requirement. In November 2004, Canada's Department of National Defence (DoND) awarded a contract for 28 aircraft to the Sikorsky Aircraft Corporation. In Canadian service the aircraft is designated the CH-148 Cyclone, and it is replacing the Westland CH-124 Sea King, which has been in operation since the early 1960s. The first production CH-148 Cyclone was flown on November 15, 2008.

The CH-148 Cyclone, a dedicated naval version, is an extremely capable machine developed for maritime surveillance, reconnaissance, anti-submarine and anti-shipping operations. For stowage on board a ship, the type is fitted with a folding tail boom and folding main rotor blades. Self-sealing fuel tanks with a capacity of 3,030kg/6,680lb are fitted, as is an air-to-air refuelling probe. The type is also fitted with emergency flotation systems positioned under the fuselage and in the tail boom; these automatically inflate and are expected to keep the helicopter afloat and upright in up to Sea State 5 conditions. In addition, a 15-man life raft is installed in each sponson. The Cyclone has a metal and composite airframe, and a number of safety features such as engine burst containment have been incorporated into the design.

Concerns with the overall weight of the aircraft has led Sikorsky to consider an engine upgrade, but deliveries of aircraft (all to be modified later to the contracted specification) began in February 2010 at Canadian Forces Base (CFB), Shearwater. The programme has been delayed mutliple times. Sea trials on board HMCS *Montréal* began in March 2018 and by 2021, 23 examples had been delivered to the Canadian military.

BELOW: **Canada operates the CH-148 Cyclone, the military version of the type, for maritime duties. Equipped with active and passive sensors, the CH-148 is armed with ASW torpedoes.**

Sikorsky Superhawk

First flight: December 23, 1998
Power: 2 x General Electric CT7-8A7 turboshaft
Armament: 7.62mm C6 machine-gun
Size: Rotor diameter – 17.12m/56ft 2in
  Length – 20.88m/68ft 6in
  Height – 4.71m/15ft 5in
Weights: Empty – 7,359kg/16,223lb
  Take-off – 12,837kg/28,300lb (maximum)
Performance: Speed – 306kph/190mph (maximum)
  Service ceiling – 4,572m/15,000ft
  Range – 1,521km/945 miles

LEFT: **The Sud-Ouest S.O.1221 Djinn has a skid-type undercarriage fitted with small retractable wheels to facilitate ground handling. The Djinn was the world's first production helicopter to make use of the cold jet principle of propulsion.**

Sud-Ouest S.O. 1221 Djinn

On May 14, 1947, two years after the end of World War II, the French company Sud-Ouest test-flew the S.O. 1100 Ariel, built with the benefit of research carried out in Nazi Germany. The machine differed from most other designs in that the single three-blade rotor was powered by tipjets.

A Mathis G7 petrol engine drove a compressor to provide low-pressure air which was then fed through ducting inside each rotor blade to the combustion chamber in each tip-mounted pulse jet, where it was mixed with fuel and electrically ignited. The thrust generated powered the rotor.

Experience gained from the various versions of this experimental machine led to the development of the S.O.1220, which was first flown on January 2, 1953.

BELOW: **High-pressure air for the rotor tipjets was bled from the compressor of the Turboméca Palouste IV turbine engine.**

ABOVE: **The torqueless propulsion system did not require the machine to be fitted with a tail rotor.**

RIGHT: **Twin fins and a central rudder provided added directional control, and the boom was left uncovered, which also saved weight.**

This led to the production of the S.O. 1221 Djinn (genie), but the crucial difference was that the rotor blades now had cold-jet propulsion, compressed air ducted from the compressor section of the Turboméca Palouste and blown from tip-mounted pods. The rotor was torqueless, and a tail rotor was not required to be fitted to the machine. Additionally, warm air ducted through the rotor blades was enough to provide de-icing.

The S.O. 1220 was used to prove the viability of the propulsion system, and Sud-Ouest used this experience to help them build five prototypes of the S.O. 1221, the first being flown on December 16, 1953. Within days, a prototype machine set an altitude record for light helicopters of 4,789m/15,712ft.

The Djinn had the appearance of a conventional helicopter, with a two-seat side-by-side cockpit enclosed by a bubble-type canopy and transparent side doors. The Turboméca Palouste gas turbine engine (originally designed as an air generator and primarily used as an engine ground starter unit) was mounted behind the cockpit bulkhead to provide forward thrust and compressed air for the tip-mounted pods on the rotor blades. No tail rotor was fitted but the short tail boom, fabricated from welded steel tubing, was fitted with two vertical fins. A centrally mounted rudder, positioned in line with the engine exhaust, provided directional control. To save weight, the tail structure was uncovered.

The French Army was very interested by the highly manoeuvrable machine, and 22 pre-production airframes were built for evaluation, followed by an order for 100 machines. The US Army became interested in the Djinn because of the type's size, excellent manoeuvrability, ease of maintenance and relatively low unit cost. Three of the pre-production machines were sent to the US Army for

evaluation (serial numbers 57-6104 to 6106) and the experimental aircraft was designated YHO-1. No orders were placed by the US Army, apparently due to both budgetary and political constraints. A further six examples were purchased for the West German Army. In French military use, the Djinn was used for liaison, observation, CASEVAC (fitted with two removable stretcher carriers) and pilot training. A Djinn was used by the French Army for firing trials with the Nord SS10 anti-tank missile.

When production ended in the mid-1960s, a total of 178 of the type, including pre-production machines, had been built. When the type was retired from military use, many were registered with civilian operators and converted for

agricultural use by being fitted with aerial spraying equipment.

The Djinn was replaced in French military service by the Aérospatiale Alouette series of helicopters.

Sud-Ouest S.O. 1221 Djinn

First flight: December 16, 1953
Power: 1 x Turboméca Palouste IV gas turbine
Armament: None
Size: Rotor diameter – 11m/36ft 1in
 Length – 5.3m/17ft 5in (fuselage)
 Height – 2.6m/8ft 6in
Weights: Empty – 360kg/794lb
 Take-off – 800kg/1,764lb (maximum)
Performance: Speed – 130kph/81mph (maximum)
 Service ceiling – 1,463m/4,800ft
 Range – 293km/180 miles

Westland Whirlwind

After World War II, service planners in the UK began to truly appreciate the potential of the helicopter as a military asset. However, design and development of the helicopter did not receive sufficient funding or production priority during the war years. Instead, the simplest way for the country to acquire a UK-produced helicopter was to build US-designed machines. Westland Aircraft Limited Helicopters of Yeovil negotiated with the Sikorsky Aircraft Corporation and agreed a licence to build the S-55 helicopter. The first aircraft to enter service with the Royal Navy were in fact built in the USA by Sikorsky and supplied under the Mutual Defense Assistance (MDA) programme. A total of 32 Sikorsky-built machines, powered by the Pratt & Whitney R01340-40 radial piston engine, were successfully trialled operationally by the Royal Navy.

The first Westland-built machine, powered by the Pratt & Whitney R-1340-40, was flown on August 15, 1953. The HAR.1, now named

Whirlwind, was delivered to the RN for use in the Air Sea Rescue (ASR) role. The almost identical HAR.2 was produced for the Royal Air Force and was deployed in the same role. The machines in RAF service were initially operated by RAF Coastal Command to provide ASR coverage for most of the UK. In reality, however, many rescue operations involved the recovery of civilians in dangerous situations.

ABOVE: Only two Westland Whirlwind HCC Mk12s powered by a Rolls-Royce Gnome turboshaft engine were built. Both were assigned to the Royal Flight, and were later replaced for these duties by the Westland Wessex.

The HAR.3 delivered to the RN was powered by the Wright R-1300-3 Cyclone 7 radial piston engine. The HAR.4 built for the RAF was equipped to operate in a hot climate and at higher

RIGHT: The Westland Whirlwind HAR.10 was fitted with the Rolls-Royce Gnome turboshaft engine. The engine was lighter and easier to maintain than a radial piston engine, and also gave an improvement in aircraft performance.

RIGHT: The Westland Whirlwind HAR.3 delivered to the Royal Navy was powered by the Wright R-1300-3 Cyclone 7 radial piston engine. This was later changed to a Pratt & Whitney R-1340-57 for the HAR.4. The HAR.5 was powered by a British-built Alvis Leonides Major radial piston engine.

altitudes, and all 24 built retained the Pratt & Whitney R-1340-57 engine. The HAR.4 first entered RAF service with No. 155 Squadron in September 1954, and operated transport and rescue missions in jungle conditions during the Malayan Emergency (1948–60). A number of HAR.4s were operated by the RAF in support of the British nuclear weapon testing programme from the base on Christmas Island in the Indian Ocean.

In 1955, the HAR.5 was fitted with the more powerful British-built Alvis Leonides Major radial piston engine, which gave the Whirlwind an improvement in overall performance.

BELOW: The Whirlwind HAR Mk1 was powered by a Bristol-Siddeley (later Rolls-Royce) Gnome turboshaft engine, which gave the machine an improvement in performance and range.

The HAR.5 was delivered to the British military and was exported to Austria.

The HAS.7, purposely built for the anti-submarine warfare role, was first flown on October 17, 1956, and entered service with No.845 Naval Air Squadron (NAS) in August 1957. The HAS.7 replaced the fixed-wing Fairey Gannet AS4 in the vital carrier-borne anti-submarine role. This version was equipped with radar and dipping ASDIC for detecting submarines, and could carry homing torpedoes. As the first British helicopter deployed in the role, this aircraft pioneered rotary wing ASW capability for the RN at a vital stage in the Cold War. Fleet Air Arm (FAA) squadrons operating the Whirlwind included No.814, 815, 820, 824, 845, 847 and 848 NAS, as well as No.705 and 771 Training Squadrons. Later, some were converted

for use in the ASR role and fitted with the much lighter and more powerful Bristol-Siddeley Gnome turboshaft engine; these were designated HAR.9.

In 1962, all HAR.2 and HAR.4 machines in RAF service were replaced by the Rolls-Royce Gnome-powered HAR.10. The first Gnome-powered Whirlwind had been flown in 1959, and can be most easily identified by the longer nose section. The HAR.10 was widely used by the RAF as a short-range tactical transport and training helicopter both in the UK and overseas, including operations over Borneo in late 1963. This version of the Whirlwind was also used extensively in supporting the British Army in Malaya, and could be equipped with four anti-tank missiles. The RAF continued to use the type in Cyprus for SAR duties until 1982.

Westland-built Whirlwinds were exported to Austria, Canada, Ghana, France, Jordan, Spain and Yugoslavia.

Westland Whirlwind HAR.3

First flight: August 15, 1953
Power: 1 x Wright R-1300-3 Cyclone 7 radial piston engine
Armament: None
Size: Rotor diameter – 16.15m/53ft
Length – 12.88m/42ft 3in
Height – 4.06m/13ft 4in
Weights: Empty – 2,381kg/5,250lb
Take-off – 3,583kg/7,900lb (maximum)
Performance: Speed – 180kph/112mph (maximum)
Service ceiling – 4,816m/15,800ft
Range – 579km/360 miles

Westland Wessex

In 1955, a year after the Sikorsky S-58 Choctaw had been first flown, the Royal Navy issued a requirement for a turbine-powered helicopter equipped for anti-submarine warfare. Westland Aircraft Limited proposed a licence-built version of the S-58 already in service with the US Navy as the HSS-1 for the basis, but converted to be powered by a Napier Gazelle NGa.1 turboshaft engine. A Sikorsky-built HSS-1 was delivered to the Westland factory at Yeovil as a pattern airframe. To accommodate the longer turboshaft engine, the nose section of the aircraft had to be completely redesigned.

The first Westland-built machine was flown at Yeovil on May 17, 1957, and the first pre-production Wessex HAS.1 was flown on June 20, 1958. The first machines for the RN were delivered in April 1961. The Wessex entered Fleet Air Arm (FAA) squadron service with No.815 Naval Air Squadron (NAS) at Culdrose (HMS *Seahawk*) in July 1961. A total of

RIGHT: **The Wessex was a considerable improvement on the original Sikorsky S-58 design. Note the starboard turbine exhaust below the cockpit.**

11 FAA squadrons were equipped with the HAS.1, the first purpose-designed ASW helicopter to be operated by the Fleet Air Arm. The only offensive weapons carried by this version were torpedoes.

The Wessex was also ordered by the Royal Air Force as the HC.2 for use as a troop transport. Seventy-four were built, and a number were later converted to HAR.2 for standard SAR duties. These also differed from the

ABOVE: **The Wessex served the British Armed Forces for three decades, seeing action with both the Royal Air Force and the Royal Navy.**

Wessex helicopters in FAA service by being powered by two Bristol Siddeley (later Rolls-Royce) Gnome Mk.110/111 turboshaft engines coupled to a common gearbox. The HC.2 could accommodate 16 fully equipped troops or lift a 1,814kg/4,000lb load in a cargo sling. The Gnome-powered versions

are easily identifiable by a large single engine exhaust on each side of the nose. A version of the HC.2, the HU.5, was ordered as a troop transport for the Royal Marines, the first was delivered in December 1963, just six months after the prototype had been flown. For operating at sea and in the event of an emergency water landing, the HU.5 was equipped with rapid-inflation flotation bags stowed in housings mounted on the hub of each main undercarriage wheel. The HU.5 was flown by six RAF squadrons until 1987, and they were used on operations in Borneo, Oman and the Falkland Islands.

The Napier Gazelle-powered HAS.3 entered FAA service in January 1967. This version was equipped with improved radar equipment, and was fitted to carry torpedoes, depth charges and wire-guided missiles. A large radome for the search radar scanner was positioned on top of the fuselage. Inevitably, this version became known to FAA personnel as the Camel. Apart from three development aircraft, all were converted or, more accurately, rebuilt HAS.1 machines. Although the HAS.3 was planned to be withdrawn from service in early 1982, the type remained in squadron service until

December 1982, having been required for ASW operations in the Falklands War.

The destroyer HMS *Antrim* (D18) reached the South Atlantic before the main British task force arrived in April 1982. On April 22, an HAS.3 (XP142) operating from the ship was deployed to rescue a Special Air Service (SAS) reconnaissance party from a glacier after their transport (two Wessex HU.5s) had crashed in blizzard conditions. On April 25, the same machine flown by Lt Cmdr I. Stanley was deployed to attack and depth-charge the Argentine submarine *Santa Fe*. Although the helicopter was subsequently damaged by enemy small arms fire and bomb splinters, this machine survived and is now preserved by the Fleet Air Arm Museum, Yeovilton.

LEFT: **In Royal Navy
service, the Wessex
was operated in the
transport, air sea rescue
and anti-submarine
warfare roles. In 1982,
the type was deployed
in action during the
Falklands War.**

Westland Wessex HAS.2

First flight: May 17, 1958
Power: 1 x Napier Gazelle NGa.1 turboshaft
Armament: None
Size: Rotor diameter – 17.07m/56ft
  Length – 27.07m/65ft 10in
  Height – 4.85m/15ft 11in
Weights: Empty – 3,583kg/7,900lb
  Take-off – 6,169kg/13,600lb (maximum)
Performance: Speed – 212kph/132mph (maximum)
  Service ceiling – 3,048m/10,000ft
  Range – 628km/390 miles

LEFT: **Although originally developed for the Egyptian Air Force, the Westland Commando HC.4 was operated by the Royal Navy, and became a key asset for amphibious operations by the Royal Marines.**

Westland Sea King

The Sea King manufactured by Westland Helicopters is a licence-built version of the Sikorsky S-61 helicopter, which is also known as the Sea King. Although these aircraft share a name, the British-built one differs considerably from the S-61 by being equipped with many British-built systems and components, including Rolls-Royce Gnome turboshaft engines, anti-submarine warfare systems and an automatic flight control system. The Westland Sea King was also developed for a much wider range of missions than the S-61s produced by Sikorsky.

A 1969 licence agreement between Westland and Sikorsky allowed the British company to use the Sea King airframe and rotor system as the basis for a machine to meet a Royal Navy requirement for a replacement for the Westland Wessex HAS.3 helicopter.

The prototype and three pre-production machines (SH-3D) were built by Sikorsky and delivered by sea in October 1966. Two pre-production development machines were used for trials and evaluation by Westland and subsequently by the Aeroplane and Armaments Experimental Establishment

(AAEE). The first Westland-built Sea King HAS.1 was flown on May 7, 1969, at Yeovil. In August 1969, the machine was delivered to No.700S Naval Air Squadron (NAS) Intensive Flight Trials Unit (IFTU), and was the first of 60 ordered by the RN. The last Westland Sea King to be built left the production line in 1990.

The basic ASW Sea King was upgraded a number of times as the HAS.2, HAS.5 and the HAS.6, which were replaced in service by the AgustaWestland Merlin MH1. A number of HAS.6 machines had the ASW equipment removed for the aircraft to be used in the transport role as part of the Commando Helicopter Force (CHF).

The Sea King HAR.3 developed for the RAF entered service from September 1977 to replace the Westland Whirlwind and, later, the Wessex, in the search and rescue role. These aircraft provide 24-hour emergency coverage around the UK and the Falkland Islands. SAR versions of the Sea King were also produced for the Royal Norwegian Air Force (RNAF), German Navy and later for the Belgian Air Force.

In 2003, during Operation Iraqi Freedom, a number of Sea King HC.4s were deployed from HMS *Ocean* (L12) to land the leading elements of the invasion force on the Al-Faw Peninsula. On return

LEFT: **Royal Navy HC.4 Sea Kings were flown repeatedly in support of the NATO (IFOR) presence in Bosnia, moving military equipment and undertaking many life-saving CASEVAC flights.**

LEFT: **To fulfil an urgent requirement for an Airborne Early Warning (AEW) aircraft, two machines were converted for this role as the Westland Sea King AEW.2A. The ASaC7 version was equipped with Thales 2000 Searchwater AEW radar, which provided accurate detection of air and ground targets.**

from operations in Iraq, all Sea King HC.4 helicopters needed to be upgraded to enable the type to be operated in the hot and high conditions found in Afghanistan. This included fitting an improved design of main rotor blade, a high-performance tail rotor and an updated Defensive Aids Suite (DAS). An improved type of Display Night Vision Goggles (DNVG) system was also fitted as part of the upgrade. This package of modifications resulted in the aircraft being redesignated as the Sea King Mk4+.

A troop-carrying version, the Commando, was originally developed for the Egyptian Air Force. Capable of transporting 27 fully equipped troops over 644km/400 miles, the type retained the foldable rotor blades and tail boom fitted to the naval variants. The Commando was fitted with an external cargo hook with a load-carrying capacity of up to 2,722kg/6,000lb. A rescue hoist was fitted as standard. In RN service, the type was designated Sea King HC.4 and remained in service with the Commando Helicopter Force until 2016. The aircraft is fitted with a Defensive Aids Suite (DAS) which offers a high standard of protection from both infra-red and radar-guided anti-aircraft weapons. It is equipped with a cabin-mounted 7.62mm General Purpose Machine Gun (GPMG) for defence and limited fire support.

During the Falklands War a number of RN warships, Royal Fleet Auxiliary (RFA) and transport ships were lost due to the lack of AEW coverage. In 1982, two Sea King HAS.2 helicopters were hastily modified to become the Sea King AEW.2A, and a total of 13 were eventually completed. The AEW.2A was fitted with the Thorn-EMI ARI-5930/3 Searchwater radar, the scanner for which was mounted on a swivelling arm attached to the side of the fuselage and protected by an inflatable dome. The radar scanner is lowered in flight and raised before landing. A further upgrade of the AEW.7 included fitting Thales 2000 Searchwater radar and LINK16 data link equipment, the type being designated as the ASaC7. The main role for the ASaC7 is the detection of low-flying attacking aircraft, interception/attack control and over-the-horizon targeting for ship-launched missiles. The radar is capable of simultaneously tracking up to 400 targets.

In 1982, during the Falklands War, Sea Kings of the RN proved to be remarkably versatile, being deployed mainly for ASW, but also for troop and supply transport, and supporting Special Air Service (SAS) forces. In 1991, during the first Gulf War, the Sea King was operated in a number of roles, including SAR and as a ship-to–ship logistics transport. During the blockade of Iraqi ports, Royal Marines (RM) were flown in Sea King helicopters to intercept any suspect ships that refused to stop or alter course.

Sea Kings operated by No.820 NAS and 845 NAS were deployed as part of the NATO intervention force in Bosnia.

Aircraft from 820 NAS were deployed from RFA ships to provided logistical support, ferrying troops and supplies across the Adriatic Sea. The squadron performed over 1,400 deck landings and flew in excess of 1,900 hours. The Sea Kings from No.845 NAS performed vital CASEVAC and other tasks, and many of these machines were damaged by hostile ground fire. Ship-based Sea Kings from No.814 NAS were deployed to the Kosovo region in the same conflict to provide SAR coverage, as well as troop and logistics transport. In 2003, during Operation Iraqi Freedom, Sea King helicopters were used to provide logistics support, and to transport Royal Marines into Kuwait from HMS *Ark Royal*, HMS *Ocean* and other ships operating offshore.

A total of 330 Westland Sea King helicopters were built, and the type was exported to Australia, Belgium, Egypt, Germany, India and Norway.

Westland Sea King HC.4

First flight: May 7, 1969
Power: 2 x Rolls-Royce Gnome H1400-1T turboshaft
Armament: None
Size: Rotor diameter – 18.9m/62ft
Length – 17.02m/55ft 10in
Height – 4.72m/15ft 6in
Weights: Empty – 5,620kg/12,390lb
Take-off – 9,752kg/21,500lb (maximum)
Performance: Speed – 245kph/152mph (maximum)
Service ceiling – 3,048m/10,000ft
Range – 1230km/764 miles

Westland Wasp and Scout

The Westland Wasp and Scout were small, gas turbine-powered, light military helicopters derived from the P.531 programme that began as a Saunders-Roe design before that company was absorbed by Westland. At one point, the naval aircraft was to be called Sea Scout. The Wasp differed from the land-based Scout by being fitted with a four-wheeled undercarriage (as opposed to a skid type) for easy manoeuvring on a flight deck. The Wasp also had increased fuel capacity for longer overwater operations, and a folding tail unit and rotor blades for easy stowage in the compact hangar on a frigate-sized ship.

The Wasp was a classic Cold War design that met a Royal Navy requirement for a small helicopter that could operate from the deck of a frigate and carry two homing torpedoes. This was to counter the improvement in speed and attack range of the Soviet submarine fleet, and to increase the range at which an enemy vessel could be detected and attacked. The Wasp was in effect a stand-off weapons system that gave the RN an anti-submarine reach beyond the range of any weapons carried on board on a warship of the time. However, the Wasp was not

equipped with sonar or radar, and had to be guided to the target by radar operators on board the ship.

The prototype of the naval version was first flown on October 28, 1962, and production of 98 Wasp helicopters began almost immediately. From mid-1963, the type began to enter squadron service with the RN. As the more capable Westland Lynx entered service in the late 1970s, the Wasp was gradually withdrawn from

ABOVE: **The Westland Scout AH Mk1 became operational with the British Army Air Corps (AAC) in 1963, and continued in service until 1994. For practicality, the machine was built with a skid-type undercarriage equipped with two small wheels as an aid to ground handling. The type was originally flown on observation and liaison duties, but was later modified to carry four Nord SS.11 anti-tank missiles. The Scout was given the name "The Flying Jeep" by army aircrew, after the famous light utility vehicle of World War II.**

ABOVE: **The Westland Wasp was developed for the Royal Navy and fitted with a four-strut, double-wishbone undercarriage. The four wheels were self-castoring for operations on the landing deck of a warship. Later in Royal Navy service, the Wasp was modified to carry the Nord SS.11 wire-guided missile to target small surface vessels.**

operational use. That was until 1982 and the Falklands War, when seven "mothballed" Type 22 frigates and their helicopters were recommissioned for active service in the South Atlantic. The Wasp was finally withdrawn from service in 1988, when the last of the frigates for which the helicopter had been designed was decommissioned.

From 1963, the Westland Scout AH Mk1 became an important element of the Army Air Corps (AAC) and, of the 150 ordered, 30 were still operational when the type was withdrawn from service in 1994. Known to aircrew as "The Flying Jeep", the Scout was used for observation, liaison and Casualty Evacuation (CASEVAC) duties. The type could also be configured as a light attack helicopter armed with two skid-mounted, forward-firing 7.62mm machine-gun packs or a single pintle-mounted machine-gun in the rear cabin. In the anti-tank role, the Scout was armed with four Nord SS.11 wire-guided missiles. In the CASEVAC role, the Scout could be fitted with two stretchers internally or two externally in pods mounted on the undercarriage.

BELOW: **The design for the type originated from the ex-Cierva team working at Saunders-Roe Limited.**

RIGHT: **The Westland Scout was used operationally by the AAC in actions in various locations around the world. These included the Falklands campaign in 1982, where the type was used for many duties, such as supply, CASEVAC and ground attack.**

The type was used operationally in Aden, Borneo, Oman and Rhodesia. In Northern Ireland, AAC Scout helicopters were used for the rapid deployment of troops to set up surprise vehicle checkpoints to disrupt terrorist activity. The type could be fitted with a Nightsun high-power searchlight as an aid to night search operations.

The Scout was very much in the front line during the Falklands campaign. Twelve of the type were used to insert Special Air Service (SAS) personnel,

as well as supplying ammunition to front-line positions and recovering casualties for treatment. Two Scout helicopters were attacked by Argentine Air Force Pucara aircraft, and one was shot down – the only Argentine air-to-air victory of the war. The Scout was also used to attack enemy strongpoints. On June 14, an Argentine artillery position which was firing on advancing British troops was attacked and destroyed by Nord SS.11 anti-tank missiles fired from Scout helicopters at a range of 3,000m/3,281yd.

Few Scouts were exported, the only customers being Bahrain (2), Jordan (3) and Uganda (2). In 1963, two Westland Scout helicopters were acquired by the Royal Australian Navy (RAN), and were operated from survey ships until 1973.

Westland Wasp HAS.1

First flight: October 28, 1962
Power: 1 x Rolls-Royce Nimbus Mk 503 turboshaft
Armament: Torpedoes, depth charges or anti-shipping missiles
Size: Rotor diameter – 9.83m/32ft 3in
Length – 9.24m/30ft 4in
Height – 3.56m/11ft 8in
Weights: Empty – 1,565kg/3,452lb (maximum)
Take-off – 2,495kg/5,500lb
Performance: Speed – 193kph/120mph (maximum)
Service ceiling – 3,813m/12,500ft
Range – 488km/303 miles

Westland Lynx

A British Army requirement for a multi-role helicopter to replace the Westland Scout was announced in 1964. The specification detailed. a machine to carry seven fully armed troops, a 6,614kg/3,000lb load, and be operated in the CASEVAC, reconnaissance or liaison role. Westland Helicopters was contracted to design, build and develop the new machine that would enter service as the Lynx. Significantly, the new helicopter also had to be compact enough to be air-transportable in a Lockheed C-130 Hercules. In addition, Westland identified a Royal Navy requirement for a second-generation helicopter to operate from ships in adverse weather. In France, the military also had a requirement for an armed reconnaissance and ASW helicopter. The result was an Anglo–French agreement under which Westland would produce 70 per cent of each aircraft and Aérospatiale in France the balance. Significantly, the Lynx was the first British aircraft designed using metric rather than imperial measurements.

The prototype Lynx was first flown in 1971. The design utilized many components previously used in the Scout and Wasp helicopters. The rotor design was, however, all new and of honeycomb sandwich construction. In 1972, a Lynx was used to break the world helicopter speed record over distance for both 15 and 25km (9 and 15.5 miles) flown at 321.73kph/199.92mph. A short time later,

ABOVE: **The Westland Lynx was in service with the Royal Navy from 1972 until 2017, and was used in combat during the Falklands campaign and both Gulf wars in Iraq. For the anti-submarine warfare role, the Lynx is armed with the Mk46 lightweight homing torpedo.**

the type was used to set a new 100km/ 62 miles closed circuit record, at a speed of 318.504kph/197.91mph.

ABOVE: **Westland proposed the Lynx 3 to the Army Air Corps as a purpose-built attack helicopter. The type was not ordered for production, and all development was cancelled.**

LEFT: **A Westland Lynx Mk3 was used as the development for the Lynx Mk8 in Royal Navy service. The type is equipped with the Sea Owl thermal imager in a turret mounting. The scanner for the Sea Spray radar is housed in a radome mounted under the nose of the aircraft.**

The first naval version, fitted with a lengthened nose to enclose a radar scanner, tricycle undercarriage and a deck restraint system, was flown in 1972. On June 29, 1973, the first landing trials at sea took place from the deck of RFA *Engadine*, a ship of the Royal Fleet Auxiliary (RFA).

An order for 113 of the Westland Lynx AH.1 (Army Helicopter Mk 1) was placed for service with the British Army to be used in the transport, anti-tank warfare (carrying eight TOW missiles) and reconnaissance roles. In 1977, deliveries of the first production Lynxes began to reach to the British Army. These machines were later upgraded to AH.7 standard with a strengthened airframe, an improved tail rotor, more sophisticated avionic and defensive equipment. Infra-red suppressors were fitted over the exhausts from each engine.

The first production Lynx HAS Mk2 was flown in 1976, and deck-handling trials at sea on HMS *Birmingham* (D86), a Type 42 destroyer, began in February 1977. In 1978, No. 702 Naval Air Squadron (NAS) based at RNAS Yeovilton, Somerset, was the first Royal Navy squadron to be equipped with the Lynx. The HAS Mk2 was developed principally for anti-submarine warfare and to be operated from the flight deck of destroyers and frigates. A total of 80 of the type were delivered to the RN, with the last 20 machines (designated HAS Mk3) being fitted with uprated engines. The type was widely used by the French Navy as the Lynx Mk2 (FN) and Mk4 (FN) respectively.

Some 25 Lynx helicopters were deployed by the Royal Navy during the Falklands War. On April 25, 1982, the type was first used in an action in an attack on the *Santa Fe*, an Argentine Navy submarine. The Lynx was deployed during Operation Desert Storm (first Gulf War), and those in RN service were used to attack ships of the Iraqi Navy with the Sea Skua anti-shipping missile.

In 1986, a modified Lynx flown by Westland test pilot John Egginton set an absolute speed record for helicopters over 15 and 25km (9 and 15.5 miles) of 400.87kph/249.09mph. The Lynx remains one of the most agile military helicopters in the world and, being cleared for aerobatics, has equipped "The Black Cats", the Royal Navy helicopter display team formed by pilots of No.702 NAS.

The Lynx Mk7 that served with the Fleet Air Arm (FAA) was operated as an attack/utility helicopter in support of the Royal Marines. The Lynx HMA Mk8 was an ASW helicopter equipped with the Sea Skua anti-shipping missile operating from RN warships. During the invasion of Iraq in 2003, a Lynx from No.847 NAS was shot down over Basra, on May 6, 2006. The Lynx began being phased out of service with the Royal Navy from 2012.

In June 2006, the Ministry of Defence awarded AgustaWestland a contract to develop a "super" Lynx helicopter, incorporating advanced technology to provide an increased operational capability. The AW159 Lynx Wildcat was designed to have a high level of commonality in airframe, avionics and cockpit equipment. More powerful engines are fitted to provide the type with an improvement in speed, endurance and economy. The most visible changes include a redesigned nose and rear fuselage, a tailplane with endplates and an improved tail rotor.

The Lynx has been operated by the navies of Argentina, Brazil, Denmark, Egypt, Germany, Portugal, Norway, the Netherlands, Nigeria and South Korea. The Army Air Corps (AAC) were the only operators of the battlefield version.

Westland Lynx HAS.8

First flight: March 21, 1971
Power: 2 x Rolls-Royce Gem 42-1 turboshaft
Armament: Torpedoes, depth charges, anti-shipping missile or anti-tank missile
Size: Rotor diameter – 12.8m/42ft
　　Length – 15.24m/50ft
　　Height – 3.76m/12ft 1in
Weights: Empty – 3,291kg/7,255lb
　　Take-off – 5,125kg/11,300lb (maximum)
Performance: Speed – 232kph/144mph (maximum)
　　Service ceiling – 2,576m/8,450ft
　　Range – 275km/171 miles

Glossary

AAC Army Air Corps (UK).

AAF Army Air Forces (US).

AAM Air-to-Air Missile.

aerodynamics Study of how gases, including air, flow and how forces act upon objects moving through air.

AEW Airborne Early Warning.

ailerons Control surfaces at the trailing edge of each wing used to make the aircraft roll.

angle of attack Angle of a wing or rotor blade to the oncoming airflow.

anti-torque To counter the effect of torque, often applied to a system.

ASDIC Anti-Submarine Detection Investigation Committee; a system that uses pulses of sound to detect objects underwater, invented during World War I and refined during World War II.

ASM Anti-Ship Missile.

ASR Air Sea Rescue; *see also* SAR.

ASW Anti-Submarine Warfare.

autorotation The movement of relative wind up through the rotor blades, causing them to turn with enough speed to generate lift and carry the aircraft aloft without an engine.

AWACS Airborne Warning and Control System.

blister A streamlined, often clear, large fairing on an aircraft body, housing guns or electronics.

BVR Beyond Visual Range.

CASEVAC Casualty Evacuation.

ceiling The maximum height at which an aircraft can operate.

coaxial Contra-rotating superimposed rotors which cancel out any torque effect.

collective/collective control Essentially the "up" or "down" control that changes, collectively, the angle of all rotor blades simultaneously, and increases or decreases the lift that the rotors provide to the aircraft, allowing the helicopter to gain or lose altitude.

control tubes Push/pull tubes that change the pitch of the rotor blades.

CSAR Combat, Search and Rescue.

cyclic Cyclic control changes the angle of attack of the main rotors unevenly – on one side of the helicopter the angle of attack (and therefore lift) is greater.

dihedral The upward angle of the wing formed where the wings connect to the fuselage.

dipping sonar Sonar that is lowered into the sea by a helicopter to listen for submarines beneath the surface.

dorsal Pertaining to the upper side of an aircraft.

drag The force that resists the motion of the aircraft through the air.

drone An unmanned aircraft controlled by radio or other means.

dynamic components The main rotating part of a helicopter airframe.

ECM Electronic Countermeasures.

elevators Control surfaces on the horizontal part of the tail that are used to alter the aircraft's pitch.

ELINT Electronic Intelligence.

eshp Equivalent shaft horsepower.

BELOW: The Sikorsky (S-49) R-6A was developed from the R-4, but in order to provide improved performance, the fuselage was completely redesigned. The R-6A was fitted with the rotor and gearbox from the R-4 and was powered by a Franklin 0-405-9 radial piston engine.

FBW Fly-By-Wire.

fin The vertical portion of the tail.

flaps Moveable parts of the trailing edge of a wing used to increase lift at slower air speeds.

FLIR Forward Looking Infra-Red.

g The force of gravity.

hp Horsepower.

hub This sits atop the mast, and connects the rotor blades to the control tubes.

HUD Head-Up Display.

jet engine An engine that works by creating a high-velocity jet of air to propel the engine forward.

JMSDF Japanese Maritime Self-Defense Force.

LCD Liquid Crystal Display.

leading edge The front edge of a wing or tailplane.

MAD Magnetic Anomaly Detection; a technique for locating submarines by detecting their metal mass.

mast Rotating shaft from the transmission, connecting the rotor blades to the helicopter.

MEDEVAC Medical Evacuation.

NATO North Atlantic Treaty Organization.

nautical mile 1.852km/1.1508 miles.

pitch Rotational motion in which an aircraft turns around its lateral axis. Alternatively, increased or decreased angle of the rotor blades to raise, lower or change the direction of the rotors' thrust force.

port Left side.

RAAF Royal Australian Air Force.

radome Protective covering for radar, made from material through which radar beams can pass.

RAF Royal Air Force.

RCAF Royal Canadian Air Force.

RN Royal Navy.

roll Rotational motion in which the aircraft turns around its longitudinal axis.

root The inner end of the blade where the rotors connect to the blade grips.

rotor The rotary wing formed of spinning blades that act as a wing to generate lift.

rudder The parts of the tail surfaces that control yaw (left and right turning).

SAAF South African Air Force.

SAM Surface-to-Air Missile.

SAR Sea Air Rescue/Search and Rescue.

shp Shaft horsepower.

SLR Side-Looking Airborne Radar.

sonar Acronym for Sound Navigation and Ranging, a technique that uses sound propagation, usually underwater, to detect other vessels.

sponson An aerodynamic fairing on the lower side of an helicopter, often housing fuel.

starboard Right side.

STOL Short Take-Off and Landing.

supersonic Indicating motion faster than the speed of sound.

tailplane Horizontal part of the tail, known as horizontal stabilizer in North America.

thrust Force produced by an engine, pushing the aircraft forward.

torque The tendency of an engine and the aircraft it is mounted in to spin around in the opposite direction, a rotor being driven by the engine.

UHF Ultra High Frequency.

USAAC United States Army Air Corps.

USAAF United States Army Air Forces.

USAF United States Air Force.

USCG United States Coast Guard.

USMC United States Marine Corps.

USN United States Navy.

ventral Pertaining to the underside of an aircraft.

VHF Very High Frequency.

V/STOL Vertical/Short Take-Off and Landing.

ABOVE: The Aérospatiale Gazelle is a light multi-role helicopter that has been in military service since the early 1970s. The tail rotor housed within the tail boom is one of its key recognition features.

Key to flags

For the specification boxes, the national flag that was current at the time of the helicopter's use is shown.

 Canada

 France

 Germany

 India

 Italy

 The Netherlands

 Poland

 South Africa

 Soviet Union

 United Kingdom

 United States of America

Index

A

Achgelis, Gerd 22
Advanced Aerial Fire
Support System
(AAFFSS) 75, 126
Aerial
Carriage 11
Top 10
Aérospatiale
Cheetal 97
Puma 61, 79
SA 321 Super Frélon
68, 98–9
SA 330 Puma 100–1
SA 341 Gazelle 104–5
SA 343M 105
SE 315B Lama 96–7
SE 3130 Alouette II
47, 63, 94
SE 316 Alouette III 95
Aerotécnica AC-12 46
Afghanistan (Soviets)
72–3
Afghanistan (UK forces)
77
AGM-114 Hellfire missile
81, 110, 124
Agusta
A101 46
A109 47
A129/T129 Mangusta
47, 110–11

AS-61 215, 217
AgustaWestland
AH-64W Apache Longbow
82–3
AW101 Merlin 112–13
AW109E Power 108–9
AW139 57
/Leonardo AW159 Wildcat
114–15
CH-149 Cormorant 41
EH101 Merlin 46, 55,
56, 58
Air Sea Rescue (ASR) 40–1
Airborne Forces Experimental
Establishment (AFEE)
21
Airborne Low-Frequency
Sonar (ALPS) 71
Airborne Target Handover
System (ATHS) 125
American Helicopter Society
(AHS) 6
Anti-Submarine Warfare
(ASW) 9, 27, 33, 54,
67, 71, 98–9, 188–9,
199, 215
anti-tank helicopters 80–3
asymmetric lift 15
Atlas Oryx M2 55
attack helicopters 74–5
Automatic Flight Control
Systems (AFCS) 109

autorotation 15

B

Baikalov, M. K. 178
BCD-1 El Cangrejo 14
Bell
AH-1 Cobra 51, 60, 63,
75, 78, 80–1, 87, 122,
126–7, 162
AH-1W SuperCobra
128–9
AH-1Z Viper 128
Bell-47 32–3, 36, 39
Bell-47 H-13 Sioux 116–
17
Bell-47B 32
Bell 412 132–3
CH-135 130–1
CH-146 Griffon 132–3
H-13 Sioux 8, 38, 84
HT-1 Griffin 41
HTL-4 38
OH-58C/D Kiowa/Kiowa
Warrior 7, 122–5
TH-67 SeaRanger
122–3
UH-1 A/B/C Iroquois
(Huey) 9, 41, 50–1, 60,
63, 74–5, 79, 118–19
UH-1 D/H Iroquois
9, 120–1
UH-1N/Y (Twin Huey)

130–1
XHSL (Model 61) 33
XV-3 (Model 200) 33, 88
XV-15 89
Bell Aircraft Company
32–3
Bell-Boeing V-22/CV-22/
MV-22 Osprey
87, 88, 134–5
Bell/Textron Eagle Eye
91
Bennett, James 19, 42
Bensen
B7 homebuild rotorkite
17
B7M autogyro 17
B8M (X-25) autogyro 17
Bensen, Igor 17
Blue Kestrel radar 113
Boeing
AH-64D/E Apache
Longbow/Apache
Guardian 144–5
Chinook CH-47 64–5,
68–9, 78–9, 86,
138–41
Chinook HC1/2 76
Boeing-Agusta BA609 7
Boeing-Sikorsky RAH-66
Comanche 80
Boeing Vertol
CH-46 Sea Knight
86, 136–7
MH-47 E/G 142–3
Boulet, Jean 97
Bravo November (Chinook)
76–7
Bréguet, Jacques 12
Bréguet, Louis 12
Bréguet-Richet Gyroplane 12

LEFT: The Bell UH-1 Iroquois
was retired from US Army
National Guard (ANG) service
on October 2, 2009. The UH-1
entered service with the US Army
in 1959, and served with the
ANG for almost 40 years.

Brennan, Louis 13
Brequet-Dorland
    Gyroplane 13
Bristol
    Belvedere 46, 48,
        148–9
    Sycamore 41, 44–5,
        46, 49, 146–7
Bristol Helicopters 46

C
Canon, William Harold
    158
Carbon Fibre Reinforced
    Polymer (CFRP)
    153, 160
Carr, Steve 77
CASEVAC 39, 45, 48, 100,
    103, 105, 107, 119,
    132, 139, 177, 187,
    200, 209
Casualty Evacuation Flight
    (CEF) 48–9
Cayley, Sir George 10–11
Changhe Z-8 99
Cierva
    autogyros/helicopters
        14–15, 16, 18–19
    C30-A (DR624) 17
    W-14 Skeeter 13, 19,
        203
Cierva "jump-start" 18
Cierva/Weir W-11 Air Horse
    19, 58
cockpits 56–7
collective pitch 15
Combat Search and Rescue
    (CSAR) 53, 70,
    102, 103
computer-aided terrain-
    following flight
    systems 194
controls 56–7
Cornu, Paul 12
Courtney, Frank 16
Curtiss Bleecker 7

D
da Vinci, Leonardo 10
D'Ascanio, Corrandino
    12, 13

D'AT3 13
de la Cierva, Juan 14–15,
    16, 18, 58
Denel AH-2 Rooivalk 150–1
detection and attack 70–1
dipping/dunking sonar 71
Discretionary Descent
    Vehicle (DDV) 17
Doblhoff WNF 342 23
Dokdo 87
Douglas 0-75 engine 18
drones 90–1
ducted fans 61, 104
Dynavert CL-84 88

E
Eden, Anthony 44
Eisenhower, Dwight D. 84
Eithalia Mari 21
engines 62–3
Eurocopter
    /Airbus UH-72 Lakota
        156–7
    AS 332 Super Puma
        55, 102–3
    AS 350 Écureuil 47, 154
    AS 355 Écureuil 2 47
    AS 360 Dauphin 106
    AS 365 Dauphin 2 106
    AS 532 Cougar 102–3
    AS 550 Fennec/Airbus
        H125M 154–5
    AS 565 Panther 106–7
    Bo105 80, 176–7
    EC665/Airbus HAD Tiger
        87, 152–3
    EC725 Caracal 103

F
Fairchild Hiller Corporation
    35
Fairchild Hiller FH-1100 35
Fairey
    Gyrodyne 19, 42
    Rotodyne 42–3
    Ultralite 42
Falklands War 76
Faulkenberry, John I. 158
flapping 15
Flettner
    Fa 330 Bachstelze 9

Fl 184 autogyro 16
Fl 282 Kolibri 6, 23
Flettner, Anton 23
Focke, Heinrich 22
Focke-Achgelis
    Fa 223 Drache 9, 22, 23
    Fa 226 Hornisse 22
    Fa 330 Bachstelze
        20–1
Focke-Wulf Fw61 22
Forlanini, Enrico 12, 62
Fortune, Ian 77
Forward Arming and
    Refuellling Points
    (FARP) 81
Forward Looking Infra-Red
    (FLIR) system 66
Franz, Anselm 63

G
Gellatly, Ron 43
Global Positioning/Inertial
    Navigation System
    (GPS/INS) 111
Gulf War, First 78–9,
    102, 165
gun spotting 38
gunships 74–5
Gyrodyne QH-50 DASH
    90
gyrodynes 42–3
gyrogliders 20

H
Hafner, Raoul 21
HAL
    Cheetah *see* Aérospatiale
        SE 315B Lama

Dhruv 160
Harbin Aircraft Corporation
    Z-9C *see* Eurocopter
        AS 565 Panther
heat suppressors 175
heavy-lift helicopters 68–9
Helical Air Screw 10
helicopter assault ships
    86–7
Hiller
    360 34
    Flying Platform 35
    H-23 Raven 36, 39
    HRJ 2B ram jet
        engines 35
    UH-5 34
    UH-12 (OH-23 Raven)
        35, 158–9
    XH-44 34–5
    YH-32 Hornet 35
    YROE-1 (Rotorcycle)
        34–5
Hiller Aircraft Corporation
    34–5
Hiller, Stanley 34–5
Hindustan Aircraft Limited
    see HAL
HMS
    Albion 86
    Endurance 55
    Hermes 76

ABOVE: The Boeing CH-47 has been in Royal Air Force service since 1980. In 2009, an upgrade programme was initiated to equip the machines with digital avionics, and the RAF currently operate 60 Chinooks with more on order from the United States.

ABOVE: The AH Mk1 Apache was the version of the Apache specifically developed for service with Britain's Army Air Corps. The machines have been deployed to Afghanistan and also Libya, where the helicopters were flown from HMS *Ocean*.

Iron Duke 55
Ocean 44, 86, 87
Theseus 44
Huey *see* Bell UH-1 A/B/C
    Iroquois (Huey)
Hughes
    AH-64 Apache 78–9, 81,
        82–3, 124, 164–5
    OH-6A Cayuse
        162–3
    TH-55 Osage 161

I
Ilya Muromets 24
Improved Cargo Helicopter
    Program (ICHP) 140
Infra-Red Signature (IRS)
    106
Instrument Landing System
    (ILS) 101

J
Jarnot, Chuck 193
Joint Experimental
    Helicopter Unit
    (JEHU) 44

K
Kaman

H-43/HH-43 Huskie
    26–7, 59, 63,
    166–7
HOK-1 Huskie 27
K-125 26, 166
K-225 26, 63
K-1200 K-MAX 27
SH-2 Seasprite 27,
    168–9
Kaman, Charles H.
    26–7
Kamov
    Ka-10 31
    Ka-15 31
    Ka-18 31
    Ka-20 170
    Ka-22 Vintokryl 30
    Ka-25 59, 70, 170–1
    Ka-27/29/31/32 54, 172–3
    Ka-50/52 174–5
    Ka-226 31
    OKB 30
    V-80Sh-1 174
Kamov, Nikolay Il'yich
    16, 30, 178
KASKR
    KASKR-1 Red Engineer
        autogyro 16, 30
    KASKR-2 autogyro 16
Kayaba Ka-1 autogyro
    16–17
KD-1 autogyro 16
Kellett KD-1A autogyro 16
Korean War 9, 35, 38–9

L
Langworthy, Sqd Ldr 76
Lawless, Flt Lt 76
Light Airborne Multi-Purpose
    System (LAMPS) 169
Ling-Temco-Vought (LTV)
    XC-142 89
Lockheed
    AH-56 Cheyenne 81, 126
    C-130P 53
Lomonosov, Mikhail 11

M
McDonnell Douglas MD
    520N 60
Magnetic Anomaly
    Detection (MAD)
    70, 93, 170, 215
Malayan conflict 48–9
Marine One 84–5
Mast-Mounted Sight (MMS)
    7, 124
MBB 46–7, 152, 175
MBB Bo105 80, 176–7
MEDEVAC 100, 103, 106,
    109, 122, 134, 156, 177
Messerchmitt-Bölkow-Blohm
    see MBB
Mikheyev, I. V. 30
Mil
    Mi-1 178–9
    Mi-2 180–1
    Mi-4 182–3
    Mi-6 59, 184–5
    Mi-8 9, 57, 72–3,

    80, 186–7
    Mi-10 69
    Mi-12 31
    Mi-14 188–9
    Mi-24 69, 72–3, 75,
        80, 190–1
    Mi-26 68, 192–3
    Mi-28 194–5
    V-12 31, 69
Mil, Mikhail 30–1, 178
Mil Moscow Helicopter
    Plant 31
mine spotting 38
Mobile Army Surgical
    Hospital (MASH) 39
Morton, John G. P. 43
MV *Atlantic Conveyor*
    76–7

N
NH Industries NH90
    196–7
Night Vision Technology
    (NVT) 66–7, 122
Nightsun 105
Nord 500 47
Northrop Grumman RQ-8A
    Fire Scout 90
NOTAR system 60–1

O
Oemichen, Etienne 13

P
Paucton, J. P. 11
Pescara, Raul Pateras 12–13
Piasecki
    16H-1 Pathfinder 29
    H-21 Workhorse/
        Shawnee 50–1, 74,
        139, 200–1
    HRP-1 Rescuer 28, 29
    HUP Retriever/UH-25
        Army Mule 199
    PV1 28
    PV2 28–9
    PV3 28
    Sea Bat 29
    XHRP-1 29
    YH-16 Transporter 198

Piasecki, Frank N. 28–9
Piasecki Helicopter
    Corporation 29
Pitcairn PAA-1 Autogyro 17
Pterosphere 11
Pullin, Cyril 18
Pullin, Raymond 19
PZL Anakonda 40
PZL W-3 Sokól 40, 202

R
rational helicopter 12
Richet, Charles 12
Robinson R22/R44 202
Rotabuggy 21
Rotachute 20–1
Rotatank 21
Rotorcycle 34–5
rotorkites 20
Rotormatic Control
    System 34
rotors 13, 15, 31, 58–61
Royal Australian Navy
    Helicopter Flight
    Vietnam (RANHFUV) 53
Russky Vityaz 24

S
Sablie, George 46
Saunders-Roe Skeeter
    19, 203
Sea Air Rescue (SAR)
    see Air Sea Rescue
    (ASR)
sea helicopters 54–5
Search and Rescue (SAR)
    41, 133, 173
Sikorsky
    CH-3C 68
    CH-34 Choctaw 53
    CH-37 Mojave 69, 138,
        210–11
    CH-46 Sea Knight 87
    CH-53 52
    CH-53 Sea Stallion
        68, 87, 220–1
    CH-53E Super Stallion
        62, 68, 79, 85, 87,
        230–1
    CH-54 Tarhe 69, 218–19

H-3 Sea King 84
H-5 36, 38
H-19 Chickasaw 38–9,
    208–9
H-34 Choctaw 54, 63,
    136, 212–13
H-92 Superhawk 236–7
HH-3 69
HH-3E (Jolly Green Giant)
    40, 52, 74, 216–17
HH-52H Sea Guard 107
HH-60G Pave Hawk
    224–5
HH-60H Seahawk 67
HMR-161 38
HO3S-1 36, 38, 54
HRS-1 38
HUS-1 50, 53, 84
MH-53 66
MH-53E Sea Dragon
    234–5
MH-53J Pave Low 232–3
MH-60G Pave Hawk
    228–9
MH-60R/S Seahawk
    71, 137
R-4 Hoverfly 9, 22, 25,
    36–7, 204–5
R-6 Hoverfly II 204
S-51 25, 40, 46, 56,
    206–7
S-52 (HOSS-1) 25
S-55 Chickasaw 62, 209
S-58 54, 63
S-61 Sea King 98, 186

S-92 43, 59
SH-3 Sea King 214–15
SH-60 Seahawk 70, 78,
    87, 226–7
UH-60 Black Hawk
    70, 74, 79, 222–3
VH-3A 85
VH-60D Nighthawk 85
VH-60N Whitehawk 85
X-2 43
XR-4 24
YH-19 38
Sikorsky, Igor 24–5
Skrzhinskii, Nikolai K.
    16, 30
slaving 67
SNCASO 1100 Ariel 1
    63
Sonar (Sound Navigation
    and Ranging) 70–1
stretcher pods 38
Stuart-Jervis, Lt 45
Sud-Aviation/Aérospatiale
    Puma 46
Sud-Est Alouette 46
Sud-Ouest
    SO 1221 Djinn 46, 63,
        238–9
    SO-120 Ariel III 46
Suez Crisis 44–5
swash plates 58

T
Target Sighting System
    (TSS) 131

Tedder, Arthur 19
Thomson-CSF Target
    radar 102–3
tilt-rotor 7, 88–9
tilt-wings 88–9
Tishchenko, Marat
    192
TsAGI 30

U
U-boat towing 20–1
United Helicopters 34
US presidential helicopters
    84–5
USS
    Bay Lander 123
    Boxer 87
    Bunker Hill 204
    Hancock 168
    Harpers Ferry 102
    McInerney 161
    Mobile Bay 102
    New Jersey 54
    Nicholson 168
    Philippine Sea 38
    Swift 55
    Taylor 54

BELOW: The Kamov Ka-52 Alligator (NATO identifier Hokum A) entered front-line service with the Russian Air Force on February 10, 2011. A naval version is being deployed on the French-built Mistral-class amphibious assault ships ordered for the Russian Navy.

Valley Forge 38
Utility Tactical Transport
    Company (UTTC)
    helicopters 74, 133

V
Vertical Replenishment
    (VertRep) 55, 197
Vertical Take-Off and
    Landing (VTOL)
    29, 35, 134
Vertical Unmanned Aircraft
    Systems (VUAS)
    90–1
Vertol VZ-2 88–9
Vietnam Helicopter Pilots
    Association (VHPA)
    51

Vietnam War 9, 50–3, 74
Viner, Dimitry 40
Von Engelhardt, Wilfried 176
Vought-Sikorsky
    VS-300 24–5
    VS-316 36–7
Vought/Hiller/Ryan XC-142
    89

W
Walker, G. E. 18
Weir autogyros/helicopters
    18–19
Weir, James George
    15, 18–19
Weir/Cierva W11 Air Horse
    19, 58
Westland

Gazelle 46, 79
HC Mk1 *see* Aérospatiale
    SA 330 Puma
Lynx 46, 55, 78–9, 248–9
S-51 Dragonfly 46,
    48–9, 63, 206–7
Scout 246–7
Sea King 40–1, 46,
    86, 244–5
Wasp 55, 246–7
Wessex 41, 55, 242–3
Whirlwind 41, 44–5,
    48–9, 63, 240–1
Wyvern 44
Wilson, Craig 77

Y
Yakovlev Yak-24 58
YO-60 autogyro 16
Yom Kippur War 81
Young, Arthur 32–3

Acknowledgements

Picture research for this book
was carried out by Jasper
Spencer-Smith, who has
selected images from JSS
Collection and the following
(key: l=left, r=right, t=top,
b=bottom, m=middle):
UK MoD Crown Copyright
2010: 2; 3; 8–9; 40br; 55tl;
58t; 65bl, 65br; 66b; 67tr;
68t; 83t, 83b; 86bl; 100, 101t,
101b; 104t, 104b; 105; 106b;
109; 113t; 114; 133t; 138t;
144t, 144b; 145t, 145b; 154b;
240t; 242t; 244t, 244b; 245;
251; 253; 254.
Every effort has been
made to acknowledge
photographs correctly,
however we apologize for
any unintentional omissions,
which will be corrected
in future editions.

BELOW: **The Bell Boeing MV-22 Osprey is operated by the US Marine Corps
(USMC) in the troop and logistical transport role. The CV-22B has been
ordered by the US Air Force for service with Special Operations Command
(SOCOM), and is equipped for long-range missions. The type has replaced
the Sikorsky MH-53 Pave Low helicopter.**